The Story of Chautauqua

Lewis Miller (1878)

# The Story of Chautauqua

By

Jesse Lyman Hurlbut, D.D.
Author of "The Story of the Bible," "Teacher Training Lessons for the Sunday School," etc.

*With 50 Illustrations*

G. P. Putnam's Sons
New York and London
The Knickerbocker Press
1921

*Printed in the United States of America*

*This book is dedicated to the honoured memory of the two Founders of Chautauqua*

**Lewis Miller**

*and*

**John Heyl Vincent**

# PREFACE

## WHY AND WHEREFORE

AN ancient writer—I forget his name—declared that in one of the city-states of Greece there was the rule that when any citizen proposed a new law or the repeal of an old one, he should come to the popular assembly with a rope around his neck, and if his proposition failed of adoption, he was to be immediately hanged. It is said that amendments to the constitution of that state were rarely presented, and the people managed to live under a few time-honored laws. It is possible that some such drastic treatment may yet be meted out to authors—and perhaps to publishers—as a last resort to check the flood of useless literature. To anticipate this impending constitutional amendment, it is incumbent upon every writer of a book to show that his work is needed by the world, and this I propose to do in these prefatory pages.

Is Chautauqua great enough, original enough, sufficiently beneficial to the world to have its history written? We will not accept the votes of the thousands who beside the lake, in the Hall of Philosophy, or under the roof of the amphitheater, have been inoculated with the Chautauqua spirit. We will seek for the testimony of sane, intelligent, and thoughtful people, and we will be guided in our conclusions by their opinions. Let us listen to the words of the wise and then determine whether a book about Chautauqua should be published. We have the utterances by word of mouth and the written statements of public men, governors, senators, presidents; of educators, professors, and college presidents; of preachers and ecclesiastics in many churches; of speakers upon many platforms; of authors whose works are read everywhere; and we present their testimonials as a sufficient warrant for the preparation and publication of *The Story of Chautauqua*.

The Hon. George W. Atkinson, Governor of West Virginia, visited Chautauqua in 1899, and in his Recognition Day address on "Modern Educational Requirements" spoke as follows:

> It (Chautauqua) is the common people's College, and its courses of instruction are so admirably arranged that it somehow induces the toiling millions to voluntarily grapple with all subjects and with all knowledge.
>
> My Chautauqua courses have taught me that what we need most is only so much knowledge as we can

assimilate and organize into a basis for action; for if more be given it may become injurious.

Chautauqua is doing more to nourish the intellects of the masses than any other system of education extant; except the public schools of the common country.

Here is the testimony of ex-Governor Adolph O. Eberhardt of Minnesota:

If I had the choice of being the founder of any great movement the world has ever known, I would choose the Chautauqua movement.

The Hon. William Jennings Bryan, from the point of view of a speaker upon many Chautauqua platforms, wrote:

The privilege and opportunity of addressing from one to seven or eight thousand of his fellow Americans in the Chautauqua frame of mind, in the mood which almost as clearly asserts itself under the tent or amphitheater as does reverence under the "dim, religious light"—this privilege and this opportunity is one of the greatest that any patriotic American could ask. It makes of him, if he knows it and can rise to its requirements, a potent human factor in molding the mind of the nation.

Viscount James Bryce, Ambassador of Great Britain to the United States, and author of ***The American Commonwealth***, the most illuminating work ever written on the American system of government, said, while visiting Chautauqua:

I do not think any country in the world but America could produce such gatherings as Chautauqua's.

Six presidents of the United States have thought it worth while to visit Chautauqua, either before, or during, or after their term of office. These were Grant, Hayes, Garfield, McKinley, Roosevelt, and Taft. Theodore Roosevelt was at Chautauqua four times. He said on his last visit, in 1905, "Chautauqua is the most American thing in America"; and also:

This Chautauqua has made the name Chautauqua a name of a multitude of gatherings all over the Union, and there is probably no other educational influence in the country quite so fraught with hope for the future of the nation as this and the movement of which it is the archtype.

Let us see what some journalists and writers have said about Chautauqua. Here is the opinion of Dr. Lyman Abbott, editor of *The Outlook*, and a leader of thought in our time:

Chautauqua has inspired the habit of reading with a purpose. It is really not much use to read, except as an occasional recreation, unless the reading inspires one to think his own thoughts, or at least make the writer's thoughts his own. Reading without reflection, like eating without digestion, produces dyspepsia. The influence and guidance of Chautauqua will long be needed in America.

The religious influence of Chautauqua has been not less valuable. Chautauqua has met the restless questioning of the age in the only way in which it can be successfully met, by converting it into a serious seeking for rest in truth.

Dr. Edwin E. Slosson, formerly professor in Columbia University, now literary editor of the *Independent*, wrote in that paper:

If I were a cartoonist, I should symbolize Chautauqua by a tall Greek goddess, a sylvan goddess with leaves in her hair—not vine leaves, but oak, and tearing open the bars of a cage wherein had been confined a bird, say an owl, labeled "Learning." For that is what Chautauqua has done for the world—it has let learning loose.

From the American *Review of Reviews*, July, 1914:

The president of a large technical school is quoted as having said that ten per cent. of the students in the institution over which he presides owe their presence to Chautauqua influence. A talk on civic beauty or sanitation by an expert from the Chautauqua platform often results in bringing these matters to local attention for the first time.

Here is an extract from *The World To-day:*

Old-time politics is dead in the States of the Middle West. The torchlight parade, the gasoline lamps, and the street orator draw but little attention. The "Republican Rally" in the court-house and the "Democratic Barbecue" in the grove have lost their potency. People turn to the Chautauquas to be taught politics along with domestic science, hygiene, and child-welfare.

Mr. John Graham Brooks, lecturer on historical, political, and social subjects, author of works widely circulated and highly esteemed, has given courses of lectures at Chautauqua, and has expressed his estimate in these words:

After close observation of the work at Chautauqua, and at other points in the country where its affiliated work goes on, I can say with confidence that it is among the most enlightening of our educational agencies in the United States.

Dr. A. V. V. Raymond, while President of Union College in New York State, gave this testimony:

Chautauqua has its own place in the educational world, a place as honorable as it is distinctive; and those of us who are laboring in other fields, by other methods, have only admiration and praise for the great work which has made Chautauqua in the best sense a household word throughout the land.

Mr. Edward Howard Griggs, who is in greater demand than almost any other lecturer on literary and historical themes, in his Recognition Day address, in 1904, on "Culture Through Vocation," said as follows:

> The Chautauqua movement as conceived by its leaders is a great movement for cultivating an avocation apart from the main business of life, not only giving larger vision, better intellectual training, but giving more earnest desire and greater ability to serve and grow through the vocation.

This from Dr. William T. Harris, United States Commissioner of Education:

> Think of one hundred thousand persons of mature age following up a well-selected course of reading for four years in science and literature, kindling their torches at a central flame! Think of the millions of friends and neighbors of this hundred thousand made to hear of the new ideas and of the inspirations that result to the workers!
>
> It is a part of the great missionary movement that began with Christianity and moves onward with Christian civilization.
>
> I congratulate all members of Chautauqua Reading Circles on their connection with this great movement which has begun under such favorable auspices and has spread so widely, is already world-historical, and is destined to unfold so many new phases.

Prof. Albert S. Cook, of Yale University, wrote in *The Forum:*

As nearly as I can formulate it, the Chautauqua Idea is something like this: A fraternal, enthusiastic, methodical, and sustained attempt to elevate, enrich, and inspire the individual life in its entirety, by an appeal to the curiosity, hopefulness, and ambition of those who would otherwise be debarred from the greatest opportunities of culture and spiritual advancement. To this end, all uplifting and stimulating forces, whether secular or religious, are made to conspire in their impact upon the person whose weal is sought. . . . Can we wonder that Chautauqua is a sacred and blessed name to multitudes of Americans?

The late Principal A. M. Fairbairn, of Mansfield College, Oxford, foremost among the thinkers of the last generation, gave many lectures at Chautauqua, and expressed himself thus:

The C. L. S. C. movement seems to me the most admirable and efficient organization for the direction of reading, and in the best sense for popular instruction. To direct the reading for a period of years for so many thousands is to affect not only their present culture, but to increase their intellectual activity for the period of their natural lives, and thus, among other things, greatly to add to the range of their enjoyment. It appears to me that a system which can create such excellent results merits the most cordial praise from all lovers of men.

Colonel Francis W. Parker, Superintendent of Schools, first at Quincy, Mass., and later at

Chicago, one of the leading educators of the land, gave this testimony, after his visit to Chautauqua:

> The New York Chautauqua—father and mother of all the other Chautauquas in the country—is one of the great institutions founded in the nineteenth century. It is essentially a school for the people.

Prof. Hjalmar H. Boyesen, of Columbia University, wrote:

> Nowhere else have I had such a vivid sense of contact with what is really and truly American. The national physiognomy was defined to me as never before; and I saw that it was not only instinct with intelligence, earnestness, and indefatigable aspiration, but that it revealed a strong affinity for all that makes for righteousness and the elevation of the race. The confident optimism regarding the future which this discovery fostered was not the least boon I carried away with me from Chautauqua.

Mrs. Alice Freeman Palmer, President of Wellesley College, expressed this opinion in a lecture at Chautauqua:

> I could say nothing better than to say over and over again the great truths Chautauqua has taught to everyone, that if you have a rounded, completed education you have put yourselves in relation with all the past, with all the great life of the present; you have reached on to the infinite hope of the future.
>
> I venture to say there is no man or woman educating

himself or herself through Chautauqua who will not feel more and more the opportunity of the present moment in a present world.

The character of Chautauqua's training has been that she has made us wiser than we were about things that last.

Rev. Charles M. Sheldon, author of *In His Steps*, a story of which three million copies were sold, said:

During the past two years I have met nearly a million people from the platform, and no audiences have impressed me as have the Chautauqua people for earnestness, deep purpose, and an honest desire to face and work out the great issues of American life.

This is from the Rev. Robert Stuart MacArthur, the eminent Baptist preacher:

I regard the Chautauqua Idea as one of the most important ideas of the hour. This idea, when properly utilized, gives us a "college at home." It is a genuine inspiration toward culture, patriotism, and religion. The general adoption of this course for a generation would give us a new America in all that is noblest in culture and character.

Dr. Edward Everett Hale, of Boston, Chaplain of the United States Senate, in his *Tarry At Home Travels*, wrote:

If you have not spent a week at Chautauqua, you do not know your own country. There, and in no other place known to me, do you meet Baddeck and Newfoundland and Florida and Tiajuara at the same table; and there you are of one heart and one soul with the forty thousand people who will drift in and out—people all of them who believe in God and their country.

More than a generation ago, the name of Joseph Cook was known throughout the continent as a thinker, a writer, and a lecturer. This is what he wrote of Chautauqua:

I keep Chautauqua in a fireside nook of my inmost affections and prayers. God bless the Literary and Scientific Circle, which is so marvelously successful already in spreading itself as a young vine over the trellis-work of many lands! What rich clusters may ultimately hang on its cosmopolitan branches! It is the glory of America that it believes that all that anybody knows everybody should know.

Phillips Brooks, perhaps the greatest of American preachers, spoke as follows in a lecture on "Literature and Life":

May we not believe—if the students of Chautauqua be indeed what we have every right to expect that they will be, men and women thoroughly and healthily alive through their perpetual contact with the facts of life—that when they take the books which have the knowledge in them, like pure water in silver urns, though they will not drink as deeply, they will drink more healthily than many of those who in the deader and more artificial life of college halls bring no such eager vitality to give value to their draught? If I understand Chautauqua, this is what it means: It finds its value in the vitality of its students. . . . It summons those who are alive with true human hunger to come and learn of that great world of knowledge of which he who knows the most knows such a very little, and feels more and more, with every increase of his knowledge, how very little it is that he knows.

Julia Ward Howe, author of the song beginning "Mine eyes have seen the glory," and honored throughout the land as one of the greatest among the women of America, wrote as follows:

I am obliged for your kind invitation to be present at the celebration of the twenty-fifth anniversary of the founding of Chautauqua Assembly. As I cannot well allow myself this pleasure, I send you my hearty congratulations in view of the honorable record of your association. May its good work long continue, even until its leaven shall leaven the whole body of our society.

The following letter was received by Dr. Vincent from one of the most distinguished of the older poets:

April 29, 1882.

J. H. VINCENT, D.D.,

DEAR FRIEND: I have been watching the progress of the Chautauqua Literary and Scientific Circle inaugurated by thyself, and take some blame to myself for not sooner expressing my satisfaction in regard to its objects and working thus far. I wish it abundant success, and that its circles, like those from the agitated center of the Lake, may widen out, until our entire country shall feel their beneficent influences. I am very truly thy friend,

JOHN G. WHITTIER.

After these endorsements, we may confidently affirm that a book on Chautauqua, its story, its principles, and its influence in the world, is warranted.

And now, a few words of explanation as to this particular book. The tendency in preparing such a work is to make it documentary, the recital of programs, speakers, and subjects. In order to lighten up the pages, I have sought to tell the story of small things as well as great, the witty as well as the wise words spoken, the record of by-play and repartee upon the platform, in those days when Chautauqua speakers were a fraternity. In fact, the title by which the body of workers was known among its members was "the Gang." Some of these stories are worth preserving, and I have tried to recall and retain them in these pages.

JESSE LYMAN HURLBUT.

Feb. 1, 1921.

## CONTENTS

# ILLUSTRATIONS

# The Story of Chautauqua

# The Story of Chautauqua

## CHAPTER I

### THE PLACE

JOHN HEYL VINCENT—a name that spells Chautauqua to millions—said: "Chautauqua is a *place*, an *idea*, and a *force*." Let us first of all look at the place, from which an idea went forth with a living force into the world.

The State of New York, exclusive of Long Island, is shaped somewhat like a gigantic foot, the heel being at Manhattan Island, the crown at the St. Lawrence River, and the toe at the point where Pennsylvania touches upon Lake Erie. Near this toe of New York lies Lake Chautauqua. It is eighteen miles long besides the romantic outlet of three miles, winding its way through forest primeval, and flowing into a shallow stream, the Chadakoin River, thence in succession into the Allegheny, the Ohio, the Mississippi, and finally resting in the bosom of the Gulf of Mexico. As we look at it upon the map, or sail upon it in the steamer, we perceive that it is about three miles across at its widest points, and moreover that it is in reality two lakes connected by a narrower channel, almost separated by two or three peninsulas. The earliest extant map of the lake, made by the way for General Washington soon after the Revolution (now in the Congressional Library at Washington), represents two separate lakes with a narrow stream between them. The lake receives no rivers or large streams. It is fed by springs beneath, and by a few brooks flowing into it. Consequently its water is remarkably pure, since none of the surrounding settlements are permitted to send their sewage into it.

The surface of Lake Chautauqua is 1350 feet above the level of the ocean; said to be the highest navigable water in the United States. This is not strictly correct, for Lake Tahoe on the boundary between Nevada and California is more than 6000 feet above sea-level. But Tahoe is navigated only by motor-boats and small steamers; while Lake Chautauqua, having a considerable town, Mayville, at its northern end, Jamestown, a flourishing city at its outlet, and its shores fringed with villages, bears upon its bosom many sizable steam-vessels.

It is remarkable that while Lake Erie falls into the St. Lawrence and empties into the Atlantic at

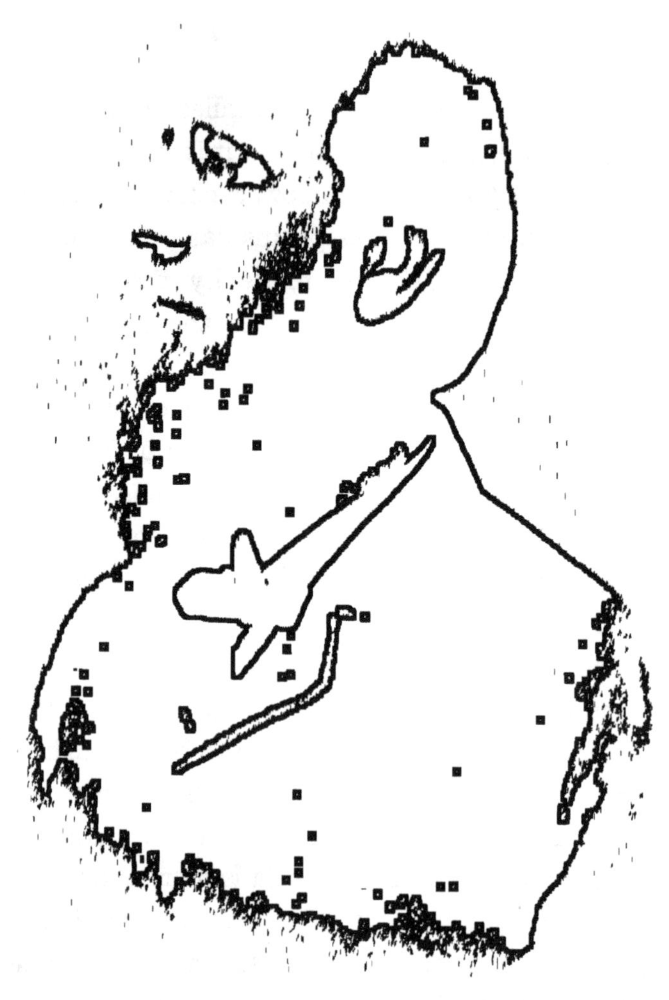

John H. Vincent (1876)

iceberg-mantled Labrador and Newfoundland, Lake Chautauqua only seven miles distant, and of more than seven hundred feet higher altitude, finds its resting place in the warm Gulf of Mexico. Between these two lakes is the watershed for this part of the continent. An old barn is pointed out, five miles from Lake Chautauqua, whereof it is said that the rain falling on one side of its roof runs into Lake Erie and the St. Lawrence, while the drops on the other side through a pebbly brook find their way by Lake Chautauqua into the Mississippi.

Nobody knows, or will ever know, how this lake got its smooth-sounding Indian name. Some tell us that the word means "the place of mists"; others, "the place high up"; still others that its form, two lakes with a passage between, gave it the name, "a bag tied in the middle," or "two moccasins tied together." Mr. Obed Edson of Chautauqua County, who made a thorough search among old records and traditions, which he embodied in a series of articles in *The Chautauquan* in 1911–12, gives the following as a possible origin. A party of Seneca Indians were fishing in the lake and caught a large muskallonge. They laid it in their canoe, and going ashore carried the canoe over the well-known portage to Lake Erie. To their surprise, they found the big fish still alive, for it leaped from the boat into the water, and escaped. Up to that time, it is said, no muskallonge had ever been caught in that lake; but the eggs in that fish propagated their kind, until it became abundant. In the Seneca language, *ga-jah* means fish; and *ga-da-quah* is "taken out" or as some say, "leaped out." Thus Chautauqua means "where the fish was taken out," or "the place of the leaping fish." The name was smoothed out by the French explorers, who were the earliest white men in this region, to "Tchadakoin," still perpetuated in the stream, Chadakoin, connecting the lake with the Allegheny River. In an extant letter of George Washington, dated 1788, the lake is called, "Jadaqua."

From the shore of Lake Erie, where Barcelona now stands, to the site of Mayville at the head of Lake Chautauqua ran a well-marked and often-followed Indian trail, over which canoes and furs were carried, connecting the Great Lakes with the river-system of the mid-continent. If among the red-faced warriors of those unknown ages there had arisen a Homer to sing the story of his race, a rival to the Iliad and the Nibelungen might have made these forests famous, for here was the borderland between that remarkable Indian confederacy of central New York, the Iroquois—Five Nations,

—after the addition of the Tuscaroras, the Six Nations—those fierce Assyrians of the Western Continent who barely failed in founding an empire, and their antagonists the Hurons around Lake Erie. The two tribes confronting each other were the Eries of the Huron family and the Senecas of the Iroquois; and theirs was a life and death struggle. Victory was with the Senecas, and tradition tells that the shores of Chautauqua Lake were illuminated by the burning alive of a thousand Erie prisoners.

It is said that the first white man to launch his canoe on Lake Chautauqua was Étienne Brule, a French voyageur. Five years before the landing of the Pilgrims at Plymouth, with a band of friendly Hurons he came over the portage from Lake Erie, and sailed down from Mayville to Jamestown, thence through the Chadakoin to the Allegheny and the Ohio, showing to the French rulers in Canada that by this route lay the path to empire over the continent.

Fifteen years later, in 1630, La Salle, the indomitable explorer and warrior, passed over the portage and down the lake to the river below. Fugitives from the French settlements in Nova Scotia, the Acadia of Longfellow's *Evangeline*, also passed over the same trail and watercourses in their search for a southern home under the French flag. In 1749, Captain Bienville de Celoron led another company of pioneers, soldiers, sailors, Indians, and a Jesuit priest over the same route, bearing with him inscribed leaden plates to be buried in prominent places, as tokens of French sovereignty over these forests and these waters. Being a Frenchman, and therefore perhaps inclined to gayety, he might have been happy if he could have foreseen that in a coming age, the most elaborate amusement park on the border of Tchadakoin (as he spelled it on his leaden plates) would hand down the name of Celoron to generations then unborn!

In order to make the French domination of this important waterway sure, Governor Duquesne of Canada sent across Lake Erie an expedition, landing at Barcelona, to build a rough wagon-road over the portage to Lake Chautauqua. Traces of this "old French road" may still be seen. Those French surveyors and toilers little dreamed that in seven years their work would become an English thoroughfare, and their empire in the new world would be exploited by the descendants of the Puritan and Huguenot!

During the American Revolution, the Seneca tribe of Indians, who had espoused the British side, established villages at Bemus and Griffiths points

Steamer in the Outlet

on Lake Chautauqua; and a famous British regiment, "The King's Eighth," still on the rolls of the British army, passed down the lake, and encamped for a time beside the Outlet within the present limits of Jamestown. Thus the redskin, the voyageur, and the redcoat in turn dipped their paddles into the placid waters of Lake Chautauqua. They all passed away, and the American frontiersman took their place; he too was followed by the farmer and the vinedresser. In the last half of the nineteenth century a thriving town, Mayville, was growing at the northern end of the lake; the city of Jamestown was rising at the end of the Outlet; while here and there along the shores were villages and hamlets; roads, such as they were before the automobile compelled their improvement, threaded the forests and fields. A region situated on the direct line of travel between the east and the west, and also having Buffalo on the north and Pittsburgh on the south, could not long remain secluded. Soon the whistle of the locomotive began to wake the echoes of the surrounding hills.

In its general direction the lake lies southeast and northwest, and its widest part is about three miles south of Mayville. Here on its northwestern shore a wide peninsula reaches forth into the water. At the point it is a level plain, covered with stately trees; on the land side it rises in a series of natural terraces marking the altitude and extent of the lake in prehistoric ages; for the present Chautauqua Lake is only the shrunken hollow of a vaster body in the geologic periods. In the early 'seventies of the last century this peninsula was known as Fair Point; but in a few years, baptized with a new name CHAUTAUQUA, it was destined to make the little lake famous throughout the world and to entitle an important chapter in the history of education.

## CHAPTER II

### THE FOUNDERS

EVERY idea which becomes a force in the world has its primal origin in a living man or woman. It drops as a seed into one mind, grows up to fruitage, and from one man is disseminated to a multitude. The Chautauqua Idea became incarnate in two men, John Heyl Vincent and Lewis Miller, and by their coördinated plans and labors made itself a mighty power. Let us look at the lives of these two men, whose names are ever one in the minds of intelligent Chautauquans.

John Heyl Vincent was of Huguenot ancestry. The family came from the canton of Rochelle, a city which was the Protestant capital of France in the period of the Reformation. From this vicinity Levi Vincent (born 1676), a staunch Protestant, emigrated to America in the persecuting days of Louis XIV., and settled first at New Rochelle, N. Y., later removed to New Jersey, and died there in 1736. For several generations the family lived in New Jersey; but at the time of John Heyl Vincent's birth on February 23, 1832, his father, John Himrod Vincent, the great-great-grandson of the Huguenot refugee, was dwelling at Tuscaloosa, Alabama. Dr. Vincent used to say that he began his ministry before he was six years old, preaching to the little negroes around his home. The family moved during his early childhood to a farm near Lewisburg, Pa., on Chillisquasque Creek, where at the age of fifteen he taught in the public school.

When not much above sixteen he was licensed as a local preacher in the Methodist Episcopal Church. He soon became a junior preacher on a four weeks' circuit along the Lehigh River, which at that time seems to have been in the bounds of the old Baltimore Conference. He rode his circuit on horseback, with a pair of saddlebags behind him, and boarded 'round among his parishioners. His saintly mother, of whose character and influence he always spoke in the highest reverence, died at this time, and soon after he went to visit relatives in Newark, N. J. There he served as an assistant in the city mission, and at the same time studied in the Wesleyan Academy on High Street. A fellow student, who became and continued through a long life one of his most intimate friends, the Rev. George H. Whitney, said that young Vincent differed from most of his classmates in his eager desire for education, his appetite for book-knowledge leading him to read almost every volume that came his way, and his visions, then supposed to be mere dreams, of plans for the intellectual uplift of humanity. It was his keenest sorrow that he could not realize his intense yearning for a course in college; but perhaps his loss in youth became a nation's gain in his maturer years.

In 1853 he was received formally as a member "on trial" in the New Jersey Conference, at that time embracing the entire State. His first charge as pastor was at North Belleville, later known as Franklin, now Nutley, where a handsome new church bears his name and commemorates his early ministry. His second charge was at a small suburb of Newark, then called Camptown, now the thriving borough of Irvington. His ministry from the beginning had been marked by an interest in childhood and youth, and a strong effort to strengthen the work of the Sunday School. At Camptown he established a definite course of Bible teaching for teachers and young people. Near the church he staked out a map of Palestine, marked its mountains and streams, its localities and battlefields, and led his teachers and older scholars on pilgrimages from Dan to Beersheba, pausing at each of the sacred places while a member of the class told its story. The lessons of that Palestine Class, taught on the peripatetic plan in the fifties, are still in print, showing the requirements for each successive grade of Pilgrim, Resident in Palestine, Dweller in Jerusalem, Explorer of other Bible Lands, and after a final and searching examination, Templar, wearing a gold medal. At each of his pastoral charges after this, he conducted his Palestine Class and constructed his outdoor map of the Holy Land. May we not find here the germ destined to grow into the Palestine Park of the Chautauqua Assembly?

After four years in New Jersey young Vincent was transferred in 1857 to Illinois, where in succession he had charge of four churches, beginning with Joliet, where he met a young lady teacher, Miss Elizabeth Dusenbury, of Portville, N. Y., who became his wife, and in the after years by her warm heart, clear head, and wise judgment greatly contributed to her husband's success. He was a year at Mount Morris, the seat of the Rock River Conference Seminary, at which he studied while pastor in the community. For two years, 1860 and '61, he was at Galena, and found in his congregation a quiet ex-army officer, named Ulysses S. Grant, who afterward said when introducing him to President Lincoln, "Dr. Vincent was my pastor at Galena,

Ill., and I do not think that I missed one of his sermons while I lived there." Long after the Civil War days Bishop Vincent expressed in some autobiographical notes his estimate of General Grant. He wrote: "General Grant was one of the loveliest and most reverent of men. He had a strong will under that army overcoat of his, but he was the soul of honor and as reverent as he was brave." After two years at Rockford—two years having been until 1864 the limit for a pastorate in American Methodism—in 1865 he was appointed to Trinity Church, Chicago, then the most important church of his denomination in that city.

Chicago opened the door of opportunity to a wider field. The pastor of Trinity found in that city a group of young men, enthusiasts in the Sunday School, and progressive in their aims. Dr. Vincent at once became a leader among them and by their aid was able to introduce a Uniform Lesson in the schools of the city. He established in 1865 a *Sunday School Quarterly*, which in the following years became the *Sunday School Teacher*, in its editorials and its lesson material setting a new standard for Sunday School instruction. His abilities were soon recognized by the authorities in his church, and he was called to New York to become first General Agent of the Sunday School

Union, the organization directing Methodist Episcopal Sunday Schools throughout the world, and in 1868, secretary and editor. He organized and set in circulation the Berean Uniform Lessons for his denomination, an important link in the chain of events which in 1873 made the Sunday School lessons uniform throughout America and the world. It is the fashion now to depreciate the Uniform Lesson Plan as unpedagogic and unpsychologic; but its inauguration was the greatest forward step ever taken in the evolution of the Sunday School; for it instituted systematic study of the Bible, and especially of the Old Testament; it brought to the service of the teacher the ablest Bible scholars on both sides of the Atlantic; it enabled the teachers of a school, a town, or a city to unite in the preparation of their lessons. Chicago, New York, Brooklyn, Boston, and many other places soon held study-classes of Sunday School teachers, of all grades, of a thousand or more gathered on a week-day to listen to the lectures of great instructors. The Plainfield (N. J.) Railroad Class was not the only group of Sunday School workers who spent their hour on the train passing to and from business in studying together their Sunday School lesson.

Soon after Dr. Vincent assumed the charge of general Sunday School work, having his office in

Old Business Block and Post-Office

New York, he took up his residence in Plainfield, N. J., a suburban city which felt his influence and responded to it for twenty years. Having led the way to one summit in his ideals, he saw other mountain-heights beyond, and continually pointed his followers upward. When he succeeded to the editorship of the *Sunday School Journal*, the teachers' magazine of his church, he found a circulation of about five thousand. With the Uniform Lesson, and his inspiring editorials, it speedily rose to a hundred thousand, and a few years later to two hundred thousand subscribers, while his lesson leaves and quarterlies went into the millions. With voice—that wonderful, awakening, thrilling voice—and with a pen on fire, he appealed everywhere for a training that should fit Sunday School teachers for their great work. He established in many places the Normal Class, and marked out a course of instruction for its students. This was the step which led directly to the *Chautauqua Assembly*, which indeed made some such institution a necessity.

The Normal Class proposed a weekly meeting of Sunday School teachers or of young people seeking preparation for teaching, a definite course of study, examinations at regular stages, and a diploma to those who met its standards. Dr. Vincent conceived the plan of bringing together a large body of teacher-students, who should spend at least a fortnight in daily study, morning and afternoon, and thus accomplish more work than in six months of weekly meetings. He aimed also to have lectures on inspiring themes, with a spice of entertainment to impart variety. While this ideal was rising before him and shaping in his mind, he found a kindred spirit, a genius in invention, and a practical, wise business man whose name was destined to stand beside his own in equal honor wherever and whenever Chautauqua is named—Lewis Miller of Akron, Ohio, the first and until his death in 1899 the only president of Chautauqua.

Lewis Miller was born on July 24, 1829, at Greentown, Ohio. He received in his childhood the limited education in "the three R's—reading, 'riting and 'rithmetic," usual in the country school; and at the age of sixteen was himself a school teacher. In 1849, twenty years old, he began work at the plastering trade, but at the same time was attending school. He became a partner in the manufacturing firm of Aultman, Ball and Co., which soon became Aultman, Miller and Co., and was removed from Greentown to Canton, Ohio. Here, about 1857, Mr. Miller invented and put into successful operation the Buckeye Mower and

Reaper, which made him famous, and with other inventions brought to him a fortune. His home was for many years, and until his death, at Akron. From his earliest years he was interested in education, and especially in education through the Sunday School. He became Sunday School Superintendent of the First Methodist Episcopal Church in Akron, and made it more than most of the Sunday Schools in that generation a *school*, and not merely a meeting for children. He organized a graded system and required his pupils to pass from grade to grade through the door of an examination in Bible knowledge. He was one of the earliest Sunday School superintendents to organize a Normal Class for the equipment and training of young people for teaching in his school. At a certain stage in the promotions every young man and young woman passed one year or two years in the Normal Grade; for which he arranged the course until one was provided by Dr. Vincent after he became Secretary of Sunday School work for the denomination in 1868; and in the planning of that early normal course, Mr. Miller took an active part, for he met in John H. Vincent one who, like himself, held inspiring ideals for the Sunday School, and the two leaders were often in consultation. It was an epoch in the history of the American

Sunday School when Mr. Miller built the first Sunday School hall in the land according to a plan originated by himself; its architectural features being wrought out under his direction by his fellow-townsman and friend, Mr. Jacob Snyder, an architect of distinction. In this building, then unique but now followed by thousands of churches, there was a domed central assembly hall, with rooms radiating from it in two stories, capable of being open during the general exercises, but closed in the lesson period so that each class could be alone with its teacher while studying.

Mr. Miller was also interested in secular education, was for years president of the Board of Education in Akron, always aiming for higher standards in teaching. He was also a trustee of Mount Union College in his own State. Two men such as Vincent and Miller, both men of vision, both leaders in education through the Sunday School, both aiming to make that institution more efficient, would inevitably come together; and it was fortunate that they were able to work hand in hand, each helping the other.

These two men had thoughts of gatherings of Sunday School workers, not in conventions, to hear reports and listen to speeches, not to go for one-day or two- or three-day institutes, but to spend weeks together in studying the Bible and methods of Sunday School work. They talked over their plans, and they found that while they had much in common in their conception each one could supplement the other in some of the details. It had been Dr. Vincent's purpose to hold his gathering of Sunday School workers and Bible students within the walls of a large church, in some city centrally located and easily reached by railroad. He suggested to Mr. Miller that his new Sunday School building, with its many classrooms opening into one large assembly hall, would be a suitable place for launching the new enterprise.

One cannot help asking the question—what would have been the result if Dr. Vincent's proposal had been accepted, and the first Sunday School Assembly had been held in a city and a church? Surely the word "Chautauqua" would never have appeared as the name of a new and mighty movement in education. Moreover, it is almost certain that the movement itself would never have arisen to prominence and to power. It is a noteworthy fact that no Chautauqua Assembly has ever succeeded, though often attempted, in or near a large city. One of the most striking and drawing features of the Chautauqua movement has been its out-of-doors and in-the-woods habitat. The two founders did not dream in those days of decision that the fate of a great educational system was hanging in the balance.

An inspiration came to Lewis Miller to hold the projected series of meetings in a forest, and under the tents of a camp meeting. Camp meetings had been held in the United States since 1799, when the first gathering of this name took place in a grove on the banks of the Red River in Kentucky led by two brothers McGee, one a Presbyterian, the other a Methodist. In those years churches were few and far apart through the hamlets and villages of the west and south. The camp meeting brought together great gatherings of people who for a week or more listened to sermons, held almost continuous prayer meetings, and called sinners to repentance. The interest died down somewhat in the middle of the nineteenth century, but following the Civil War, a wave of enthusiasm for camp meetings swept over the land. In hundreds of groves, east and west, land was purchased or leased, lots were sold, tents were pitched, and people by the thousand gathered for soul-stirring services. In one of the oldest and most successful of these camp meetings, that on Martha's Vineyard, tents had largely given place to houses, and a city had arisen in the forest. This example had been followed, and on many camp-meeting grounds houses of a primitive sort straggled around the open circle where the preaching services were held. Most of these buildings were mere sheds, destitute of architectural beauty, and innocent even of paint on their walls of rough boards. Many of these antique structures may still be seen at Chautauqua, survivals of the camp-meeting period, in glaring contrast with the more modern summer homes beside them.

At first Dr. Vincent did not take kindly to the thought of holding his training classes and their accompaniments in any relationship to a camp meeting or even upon a camp ground. He was not in sympathy with the type of religious life manifested and promoted at these gatherings. The fact that they dwelt too deeply in the realm of emotion and excitement, that they stirred the feelings to the neglect of the reasoning and thinking faculties, that the crowd called together on a camp-meeting ground would not represent the sober, sane, thoughtful element of church life—all these repelled Dr. Vincent from the camp meeting.

Mr. Miller had recently become one of the trustees of a camp meeting held at Fair Point on Lake Chautauqua, and proposed that Dr. Vincent should visit the place with him. Somewhat unwillingly, yet with an open mind, Vincent rode with Miller by train to Lakewood near the foot of the lake, and then in a small steamer sailed to Fair Point. A small boy was with them, sitting in the prow of the boat, and as it touched the wharf he was the first of its passengers to leap on the land—and in after years, George Edgar Vincent, LL.D., was wont to claim that he, at the mature age of nine years, was the original discoverer of Chautauqua!

It was in the summer of 1873, soon after the fourth session of the Erie Conference Camp Meeting of the Methodist Episcopal Church, that Dr. Vincent came, saw, and was conquered. His normal class and its subsidiary lectures and entertainments should be held under the beeches, oaks, and maples shading the terraced slopes rising up from Lake Chautauqua.

A lady who had attended the camp meeting in 1871, its second session upon the grounds at Fair Point, afterward wrote her first impressions of the place. She said that the superintendent of the grounds, Mr. Pratt (from whom an avenue at Chautauqua received its name some years afterward), told her that until May, 1870, "the sound of an axe had not been heard in those woods." This lady (Mrs. Kate P. Bruch) wrote:

Old Amphitheater

Old Auditorium in Miller Park

Many of the trees were immense in size, and in all directions, from the small space occupied by those who were tenting there, we could walk through seas of nodding ferns; while everywhere through the forest was a profusion of wild flowers, creeping vines, murmuring pine, beautiful mosses and lichens. The lake itself delighted us with its lovely shores; where either highly cultivated lands dotted with farmhouses, or stretches of pine forest, met on all sides the cool, clear water that sparkled or danced in the sunlight, or gave subdued but beautiful reflection of the moonlight. We were especially charmed with the narrow, tortuous outlet of the lake—then so closely resembling the streams of tropical climes. With the trees pressing closely to the water's edge, covered with rich foliage, tangled vines clinging and swaying from their branches; and luxuriant undergrowth, through which the bright cardinal flowers were shining, it was not difficult to fancy one's self far from our northern clime, sailing over water that never felt the cold clasp of frost and snow.

The steamers winding their way through the romantic outlet were soon to be laden with new throngs looking for the first time upon forest, farms, and lake. Those ivy-covered and moss-grown terraces of Fair Point were soon to be trodden by the feet of multitudes; and that camp-meeting stand from which fervent appeals to repentance had sounded forth, to meet responses of raptured shouts from saints, and cries for mercy from seekers, was soon to become the arena for religious thought and aspiration of types contrasted with those of the camp meeting of former years.

## CHAPTER III

### SOME PRIMAL PRINCIPLES

WE have looked at the spot chosen for this new movement, and we have become somewhat acquainted with its two leaders. Let us now look at its foundations, and note the principles upon which it was based. We shall at once perceive that the original plans of the Fair Point Assembly were very narrow in comparison with those of Chautauqua to-day. Yet those aims were of such a nature, like a Gothic Church, as would readily lend themselves to enlargement on many sides, and only add to the unique beauty of the structure.

In this chapter we are not undertaking to set forth the Chautauqua Idea, as it is now realized—education for everybody, everywhere, and in every department of knowledge, inspired by a Christian faith. Whatever may have been in the mind of either founder, this wide-reaching aim was not in those early days made known. Both Miller and Vincent were interested in education, and each of them felt his own lack of college training, but during the first three or four years of Chautauqua's history all its aims were in the line of religious education through the Sunday School. We are not to look for the traits of its later development, in those primal days. Ours is the story of an evolution, and not a philosophical treatise.

The first assembly on Chautauqua Lake was held under the sanction and direction of the governing Sunday School Board of the Methodist Episcopal Church, by resolution of the Board in New York at its meeting in October, 1873, in response to a request from the executive committee of the Chautauqua Lake Camp Ground Association, and upon the recommendation of Dr. Vincent, whose official title was Corresponding Secretary of the Sunday School Union of the Methodist Episcopal Church. The Normal Committee of the Union was charged with the oversight of the projected meetings; Lewis Miller was appointed President, and John H. Vincent, Superintendent of Instruction.

Although held upon a camp ground and inheriting some of the camp-meeting opportunities, the gathering was planned to be unlike a camp meeting in its essential features, and to reach a constituency outside that of the camp ground. Its name was a new one, "The Assembly," and its sphere was announced to be that of the Sunday School. There was to be a definite and carefully prepared program of a distinctly educational cast, with no opening for spontaneous, go-as-you-please meetings to be started at any moment. This was arranged to keep a quietus on both the religious enthusiast and the wandering Sunday School orator who expected to make a speech on every occasion. On my first visit to Fair Point—which was not in '74 but in '75—I found a prominent Sunday School talker from my own State, gripsack in hand, leaving the ground. He explained, "This is no place for me. They have a cut-and-dried program, and a fellow can't get a word in anywhere. I'm going home. Give me the convention where a man can speak if he wants to."

In most of the camp meetings, but not in all, Sunday was the great day, a picnic on a vast scale, bringing hundreds of stages, carryalls, and wagons from all quarters, special excursion trains loaded with visitors, fleets of boats on the lake or river, if the ground could be reached by water route. No doubt some good was wrought. Under the spell of a stirring preacher some were turned from sin to righteousness. But much harm was also done, in the emptying of churches for miles around, the bringing together of a horde of people intent on pleasure, and utter confusion taking the place of a sabbath-quiet which should reign on a ground consecrated to worship. Against this desecration of the holy day, Miller and Vincent set themselves firmly. As a condition of accepting the invitation of the Camp Meeting Association to hold the proposed Assembly at Fair Point, the gates were to be absolutely closed against all visitors on Sunday; and notice was posted that no boats would be allowed to land on that day at the Fair Point pier. In those early days everybody came to Fair Point by boat. There was indeed a back-door entrance on land for teams and foot passengers; but few entered through it. In these modern days of electricity, now that the lake is girdled with trolley lines, and a hundred automobiles stand parked outside the gates, the back door has become the front door, and the steamboats are comparatively forsaken.

In addition to the name Assembly, the exact order of exercises, and the closed ground on Sunday, there was another startling departure from camp-meeting usages—a gate fee. The overhead expenses of a camp meeting were comparatively light. Those were not the days when famous evangelists like Sam Jones and popular preachers such as DeWitt Talmage received two hundred dollars for a Sunday sermon. Board and keep were the rewards of the ministers, and the "keep" was a bunk in the preachers' tent. The needed funds were raised by collections, which though nominally "voluntary" were often obtained under high-pressure methods. But the Assembly, with well-known lecturers, teachers of recognized ability, and the necessary nation-wide advertising to awaken interest in a new movement would of necessity be expensive. How should the requisite dollars by the thousand be raised? The two heads of the Assembly resolved to dispense with the collections, and have a gate fee for all comers. Fortunately the Fair Point grounds readily lent themselves to this plan, for they were already surrounded on three sides by a high picket-fence, and only the small boys knew where the pickets were loose, and they didn't tell.

The Sunday closing and the entrance charge raised a storm of indignation all around the lake. The steamboat owners—in those days there were no steamer corporations; each boat big or little, was owned by its captain—the steamboat owners saw plainly that Sunday would be a "lost day" to them if the gates were closed; and the thousands of visitors to the camp meeting who had squeezed out a dime, or even a penny, when the basket went around, bitterly complained outside the gates at a quarter for daily admission, half of what they had cheerfully handed over when the annual circus came to town. During the first Assembly in 1874, the gatekeepers needed all their patience and politeness to restrain some irate visitors from coming to blows over the infringement of their right to free entrance upon the Fair Point Camp Ground. There were holders of leases upon lots who expected free entrance for themselves and their families—and "family" was stretched to include visitors. Then there were the preachers who could not comprehend why *they* should buy a ticket for entrance to the holy ground! The financial and restrictive regulations were left largely to Lewis Miller, who possessed the *suaviter in modo* so graciously that many failed to realize underneath it the *fortiter in re*. Behind that smiling countenance of the President of Chautauqua was an uncommonly stiff backbone. Rules once fixed were kept in the teeth of opposition from both sinners and saints.

Let me anticipate some part of our story by saying that at the present time there are from six to eight hundred all-the-year residents upon Chautauqua grounds. Before the Assembly opens on July 1st, every family must obtain season

The Old Guest House. "The Ark"

Old Children's Temple

tickets to the public exercises for all except the very youngest members and bedridden invalids. A lease upon Chautauqua property does not entitle the holder to admission to the grounds. If he owns an automobile, it must be parked outside, and cannot be brought through the gates without the payment of an entrance fee, and an officer riding beside the chauffeur to see that in Chautauqua's narrow streets and thronged walks all care is taken against accident. The only exception to this rule is in favor of physicians who are visiting patients within the enclosure.

The catholicity of the plans for the first Assembly must not be forgotten. Both its founders were members of the Methodist Episcopal Church and loyal to its institutions. But they were also believers in and members of the Holy Catholic Church, the true church of Christ on earth, wherein every Christian body has a part. They had no thought to ignore the various denominations, but aimed to make every follower of Christ at home. Upon the program appeared the names of men eminent in all the churches; and it was a felicitous thought to hold each week on one evening the prayer meetings of the several churches, each by itself, also to plan on one afternoon in different places on the ground, for denominational conferences where the members of each church could freely discuss their own problems and provide for their own interests. This custom established at the first assembly has become one of the traditions of Chautauqua. Every Wednesday evening, from seven to eight, is assigned for denominational prayer meetings, and on the second Wednesday afternoon in August, two hours are set apart for the Denominational Conferences. The author of this volume knows something about one of those meetings; for year after year it has brought him to his wit's end, to provide a program that will not be a replica of the last one, and then sometimes, to persuade the conferences to confer. But if a list were made of the noble names that have taken part in these gatherings, it would show that the interdenominational plan of the founders has been justified by the results. It is a great fact that for nearly fifty years the loyal members of almost every church in the land have come together at Chautauqua, all in absolute freedom to speak their minds, yet with never the least friction or controversy. And this relation was not one of an armed neutrality between bodies in danger of breaking out into open war. It did not prevent a good-natured raillery on the Chautauqua platform between speakers of different denominations.

If anyone had a joke at the expense of the Baptists or the Methodists or the Presbyterians, he never hesitated to tell it before five thousand people, even with the immediate prospect of being demolished by a retort from the other side.

A conversation that occurred at least ten years after the session of '74 belongs here logically, if not chronologically. A tall, long-coated minister whose accent showed his nativity in the southern mountain-region said to me, "I wish to inquire, sir, what is the doctrinal platform of this assembly." "There is none, so far as I know," I answered. "You certainly do not mean, sir," he responded, "that there is not an understanding as to the doctrines allowed to be taught on this platform. Is there no statement in print of the views that must or must not be expressed by the different speakers?" "I never heard of any," I said, "and if there was such a statement I think that I should know about it." "What, sir, is there to prevent any speaker from attacking the doctrines of some other church, or even from speaking against the fundamental doctrines of Christianity?" "Nothing in the world," I said, "except that nobody at Chautauqua ever wishes to attack any other Christian body. If anyone did such a thing, I don't believe that it would be thought necessary to disown or even to answer him. But I am quite certain that it would be his last appearance on the Chautauqua platform."

In this chapter I have sought to point out the foundation stones of Chautauqua, as they were laid nearly half a century ago. Others were placed later in the successive years; but these were the original principles, and these have been maintained for more than a generation. Let us fix them in memory by a restatement and an enumeration. First, Chautauqua, now an institution for general and popular education, began in the department of religion as taught in the Sunday School. Second, it was an out-of-doors school, held in the forest, blazing the way and setting the pace of summer schools in the open air throughout the nation and the world. Third, although held upon a camp-meeting ground it was widely different in aim and method, spirit and clientele from the old-fashioned camp meeting. Fourth, it maintained the sanctity of the Sabbath, closed its gates, and frowned upon every attempt to secularize or commercialize the holy day, or to make it a day of pleasure. Fifth, the enterprise was supported, not by collections at its services, or by contributions from patrons, but by a fee upon entrance from every comer. Sixth, it was to represent not one branch of the church, but to bring together all the churches in acquaintance and friendship, to promote, not church union, but church unity. And seventh, let it be added that it was to be in no sense a money-making institution. There were trustees but no stockholders, and no dividends. If any funds remained after paying the necessary expenses, they were to be used for improvement of the grounds or the enlargement of the program. Upon these foundations Chautauqua has stood and has grown to greatness.

## CHAPTER IV

### THE BEGINNINGS

But let us come to the opening session of the Assembly, destined to greater fortune and fame than even its founders at that time dreamed. It was named "The Sunday School Teachers' Assembly," for the wider field of general education then lay only in the depths of one founder's mind. For the sake of history, let us name the officers of this first Assembly. They were as follows:

Chairman—Lewis Miller, Esq., of Akron, Ohio.
Department of Instruction—Rev. John H. Vincent, D.D., of New York.
Department of Entertainment—Rev. R. W. Scott, Mayville, N. Y.
Department of Supplies—J. E. Wesener, Esq., Akron, Ohio.
Department of Order—Rev. R. M. Warren, Fredonia, N. Y.
Department of Recreation—Rev. W. W. Wythe, M.D., Meadville, Pa.
Sanitary Department—J. C. Stubbs, M.D., Corry, Pa.

The property of the Camp Meeting Association, leased for the season to the Assembly, embraced less than one fourth of the present dimensions of Chautauqua, even without the golf course and other property outside the gates. East and west it extended as it does now from the Point and the Pier to the public highway. But on the north where Kellogg Memorial Hall now stands was the boundary indicated by the present Scott Avenue, though at that time unmarked. The site of Normal Hall and all north of it were outside the fence. And on the south its boundary was the winding way of Palestine Avenue. The ravine now covered by the Amphitheater was within the bounds, but the site of the Hotel Athenæum was without the limit.

He who rambles around Chautauqua in our day sees a number of large, well-kept hotels, and many inns and "cottages" inviting the visitor to comfortable rooms and bountiful tables. But in those early days there was not one hotel or boarding-house at Fair Point. Tents could be rented, and a cottager might open a room for a guest, but it was forbidden to supply table board for pay. Everybody, except such as did their own cooking, ate their meals at the dining-hall, which was a long tabernacle of rough unpainted boards, with a leaky roof, and backless benches where the feeders sat around tables covered with oilcloth. And as for the meals—well, if there was high thinking at Chautauqua there was certainly plain living. Sometimes it rained, and D.D.'s, LL.D.'s, professors, and plain people held up umbrellas with one hand and tried to cut tough steaks with the other. But nobody complained at the fare, for the feast of reason and flow of soul made everybody forget burnt potatoes and hard bread.

What is now Miller Park, the level ground and lovely grove at the foot of the hill, was then the Auditorium, where stood a platform and desk sheltered from sun on some days and rain on others. Before it was an array of seats, lacking backs, instead of which the audience used their own backbones. Perhaps two thousand people could find sitting-room under the open sky, shaded by the noble trees. A sudden shower would shoot up a thousand umbrellas. One speaker said that happening to look up from his manuscript he perceived that an acre of toadstools had sprouted in a minute. At the lower end of this park stood the tent wherein Dr. Vincent dwelt during many seasons; at the upper end was the new cottage of the Miller family with a tent frame beside it for guests. At this Auditorium all the great lectures were given for the

Lewis Miller, Cottage and Tent

Bishop Vincent's Tent-Cottage

first four years of Chautauqua history, except when continued rain forbade. Then an adjournment, sometimes hasty, was made to a large tent up the hill, known as the Tabernacle.

One day, during the second season of the Assembly in 1875, Professor William F. Sherwin, singer, chorus leader, Bible teacher, and wit of the first water, was conducting a meeting in the Auditorium. The weather had been uncertain, an "open and shut day," and people hardly knew whether to meet for Sherwin's service in the grove or in the tent on the hill. Suddenly a tall form, well known at Chautauqua, came tearing down the hill and up the steps of the platform, breathless, wild-eyed, with mop of hair flying loose, bursting into the professor's address with the words, "Professor Sherwin, I come as a committee of fifty to invite you to bring your meeting up to the Tabernacle, safe from the weather, where a large crowd is gathered!" "Well," responded Sherwin, "you may be a committee of fifty, but you look like sixty!" And from that day ever after at Chautauqua a highly respected gentleman from Washington, D. C., was universally known as "the man who looks like sixty."

When we speak of Sherwin, inevitably we think of Frank Beard, the cartoonist, whose jokes were as original as his pictures. He would draw in presence of the audience a striking picture, seemingly serious, and then in a few quick strokes transform it into something absurdly funny. For instance, his "Moses in the Bulrushes" was a beautiful baby surrounded by waving reeds. A sudden twist of the crayon, and lo, a wild bull was charging at the basket and its baby. This was "The Bull Rushes." Beard was as gifted with tongue as with pen, and in the comradeship of the Chautauqua platform he and Sherwin were continually hurling jokes at each other. Oftentimes the retort was so pat that one couldn't help an inward question whether the two jesters had not arranged it in advance.

Frank Beard used to hold a question drawer occasionally. There was a show of collecting questions from the audience, but those to be answered had been prepared by Mr. Beard and his equally witty wife, and written on paper easily recognized. One by one, these were taken out, read with great dignity, and answered in a manner that kept the crowd in a roar. On one occasion Professor Sherwin was presiding at Mr. Beard's question drawer—for it was the rule that at every meeting there must be a chairman as well as the speaker. The question was drawn out, "Will Mr.

Beard please explain the difference between a natural consequence and a miracle?" Mr. Beard *did* explain thus: "This difficult question can be answered by a very simple illustration. There is Professor Sherwin. If Professor Sherwin says to me, 'Mr. Beard, lend me five dollars,' and I should let him have it, that would be *a natural consequence*. If Professor Sherwin should ever pay it back, *that* would be a miracle!" It is needless to say that the opportunity soon arrived for Mr. Sherwin to repay Mr. Beard for full value of debt with abundant interest.

Mention has been made that at each address or public platform meeting a chairman must be in charge. In the old camp-meeting days all the ministers had been wont to sit on the platform behind the preacher; and some of them could not reconcile themselves to Dr. Vincent's rule that *only* the chairman and the speaker of the hour should occupy "the preachers' stand." Notwithstanding repeated announcements, some clergymen continued to invade the platform. The head of the Department of Order once pointed to a well-known minister and said to the writer, "Four times I have told that man—and a good man he is—that he must not take a seat on the platform." Whoever casts his eyes on the platform of the Amphitheater may notice that before every public service, the janitor places just the number of chairs needed, and no more. This is one of the Chautauqua traditions, begun under the Vincent régime.

Before we come to the more serious side of our story let us notice another instance of the contrast between the camp meeting and Chautauqua. A widely known Methodist came, bringing with him a box of revival song-books, compiled by himself. He was a leader of a "praying band," and accustomed to hold meetings where the enthusiasm was pumped up to a high pitch. One Sunday at a certain hour he noticed that the Auditorium in the grove was unoccupied; and gathering a group of friends with warm hearts and strong voices, he mounted the platform and in stentorian tones began a song from his own book. The sound brought people from all the tents and cottages around, and soon his meeting was in full blast, with increasing numbers responding to his ardent appeals. Word came to Dr. Vincent who speedily marched into the arena. He walked upon the platform, held up his hand in a gesture compelling silence, and calling upon the self-appointed leader by name, said:

"This meeting is not on the program, nor appointed by the authorities, and it cannot be held."

"What?" spoke up the praying-band commander. "Do you mean to say that we can't have a service of song and prayer on these grounds?"

"Yes," replied Dr. Vincent, "I do mean it. No meeting of any kind can be held without the order of the authorities. You should have come to me for permission to hold this service."

The man was highly offended, gathered up his books, and left the grounds on the next day. He would have departed at once, but it was Sunday, and the gates were closed. Let it be said, however, that six months later, when he had thought it over, he wrote to Dr. Vincent an ample apology for his conduct and said that he had not realized the difference between a camp meeting and a Sunday School Assembly. He ended by an urgent request that Dr. Vincent should come to the camp ground at Round Lake, of which he was president, should organize and conduct an assembly to be an exact copy of Chautauqua in its program and speakers, with all the resources of Round Lake at his command. His invitation was accepted. In due time, with this man's loyal support, Dr. Vincent organized and set in motion the Round Lake Assembly, upon the Chautauqua pattern, which continues to this day, true to the ideals of the founder.

One unique institution on the Fair Point of those early days must not be omitted—the Park of Palestine. Following the suggestion of Dr. Vincent's church lawn model of the Holy Land, Dr. Wythe of Meadville, an adept in other trades than physic and preaching, constructed just above the pier on the lake shore a park one hundred and twenty feet long, and seventy-five feet wide, shaped to represent in a general way the contour of the Holy Land. It was necessary to make the elevations six times greater than longitudinal measurements; and if one mountain is made six times as large as it should be, some other hills less prominent in the landscape or less important in the record must be omitted. The lake was taken to represent the Mediterranean Sea, and on the Sea-Coast Plain were located the cities of the Philistines, north of them Joppa and Cæsarea, and far beyond them on the shore, Tyre and Sidon. The Mountain Region showed the famous places of Israelite history from Beersheba to Dan, with the sacred mountains Olivet and Zion, Ebal and Gerizim having Jacob's Well beside them, Gilboa with its memories of Gideon's victory and King Saul's defeat, the mountain on whose crown our Lord preached his sermon, and overtopping all, Hermon, where he was transfigured. From two springs flowed little rills to represent the sources of the River Jordan which wound its way down the valley, through the two lakes, Merom and the Sea of Galilee, ending its course in the Dead Sea. There were Jericho and the Brook Jabbok, the clustered towns around the Galilean Sea, and at the foot of Mount Hermon, Cæsarea-Philippi. Across the Jordan rose the Eastern Tableland, with its mountains and valleys and brooks and cities even as far as Damascus.

As the Assembly was an experiment, and might be transferred later to other parts of the country, the materials for this Palestine Park were somewhat temporary. The mountains were made of stumps, fragments of timber, filled in with sawdust from a Mayville mill, and covered with grassy sods. But the park constructed from makeshift materials proved one of the most attractive features of the encampment. Groups of Bible students might be seen walking over it, notebooks in their hands, studying the sacred places. A few would even pluck and preserve a spear of grass, carefully enshrining it in an envelope duly marked. A report went abroad, indeed, that soil from the Holy Land itself had been spread upon the park, constituting it a sort of Campo Santo, but this claim was never endorsed by either its architect or its originator.

The park of Palestine still stands, having been rebuilt several times, enlarged to a length of 350 feet, and now, as I write, with another restoration promised.

One fact in this sacred geography must needs be stated, in the interests of exact truth. In order to make use of the lake shore, north had to be in the south, and east in the west. Chautauqua has always been under a despotic though paternal government, and its visitors easily accommodate themselves to its decrees. But the sun persists in its independence, rises over Chautauqua's Mediterranean Sea where it should set, and continues its sunset over the mountains of Gilead, where it should rise. Dr. Vincent and Lewis Miller could bring to pass some remarkable, even seemingly impossible, achievements, but they were not able to outdo Joshua, and not only make the sun stand still, but set it moving in a direction opposite to its natural course.

In one of his inimitable speeches, Frank Beard said that Palestine Park had been made the model for all the beds on Fair Point. He slept, as he asserted, on Palestine, with his head on Mount Hermon, his body sometimes in the Jordan valley, at other times on the mountains of Ephraim; and one night when it rained, he found his feet in the Dead Sea.

In the early days of Chautauqua a tree was standing near Palestine Park, which invited the attention of every child, and many grown folks. It was called "the spouting tree." Dr. Wythe found a tree with one branch bent over near the ground and hollow. He placed a water-pipe in the branch and sent a current of fresh water through it, so that the tree seemed to be pouring forth water. At all times a troop of children might be seen around it. At least one little girl made her father walk down every day to the wonder, to the neglect of other walks on the Assembly ground. Afterward at home from an extended tour, they asked her what was the most wonderful thing that she had seen in her journey. They expected her to say, "Niagara Falls," but without hesitation she answered, "The tree that spouted water at Chautauqua." The standards of greatness in the eyes of childhood differ from those of the grown-up folks.

The true Chautauqua, aided as it was by the features of mirth and entertainment and repartee, was in the daily program followed diligently by the assembled thousands. Here is in part the schedule, taken from the printed report. It was opened on Tuesday evening, August 4, 1874, in the out-of-doors auditorium, now Miller Park, beginning with a brief responsive service of Scripture and song, prepared by Dr. Vincent. Chautauqua clings to ancient customs; and that same service, word for word, has been rendered every year on the first Tuesday evening in August, at what is known as "Old First Night."

Bishop Vincent afterward wrote of that memorable first meeting:

> The stars were out, and looked down through trembling leaves upon a goodly well-wrapped company, who sat in the grove, filled with wonder and hope. No electric light brought platform and people face to face that night. The old-fashioned pine fires on rude four-legged stands covered with earth, burned with unsteady, flickering flame, now and then breaking into brilliancy by the contact of a resinous stick of the rustic fireman, who knew how to snuff candles and how to turn light on the crowd of campers-out. The white tents around the enclosure were very beautiful in that evening light.

At this formal opening on August 4, 1874, brief addresses were given by Dr. Vincent and by a Baptist, a Presbyterian, a Methodist, and a Congregational pastor. This opening showed the broad brotherhood which was to mark the history of Chautauqua.

On the next day, Wednesday, began what might be called the school sessions of the Assembly. The fourteen days were divided into three terms.

Old Steamer "Jamestown"

Oriental House; Museum

Every morning at 8 o'clock a brief service of prayer and Bible reading began the day in the auditorium, now Miller Park. At 8:15 during the first term, August 4th–9th, a conference was held of Normal Class and Institute conductors, at which reports were rendered of work done, courses of study, and methods of work, and results obtained. In those days when training classes for Sunday School teachers were almost unknown, this series of conferences, attended by hundreds of workers, proved of infinite value, and set in motion classes in many places. At 9 o'clock, section meetings were held for superintendents and pastors, and teachers of the different grades, from the primary class to the adult Bible class.

The Normal Class held its sessions during the second term, from August 10th–13th, and the third term, August 14th–18th. Four classes were held simultaneously in different tents, with teachers changed each day. At these classes most of the lessons were on the Bible—its Evidences, Books and Authors, Geography, History, and Interpretation. The topics pertaining to the teacher and the class were taken up in the different conferences. The Normal Class was held to be the core and life of the Assembly, and everybody was urged to attend its sessions. All whose names began with letters from

A to G were to attend regularly Tent A. Those with initials from H to M were to go to Tent B, and so on through the alphabet, to the four Normal Tents. But the students soon found their favorite teachers, would watch for them, and follow them into their different tents. There was another infraction of the program. The blackboard was a new feature in Sunday School work, and not enough blackboards of good quality had been secured. Some were too small, some were not black enough, and one was painted with the lines for music. It is reported that some of the teachers bribed the janitor to provide for their use the good boards. There is even the tale that a Sunday School leader was seen stealing a blackboard and replacing it in another's tent by an inferior one. We humbly trust that this report was false.

That the Normal Class, the conferences, and the lectures on Sunday School work were taken seriously is shown by the report of the written examination, held on Monday, August 17th, the day before the Assembly closed. More than two hundred people sat down in the Tabernacle on the hill, each furnished with fifty questions on the Bible and the Sunday School. Twenty or more dropped out, but at the end of the nearly five hours' wrestling one hundred and eighty-four papers were handed in. Three of these were marked absolutely perfect, those of the Rev. C. P. Hard, on his way to India as a missionary, Mr. Caleb Sadler of Iowa, and the Rev. Samuel McGerald of New York. Ninety-two were excellent, fifty more were passed, making one hundred and forty-five accepted members of the Normal Alumni Association; eighteen had their papers returned to be rewritten after further study, and the lowest fourteen were consigned to the wastebasket.

The *Western Christian Advocate* gave a picture of the first normal examination at Chautauqua, which we republish.

The tent is a very large one, and was plentifully supplied with benches, chairs, camp-stools, etc. The spectacle was very imposing. The ladies seemed a little in the majority. There were two girls under fifteen, and one boy in his fourteenth year. Each was provided with paper, and each wore a more or less silent and thoughtful air. There was no shuffling, no listlessness, no whispering. The conductor, with a big stump for his table, occupied a somewhat central position, ready to respond to the call of any uplifted hand. We stood just back of Dr. Vincent, with the scene in full view. To our right, but a little on the outside of the tent, were Bishop Simpson and Dr. Thomas M. Eddy, who remained only a few minutes, as the latter was compelled to take the ten o'clock train for New York. On the same side, and a little nearer to us, were groups of visitors, mostly from the country adjacent, who gazed in rapt astonishment at the sight before them, not daring to inquire the meaning of all this mute array of paper and pencil. A little to our left was a lawyer of large experience and almost national fame, who had removed his hat, collar, coat and cuffs; just by his side was an ex-State senator; and a little further on was a boy from Iowa. He had improvised for his table a small round log, and had gathered together for the better resting of his knees, a good-sized pile of dry beech-leaves. This lad, we learned, had been studying the Normal course during the last year; and we further discovered that he succeeded in answering accurately all but ten or twelve of the fifty questions, one of the to him insoluble and incomprehensible being, "What is the relation of the church to the Sunday School?" Nearly in front of the conductor were two veteran spectacled sisters, who at no time whispered to each other, but kept up a strong thinking and a frequent use of the pencil. Near these sat a mother and daughter from Evanston, Illinois, silent and confident. On the outer row of seats we observed three doctors of divinity, a theological student, the president of an Ohio college, a gentleman connected with the internal revenue, and a lady principal of a young ladies' seminary, all with their thinking-caps admirably adjusted.

At the end of an hour and forty minutes a New York brother, who had been especially active in sectional work, held up his hand in token of success, and his paper was passed up to Dr. Vincent. Shortly afterward another made a similar signal; but nearly all occupied over three hours in the work. Over one half attained to seventy-five or eighty per cent.

Let it be remembered that no matter how long the student was compelled to remain, even long past the dinner hour, he was not permitted to take a recess for his midday meal. He must stay to the end, or give up his examination.

The report of the Assembly shows twenty-two lectures on Sunday School work, theory, and practice; sectional meetings—nine primary, six intermediate, one senior, five of pastors and superintendents, eight normal class and institute conductors' conferences; six Normal Classes in each of the four tents—twenty-four in all; three teachers' meetings for preparation of the Sunday School lesson; four Bible readings; three praise services; two children's meetings; and six sermons. All the leading Protestant churches were represented; and twenty-five States in the Union, besides Ontario, Montreal, Nova Scotia, Ireland, Scotland, and India. Among the preachers we find the names of Dr. H. Clay Trumbull, editor of the *Sunday School Times*, John B. Gough, Bishops Simpson and Janes, Dr. James M. Buckley, Dr. Charles F. Deems, Dr. T. DeWitt Talmage, and four ministers who later became bishops in the Methodist Episcopal Church:—Drs. H. W. Warren, J. F. Hurst, E. O. Haven, and C. H. Fowler.

The two Sundays, August 9th and 16th, were

golden days in the calendar. An atmosphere of quiet and peace reigned throughout the grounds. No steamboats made the air discordant around the pier; the gates were closed and the steamers sailed by to more welcome stations; no excursion trains brought curious and noisy throngs of sightseers. Tents and cottages lay open while their dwellers worshiped under the trees of the Auditorium, for no one was required to watch against thieves in the crowd. The world was shut out, and a voice seemed to be saying, "Come ye yourselves apart and rest awhile."

The day began with a Sundav School graded to embrace both young and old. The riches of officers and teachers formed an embarrassment. For once, nay twice (for there were two Sundays), a Superintendent had at call more instructors than he could supply with classes. On each Sunday the attendance at the school was fifteen hundred.

At the sunset hour each evening an "Eventide Conference" was held on the lake side. The dying day, the peaceful surroundings, the calm sheet of water, the mild air, combined to impart a tone of thoughtful, uplifting meditation. I have heard old Chautauquans speak many times of the inspiring spiritual atmosphere breathed in the very air of the first Chautauqua.

Never before had been brought together for conference and for study so many leaders in the Sunday School army, representing so large a variety of branches in the church catholic. And it was not for a day or two days as in conventions and institutes, but for a solid fortnight of steady work. The Chautauqua of to-day is a widely reaching educational system, embracing almost every department of knowledge. But it must not be forgotten that all this wide realm has grown out of a school to awaken, instruct, and inspire Sunday School workers. In their conception, however, the two famous founders realized that all truth, even that looked upon as secular, is subsidiary, even necessary for successful teaching of the word of God. Hence with the courses of study and conferences upon practical details, we find on the program, some literature and science, with the spice of entertainment and amusement.

The conception of Dr. Vincent was not to locate the Assembly in one place, but from time to time to hold similar meetings on many camp grounds, wherever the opportunity arose. There is a suspicion that Lewis Miller held his own secret purpose to make it so successful on Chautauqua Lake as to insure its permanent location at Fair Point. That was a wise plan, for with settlement in one place, buildings could be erected, and features like Palestine Park could be increased and improved. Whether it was by a suggestion or a common impulse, on the last day of the Assembly a meeting was held and a unanimous appeal was presented to make Fair Point the home of the Assembly. The trustees of the camp meeting shared in the sentiment and offered to receive new members representing the Assembly constituency. As a result, the officiary was reorganized, no longer as a camp meeting but as an Assembly Board. For two years Fair Point was continued as the name of the Post Office, although the title "Chautauqua Sunday School Assembly" was adopted. But soon Fair Point became "Chautauqua" on the list of the Post Office Department, and the old name lingers only in the memory of old Chautauquans.

Before we leave that pioneer Chautauqua, we must recall some of its aspects, which might be forgotten in these later days, at once amusing, perplexing, and sometimes trying. More steamers, great and small, were plying Chautauqua's waters than at the present under the steamboat corporation system. Old Chautauquans will remember that ancient three-decker, *The Jamestown*, with its pair of stern wheels, labeled respectively "Vincent" and "Miller." Each steamer was captained by its owner; and there was often a congestion of boats at the pier, especially after the arrival of an excursion train. Those were not the days of standard time, eastern and central, with watches set an hour fast or slow at certain well-known points. Each boat followed its own standard of time, which might be New York time, Buffalo or Pittsburgh time, forty minutes slower, or even Columbus or Cincinnati time, slower still. Railroads crossing Ohio were required to run on Columbus time. When you were selecting a steamer from the thirty placards on the bulletin board at the Fair Point Post office, in order to meet an Erie train at Lakewood, unless you noticed the time-standard, you might find at the pier that your steamer had gone forty minutes before, or on arriving at Lakewood learn that your boat was running on Cincinnati time, and you were three quarters of an hour late for the train, for even on the Erie of those days, trains were not *always* an hour behind time.

Nor was this variety of "time, times, and half-time" all the drawbacks. When news came that an excursion train was due from Buffalo, every steamboat on the lake would ignore its time-table and the needs of the travelers; and all would be bunched at the Mayville dock and around it to catch the passengers. Or it might be a similar but more tangled crowd of boats in the Outlet at Jamestown to meet a special train from Pittsburgh. Haven't I seen a bishop on the Fair Point pier, who *must* get the train at Lakewood to meet his conference in Colorado, scanning the landscape with not a boat in sight, all piled up three miles away?

Nor were the arrangements for freight and baggage in those early years any more systematic than those for transportation. Although Chautauqua Lake is on the direct line of travel east and west, between New York and Chicago, and north and south between Buffalo and Pittsburgh, Fair Point, the seat of the Assembly, was not a railroad station. Luggage could be checked only to Jamestown, Lakewood, or Mayville, and thence must be sent by boat. Its destination might be indicated by a tag or a chalk mark, or it might remain unmarked. Imagine a steamer deck piled high with trunks, valises, bundles of blankets, furniture, tent equipment, and things miscellaneous, stopping at a dozen points along the lake to have its cargo assorted and put ashore—is it strange that some baggage was left at the wrong place, and its owner wandered around looking vainly for his property? One man remarked that the only way to be sure of your trunk was to sit on it; but what if your

Palestine Park, Looking North

Dead Sea in foreground. Mount Hermon in distance

Tent-Life in 1875

J L. Hurlbut, J A Worden, Frank Beard, J L. Hughes

trunk was on the top or at the bottom of a pile ten feet high? Considering all the difficulties and discomforts of those early days—travel, baggage, no hotels nor boarding houses, a crowded dining hall with a hungry procession outside perhaps in the rain waiting for seats at the tables, the food itself none of the best—it is surprising that some thousands of people not only found the Assembly, but stayed to its conclusion, were happy in it, lived in an enchanted land for a fortnight, and resolved to return the very next year! More than this, they carried its enthusiasm and its ideals home with them and in hundreds of places far apart, the Sunday Schools began to assume a new and higher life. Some time after this, but still early in Chautauqua's history, a prominent Sunday School man expressed to the writer his opinion that "people who came home from Chautauqua became either a mighty help or a mighty nuisance. They brought with them more new ideas than could be put into operation in ten years; and if they couldn't get them, one and all, adopted at once they kicked and growled incessantly."

Before we leave the Assembly of 1874, we must not forget to name one of its most powerful and far-reaching results—the Woman's Christian Temperance Union. This assembly was held soon after the great crusade of 1874 in Ohio, when multitudes of women, holding prayer meetings on the sidewalk in front of liquor saloons literally prayed thousands of them out of existence. While the fire of the crusade was still burning, a number of women held meetings at Chautauqua during the Assembly, and took counsel together concerning the best measures to promote the temperance reform. They united in a call signed by Mrs. Mattie McClellan Brown, Mrs. Jennie Fowler Willing, Mrs. Emily Huntington Miller, and others, for a convention of women to be held in Cleveland, Ohio, November 17, 1874. At this convention, sixteen States were represented, and the national Woman's Christian Temperance Union was organized, an institution which did more than any other to form public sentiment, to make State after State "dry," and finally to establish nation-wide constitutional prohibition. It may not be generally known that this mighty movement began at the first Chautauqua Assembly.

## CHAPTER V

### THE EARLY DEVELOPMENT

CHAUTAUQUA was a lusty infant when it entered upon life in 1874, and it began with a penetrating voice, heard afar. Like all normal babies (normal seems to be the right word just here) it began to grow, and its progress in the forty-seven years of its life thus far (1920) has been the growth of a giant. Territorially, on Chautauqua Lake, it has enlarged at successive stages from twenty acres to more than three hundred and thirty acres, impelled partly by a demand of its increasing family for house-room, educational facilities, and playgrounds, partly from the necessity of controlling its surroundings to prevent occupation by undesirable neighbors. There has been another vast expansion in the establishment of Chautauquas elsewhere, until the continent is now dotted with them. A competent authority informs the writer that within twelve months ten thousand assemblies bearing the generic name Chautauqua have been held in the United States and the Dominion of Canada. There has been a third growth in the intellectual sweep of its plans. We have seen how it began as a system of training for teachers in the Sunday School. We shall trace its advancement into the wider field of general and universal education, a school in every department and for everybody everywhere.

To at least one pilgrim the Assembly of 1875 was monumental, for it marked an epoch in his life. That was the writer of this volume, who in that year made his first visit to Chautauqua. (The general reader who has no interest in personal reminiscences may omit this paragraph.) He traveled by the Erie Railroad, and that evening for the first time in his life saw a berth made up in a sleeping-car, and crawled into it. If in his dreams that night, a vision could have flashed upon his inward eye of what that journey was to bring to him in the coming years, he might have deemed it an Arabian Night's dream. For that visit to Chautauqua, not suddenly but in the after years, changed the entire course of his career. It sent him to Chautauqua thus far for forty-six successive seasons, and perhaps may round him out in a semi-centennial. It took him out of a parsonage, and made him an itinerant on a continent-wide scale. It put him into Dr. Vincent's office as an assistant, and later in his chair as his successor. It dropped him down through the years at Chautauqua assemblies in almost half of the States of this Union. On Tuesday morning, August 3, 1875, I left the train at Jamestown, rode across the city, and embarked in a steamer for a voyage up the lake. As we slowly wound our way through the Outlet—it was on the old steamer *Jamestown* which was never an ocean-greyhound—I felt like an explorer in some unknown river. Over the old pier at Fair Point was the sign, "National S. S. Assembly," and beneath it I stepped ashore on what seemed almost a holy ground, for my first walk was through Palestine Park. On Friday, August 6th, I gave a normal lesson, the first in my life, with fear and trembling. It was on "the city of Jerusalem," and I had practiced on the map until I thought that I could draw it without a copy. But, alas, one of the class must needs come to the blackboard and set my askew diagram in the right relations. Twenty years afterward, at an assembly in Kansas, an old lady spoke to me after a lesson, "I saw you teach your first lesson at Chautauqua. You said that you had never taught a normal class before, and I thought it was the solemn truth. You've improved since then!"

Some new features had been added to the

grounds since the first Assembly. Near Palestine Park was standing a fine model of modern Jerusalem and its surrounding hills, so exact in its reproduction that one day a bishop pointed out the identical building wherein he had lodged when visiting the city—the same hostel, by the way, where this writer stayed afterward in 1897, and from whose roof he took his first view of the holy places. Near Palestine Park, an oriental house had been constructed, with rooms in two stories around an open court. These rooms were filled with oriental and archæological curiosities, making it a museum; and every day Dr. A. O. Von Lennep, a Syrian by birth, stood on its roof and gave in Arabic the Mohammedan call to prayer. I failed to observe, however, the people at Chautauqua prostrating themselves at the summons. Indeed, some of them actually mocked the make-believe muezzin before his face. On the hill, near the Dining Hall, stood a sectional model of the great pyramid, done in lath and plaster, as if sliced in two from the top downward, half of it being shown, and the room inside of it indicated. Also there was a model of the Tabernacle in the Wilderness, covered with its three curtains, and containing within an altar, table, and candlestick. Daily lectures were given before it by the Rev. J. S.

Ostrander, wearing the miter, robe, and breastplate of the high priest.

The evolution of the Chautauqua Idea made some progress at the second Assembly. Instead of eight sessions of the Normal Class, two were held daily. The program report says that fifty normal sessions were held; regularly two each day, one at 8 o'clock in the morning on a Bible topic. Breakfast must be rushed through at seven to brace up the students for their class. Another was held at 3:30, on some subject pertaining to the pupil or the teacher; with extra sessions in order to complete the specified course. A class in Hebrew was held daily by Dr. S. M. Vail, and attended by forty students. Dr. Vail had been for many years professor of Hebrew in the earliest Methodist theological school, the Biblical Institute at Concord, New Hampshire, which afterward became the School of Theology in Boston University. Dr. Vail was an enthusiast in his love of Hebrew language and literature. One who occupied a tent with him—all the workers of that season were lodged in a row of little tents on Terrace Avenue, two in each tent—averred that his trunk contained only a Hebrew Bible (he didn't need a lexicon) and a clean shirt.

Besides the class in Hebrew, Madame Kriege of

New York conducted a class in kindergarten teaching, and Dr. Tourjee of Boston, W. F. Sherwin, and C. C. Case held classes in singing. All these were supposedly for Sunday School teachers, but they proved to be the thin end of the wedge opening the way for the coming summer school.

Even more strongly than at the earlier session, the Normal Class, with a systematic course of instruction in the Bible and Sunday School work, was made the center of the program. It is significant of the importance assigned to this department that for several years, no other meeting, great or small, was permitted at the normal hours. The camp must either attend the classes or stay in its tents.

At this session, Mrs. Frank Beard, noting the insistent announcement of the Normal Classes, and the persistent urging that everybody attend them, was moved to verse. As true poetry is precious, her effusion is here given:

> To Chautauqua went
> On pleasure bent
> A youth and maiden fair.
> Working in the convention
> Was not their intention,
> But to drive away dull care.
> Along came John V—
> And what did he see
> But this lover and his lass.

Says he, "You must
Get up and dust
And go to the Normal Class."

The great event in the Assembly of '75 was the visit of General U. S. Grant, then President of the United States on his second term. It was brought about partly because of the long-time friendship of the General with Dr. Vincent, dating back to the Galena pastorate of 1860 and '61, but also through the influence and activity of the Rev. Dr. Theodore L. Flood, who though a successful Methodist minister was also somewhat of a politician. The President and his party came up from Jamestown on a steamer-yacht, and at Fair Point were lodged in the tent beside the Lewis Miller cottage. True to his rule while General and President, Grant made no speech in public, not even when a handsomely bound Bagster Bible was presented to him in behalf of the assembly. Those were the palmy days of "Teachers' Bibles," with all sorts of helps and tables as appendices; and at that time the Bagster and the American Tract Society were rivals for the Sunday School constituency. Not to be outdone by their competitors, the Tract Society's representative at Chautauqua also presented one of his Bibles to the President. One can scarcely have too many

Bibles, and the General may have found use for both of them. He received them with a nod but never a word. Yet those who met him at dinners and in social life said that in private he was a delightful talker and by no means reticent. The tents and cottages on the Chautauqua of those days were taxed to almost bursting capacity to house the multitude over the Sunday of the President's visit. As many more would have come on that day, if the rules concerning Sabbath observance had been relaxed, as some had expected. But the authorities were firm, the gates by lake and land were kept closed, and that Sunday was like all other Sundays at Chautauqua.

At the close of the Assembly, the normal examinations were given to 190 students; some left the tent in terror after reading over the questions, but 130 struggled to the end and handed in their papers, of which 123 were above the passing grade. There were now two classes of graduates, and the Chautauqua Normal Alumni Association was organized. Mr. Otis F. Presbrey of Washington, D. C. (the man who on a certain occasion "looked like sixty"), was its first president. The secretary chosen was the Rev. J. A. Worden, a Presbyterian pastor at Steubenville, Ohio, and one of the normal teachers at Chautauqua; who afterward, and for

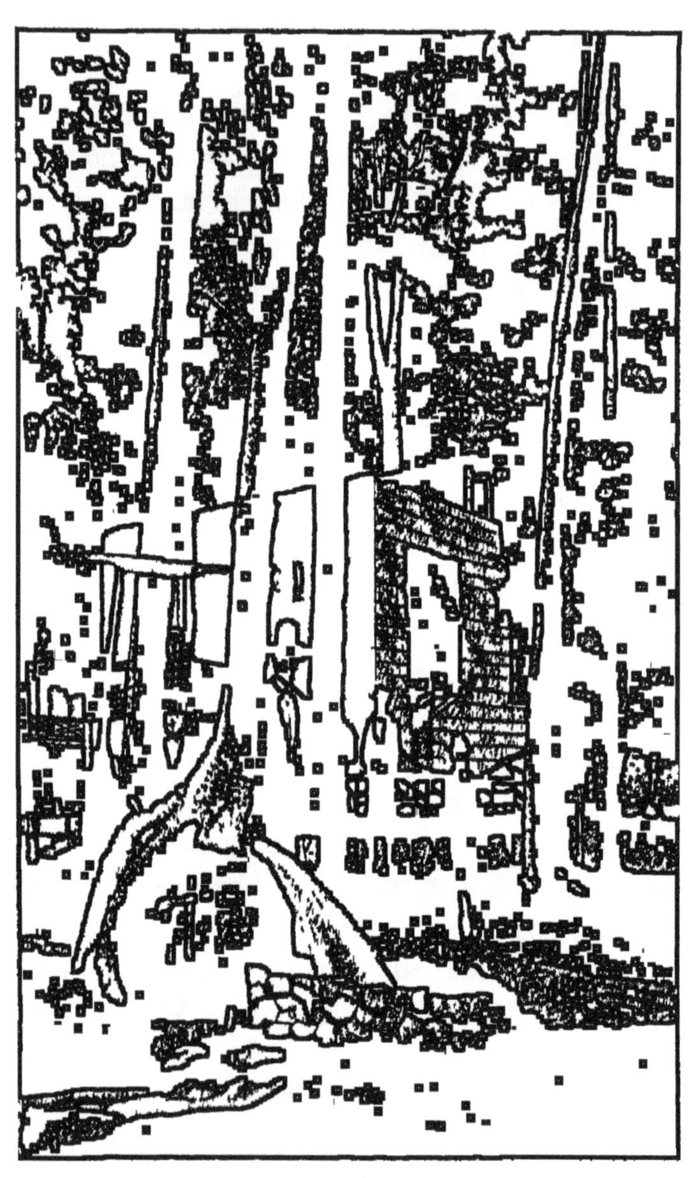

Spouting Tree and Oriental House

many years, was general secretary and superintendent of Sabbath School work in the Presbyterian Church.

At the Assembly of 1875, a quiet, unassuming little lady was present, who was already famous, and helped to increase the fame of Chautauqua. This was Mrs. G. R. Alden, the wife of a Presbyterian pastor, but known everywhere as "Pansy," whose story-books were in almost every Sunday School library on the continent. She wrote a book, *Four Girls at Chautauqua*, which ingeniously wove into the account of the actual events of the season, including some of its rainy days—that was the year when it rained more or less on fourteen of the seventeen days of the Assembly—her four girls, so well imagined that they seemed real. Indeed when one read the account of one's own speech at a children's meeting, he could not doubt that the Flossie of the story who listened to it was a veritable flesh and blood girl in the audience. The story became one of the most popular of the Pansy books, brought Chautauqua to the attention of many thousands, and led large numbers of people to Fair Point. Pansy has ever been a true friend of Chautauqua, and has written several stories setting forth its attractions.

## CHAPTER VI

### THE NATIONAL CENTENNIAL YEAR

THE founders of Chautauqua looked forward to its third session with mingled interest and anxiety. It was the centennial year of American Independence, and an exposition was opening in Philadelphia, far more noteworthy in its buildings and exhibits than any previous effort in the annals of the nation. The World's Fair in the Crystal Palace of New York, in 1855, the first attempt in America to hold an universal exposition, was a pigmy compared with the immense display in the park of Philadelphia on the centennial year. Could the multitudes from every State and from foreign lands be attracted from Philadelphia five hundred miles to Chautauqua Lake? Had the quest of the American people for new interests been satisfied by two years at the Assembly? Would it be the wiser course in view of the competition to hold merely a modest little gathering at Fair Point, or to venture boldly upon greater endeavors than ever before; to enlarge the program, to advertise more widely, and to compel attention to the new movement? Anyone who knew the adventurous, aspiring nature of both Miller and Vincent would unhesitatingly answer these questions.

The Assembly of 1876 was planned upon a larger scale than ever before. The formal opening took place on Tuesday evening, August 1st, in the forest-sheltered Auditorium, but two gatherings were held in advance and a third after its conclusion, so that the entire program embraced twenty-four days instead of seventeen.

The first meeting was the Scientific Conference, July 26th to 28th, aiming both to present science from the Christian point of view, and Christianity from the scientific point of view, showing the essential harmony between them, without either subjecting conclusions of science to church-authority or cutting up the Bible at the behest of the scientists. There had been frequent battles between the theologians and the students of nature and the "conflict of science and religion" had been strongly in evidence, ever since the publication of Darwin's *Origin of Species* in 1859. Most pulpits had uttered their thunders against "Darwinism," even though some of the pulpiteers had never read Darwin's book, nor could have understood it if they had tried. And many professors who had never listened to a gospel sermon, and rarely opened their Bibles, had launched lightnings at the camp of the theologians. But here was something new; a company of scholars including Dr. R. Ogden Doremus of New York, Professor A. S. Lattimore of Rochester, Dr. Alexander Winchell of Michigan, and others of equal standing, on the same platform with eminent preachers, and no restraint on either side, each free to utter his convictions, and all certain that the outcome would be peace and not war.

The writer of these pages was present at most of those lectures, and remembers one instance showing that the province of science is in the past and the present and not in the future. Dr. Doremus was giving some brilliant experiments in the newer developments of electricity. Be it remembered that it was the year 1876, and in the Centennial Exposition of that year there was neither an automobile, a trolley-car, nor an electric light. He said, "I will now show you that remarkable phenomenon—the electric light. Be careful not to gaze at it too steadily, for it is apt to dazzle the beholder and may injure the eyesight." Then as an arc-light of a crude sort flashed and sputtered, and fell and rose again only to sputter and fall, the lecturer said, "Of course, the electric light is only an interesting experiment, a sort of toy to amuse spectators. Every effort to ulitize it has failed, and always will fail. The electric light in all probability will never be of any practical value."

Yet at that very time, Thomas A. Edison in Menlo Park, New Jersey, was perfecting his incandescent light, and only three years later, 1879, Chautauqua was illuminated throughout by electricity. When the scientist turns prophet he becomes as fallible as the preacher who assumes to prescribe limitations to scientific discovery. We live in an age of harmony and mutual helpfulness between science and religion; and Chautauqua has wrought mightily in bringing to pass the new day.

It is worthy of mention that Chautauqua holds a connecting link with "the wizard of Llewellyn Park" and his electric light; for some years later Mr. Edison married Miss Mina Miller, daughter of the Founder Lewis Miller. The Miller family, Founder, sons, daughters, and grandchildren, have maintained a deep interest in Chautauqua; and the Swiss Cottage at the head of Miller Park has every year been occupied. Representatives of the Miller family are always members of the Board of Trustees.

After the Scientific Conference came a Temperance Congress, on July 29th and 30th. A new star had arisen in the firmament. Out of a little meeting at Chautauqua in 1874, had grown the Woman's Christian Temperance Union, already in 1876 organized in every State and in pretty nearly every town. Its founders had chosen for President of the Union a young woman who combined in one personality the consummate orator and the wise executive, Miss Frances Elizabeth Willard of Evanston, Illinois, who resigned her post as Dean of the Woman's Department of the Northwestern University to enter upon an arduous, a lifelong and world-wide warfare to prohibit intoxicants, and as a means to that end, to obtain the suffrage for women. Frances Willard died in 1898, but if she could have lived until 1920 she would have seen both her aims accomplished in the eighteenth and nineteenth amendments to the Constitution of the United States; one forbidding the manufacture and sale of all alchoholic liquors, the other opening the door of the voting-booth to every woman in the land. In Statuary Hall, Washington, the only woman standing in marble is Frances E. Willard (there will be others later), and her figure is there among the statesmen and warriors of the nation's history, by vote of the Legislature of the State of Illinois.

Rustic Bridge over Ravine

At every step in the progress of Chautauqua the two Founders held frequent consultations. Both of them belonged to the progressive school of thought, but on some details they differed, and woman's sphere was one of their points of disagreement. Miller favored women on the Fair Point platform, but Vincent was in doubt on the subject. Of course some gifted women came as teachers of teachers in the primary department of the Sunday School, but on the program their appearance was styled a "Reception to Primary Teachers by Mrs. or Miss So-and-So." Dr. Vincent knew Frances E. Willard, admired her, believed honestly that she was one of the very small number of women called to speak in public, and he consented to her coming to Chautauqua in the Temperance Congress of 1876. From the hour of her first appearance there was never after any doubt as to her enthusiastic welcome at Chautauqua. No orator drew larger audiences or bound them under a stronger spell by eloquent words than did Frances Elizabeth Willard. Frances Willard was the first but by no means the last woman to lecture on the Chautauqua platform. Mrs. Mary A. Livermore soon followed her, and before many summers had passed, Dr. Vincent was introducing to the Chautauqua constituency women as freely as men, to speak on the questions of the time.

Another innovation began on this centennial season—*The Chautauqua Assembly Herald.* For two years the Assembly had been dependent upon reports by newspaper correspondents, who came to the ground as strangers, with no share in the Chautauqua spirit, knowing very little of Chautauqua's aims, and eager for striking paragraphs rather than accurate records. A lecturer who is wise never reads the report of his speech in the current newspapers; for he is apt to tear his hair in anguish at the tale of his utterances. Chautauqua needed an organ, and Dr. Theodore L. Flood, from the first a staunch friend of the movement, undertook to establish a daily paper for the season. The first number of the *Herald* appeared on June 29, 1876, with Dr. Flood as editor, and Mr. Milton Bailey of Jamestown as publisher. The opening number was published in advance of the Assembly and sent to Chautauquans everywhere; but the regular issue began on July 29th with the Scientific Conference, and was continued daily (except Sunday) until the close of the Assembly. Every morning sleepers (who ought to have arisen earlier in time for morning prayers at 6:40) were awakened by the shrill voices of boys calling out "*Daily Assembly Herald!*" The *Daily* was a success from the start, for it contained accurate and complete reports of the most important lectures, outlines of the Normal lessons, and the items of information needed by everybody. All over the land people who could not come to Chautauqua kept in touch with its life through the *Herald*. More than one distinguished journalist began his editorial career in the humble quarters of *The Chautauqua Daily Assembly Herald*. For two seasons the *Daily* was printed in Mayville, though edited on the ground. In 1878 a printing plant was established at the Assembly and later became the Chautauqua Press. Almost a generation after its establishment, its name was changed to *The Chautauquan Daily*, which throughout the year is continued as *The Chautauquan Weekly*, with news of the Chautauqua movement at home and abroad.

Visitors to Chautauqua in the centennial year beheld for the first time a structure which won fame from its inhabitants if not from its architecture. This was the Guest House, standing originally on the lake shore near the site of the present Men's Club building; though nobody remembers it by its official name, for it soon became known as "The Ark." No, gentle reader, the report is without foundation that this was the original vessel in which Noah traveled with his menagerie, and that after reposing on Mount Ararat it went adrift on Lake Chautauqua. "The Ark" was built to provide a comfortable home for the speakers and workers at the Assembly who for two years had been lodged in tents, like the Israelites in the Wilderness. It was a frame building of two stories, shingle-roofed, with external walls and internal partitions of tent-cloth. Each room opened upon a balcony, the stairs to the upper floor being on the outside and the entire front of each cell a curtain, which under a strong wind was wont to break loose, regardless of the condition of the people inside. After a few years a partition between two rooms at one end was taken down, a chimney and fireplace built, and the result was a living room where the arkites assembled around a fire and told stories. Ah, those *noctes ambrosianæ* when Edward Everett Hale and Charles Barnard and Sherwin and the Beards narrated yarns and cracked jokes! Through the thin partitions of the bedrooms, every sneeze could be heard. The building was soon dubbed Noah's Ark, then "Knowers' Ark," from the varied learning of its indwellers; and sometimes from the reverberations sounding at night, "Snorers' Ark."

Frank Beard was a little deaf, and was wont to sit at these *conversazioni* in the parlor of the Ark with his hand held like an ear-trumpet. Mrs. Beard used to say that whenever she wished to hold a private conversation with him, they hired a boat and rowed out at least a mile from the shore. When the Assembly enlarged its boundaries by a purchase of land, the Ark was moved up to higher ground in the forest near where the Normal Hall now stands, and there served almost a generation of Chautauqua workers, until its frail materials were in danger of collapse, and it was taken down. Less famous buildings have been kept in memory by tablets and monuments; but it would require no small slab of marble to contain the names of the famous men and women who dwelt in that old Guest House; and what a book might have been made if some Boswell had kept the record of its stories and sayings! After spending two nights in the Ark, the Rev. Alfred Taylor's poetic muse was aroused to sing of the place and its occupants after this fashion:

This structure of timber and muslin contained
Of preachers and teachers some two or three score;
Of editors, parsons a dozen or more.
There were Methodists, Baptists, and 'Piscopals, too
And grave Presbyterians, a handful or two.

There were lawyers, and doctors and various folks,
All full of their wisdom, and full of their jokes.
There were writers of lessons, and makers of songs,
And shrewd commentators with wonderful tongues;
And all of these busy, industrious men
Found it hard to stop talking at just half-past ten.
They talked, and they joked, and they kept such a
clatter
That neighboring folks wondered what was the matter
But weary at last, they extinguished the light,
And went to their beds for the rest of the night.

The formal opening of the Assembly in 1876 took place after the Scientific and Temperance gatherings, on Tuesday evening, August 1st, in the leaf-roofed Auditorium, but the benches were now provided with backs for the comfort of the thousands. The platform had been enlarged to make room, for a choir, under the leadership in turn of W. F. Sherwin and Philip P. Bliss, whose gospel songs are still sung around the world. Only a few months later, that voice was hushed forever on earth, when the train bearing the singer and his wife crashed through a broken bridge at Ashtabula, Ohio. The record of that evening shows that fifteen speakers gave greetings, supposedly five minutes in length, although occasionally the flow of language overpassed the limit. Among the speakers we read the names of Dr. Henry M. Sanders of New York, Mr. John D. Wattles of the *Sunday School Times*, Dr. Henry W. Warren of Philadelphia, soon to become a bishop in the Methodist Episcopal Church, Dr. C. F. Burr, the author of *Ecce Cœlum*, a book of astronomy ministering to religion, famous in that day, though almost forgotten in our time; Dr. Lyman Abbott, who came before the audience holding up his pocket-Bible, with the words, "I am here tonight, because here this book is held in honor," Dr. Warren Randolph, the head of Sunday School work among the Baptist churches, and Mr. A. O. Van Lennep, in Syrian costume and fez-cap. He made two speeches, one in Arabic, the other in English.

Normal work for Sunday School teachers was kept well in the foreground. The subjects of the course were divided into departments, each under a director, who chose his assistants. Four simultaneous lessons were given in the section tents, reviewed later in the day by the directors at a meeting of all the classes in the pavilion. In addition, Dr. Vincent held four public platform reviews, covering the entire course. The record states that about five hundred students were present daily in the Normal department. About one hundred undertook the final examinations for membership in the Normal Alumni Association. The writer of these pages well remembers those hours in the pavilion, for he was one of those examined, and Frank Beard was another. The first question on the paper was, "What is your name and address?" Mr. Beard remarked audibly, that he was glad he could answer at least one of the questions. To dispel the doubts of our readers, we remark that both of us passed, and were duly enrolled among the Normal Alumni.

The list of the lecturers and their subjects show that Bible study and Bible teaching still stood at the fore. The program contained with many others the following names: Dr. W. E. Knox on "The Old Testament Severities," Dr. Lyman Abbott, "Bible Interpretation," Dr. R. K. Hargrove of Tennessee, later a bishop in the Methodist Episcopal Church, South, "Childhood and the Sunday School Work," Dr. George P. Hays, then President of Washington and Jefferson College, "How to Reason," Frank Beard, a caricature lecture with crayon on "Our School," showing types of teachers and scholars, Dr. George W. Woodruff, a most entertaining lecture on "Bright Days in Foreign Lands," Dr. A. J. Baird of Tennessee, "Going Fishing with Peter," Rev. J. A. Worden, "What a Presbyterian Thinks of

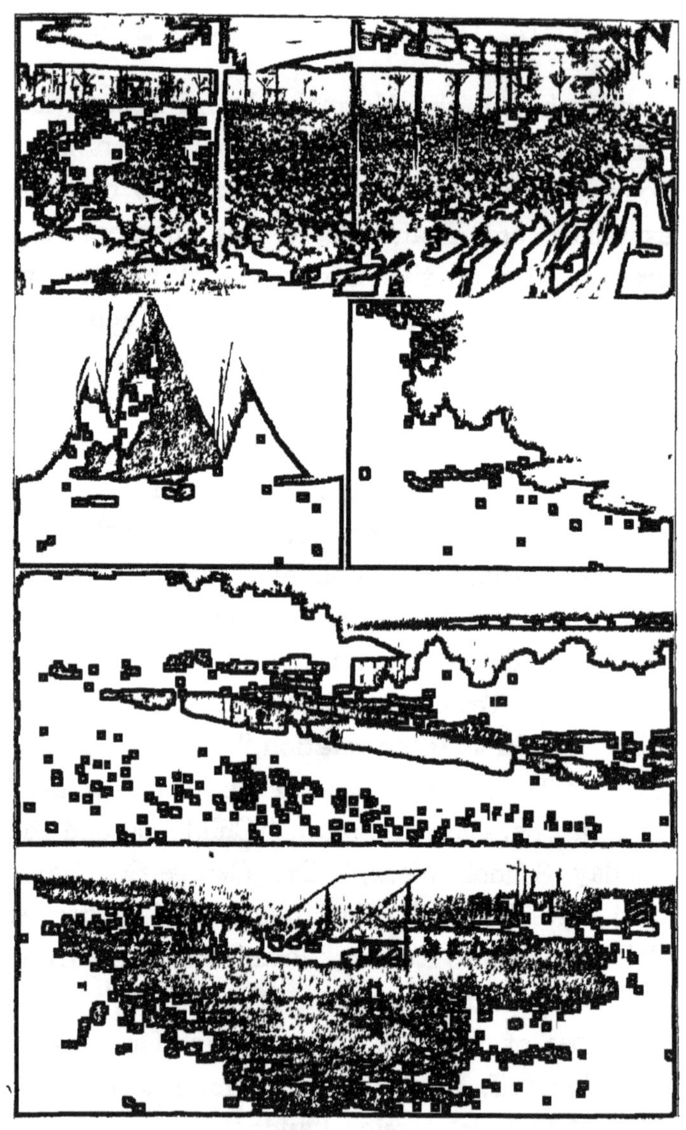

Amphitheater Audience

On the Lake By the Lake

Tennis Courts

In the Lake

John Wesley,"—a response to Rev. J. L. Hurlbut's lecture in 1875 on "What a Methodist Thinks of John Knox,"—Prof. L. T. Townsend, "Paul's Cloak Left at Troas"; also Dr. Richard Newton, M. C. Hazard, editor of the *National Sunday School Teacher*, Rev. Thomas K. Beecher of Elmira, and Bishop Jesse T. Peck. These are a few samples of the repast spread on the lecture platform of the Assembly.

The Centennial of American Independence was duly commemorated on Saturday, August 5th. Bishop Simpson had been engaged to deliver the oration, but was kept at home by illness and the hour was filled with addresses by different speakers, one of whom, Mr. W. Aver Duncan of London, presented the congratulations of Old England to her daughter across the sea. A children's centennial was held in the afternoon, at which the writer of this story spoke, and Frank Beard drew funny pictures. We will not tell, though we know, which of the two orators pleased the children most. At the sunset hour an impressive Bible service was held on the shore of the lake by Professor Sherwin, followed in the Auditorium by a concert of slave-songs from "The North Carolinians," a troupe of negro college students. Late in the evening came a gorgeous display on the lake, the Illuminated

Fleet. Every steam vessel plying Chautauqua waters marched in line, led by the old three-decker *Jamestown* all hung with Chinese lanterns, and making the sky brilliant with fireworks. A week later there was a commemorative tree-planting on the little park in the angle between the present Post Office building and the Colonnade. President Lewis Miller, Dr. C. H. Payne, President of Ohio Wesleyan University, Drs. Vail and Strong, teachers of Hebrew and Greek at the Assembly, Drs. O. H. Tiffany, T. K. Beecher, Richard Newton, J. A. Worden, Beard and Sherwin, Dr. Wythe, builder of Palestine Park and Director of Recreations at the Assembly, and Prof. P. P. Bliss were some, but not all of those who planted trees. Afterward each tree was marked by a sign bearing the name of its planter. These signs were lost in the process of the years, and not all the trees are now living. I think that I can identify the tree planted by Frank Beard, but am not sure of any other in the little group remaining at the present time.

A noteworthy event at the Assembly of 1876 was the establishment of the Children's Meeting as a daily feature. Meetings for the younger people had been held from time to time in '74 and '75 but this year Frank Beard suggested a regular

"Children's Hour," and the meetings were at first conducted by him, mingling religion and humor. Underneath his fun, Mr. Beard had a serious soul. He read strong books, talked with his friends on serious subjects, always sought to give at least one illustrated Bible reading during the Assembly, and resented the popular expectation that he should be merely the funny man on the program. He was assisted in his children's meeting by the Rev. Bethuel T. Vincent, a brother of the Founder, who was one of the most remarkable teachers of children and young people whom I have ever known. He could arrange the facts of Bible knowledge in outline, could present them in a striking manner, and drill them into the minds of the boys and girls in an enduring way that few instructors could equal and none surpass. Before many sessions, Mr. Vincent's lesson became the major feature and Beard's pictures the entertainment of the meeting. The grown-ups came to the meetings in such numbers as threatened to crowd out the children, until the rule was made that adults must take the rear seats,—no exception being made even for the row of ear-trumpets—leaving the front to the little people. Following the custom of the Normal Class, an examination in writing that would tax the brains of many ministers was held at the close, limited to all below a certain age, and prizes were awarded to the best papers presented. As after forty years I read the list of graduates in those early classes, I find the names of men and women who have distinguished themselves as ministers and missionaries in the churches.

Early in the Assembly season, on August 7, 1876, a momentous step was taken in the appointment by the instructors and students of the Normal Class, of a committee to prepare a course of study for the preparation of Sunday School teachers. Eleven men, present at Chautauqua, representing ten different denominations, were chosen as the committee, and their report constituted the first attempt at a *union* normal course. Hitherto each church had worked out its own independent course of study, and the lines laid down were exceedingly divergent. This new course prescribed forty lessons, a year's work divided between the study of the Bible, the Sunday School, the pupil, and the principles of teaching. Comparing it with the official course now adopted by the International Sunday School Association, we find it for a year's study remarkably complete and adapted to the teacher's needs. For years it stood as the basis of the teacher-training work at Chautauqua, was followed in the preparation of text-books and pursued by many classes in the United States and Canada.

The Centennial Year marked a note of progress in the music at the Assembly. Up to this time scarcely any music had been attempted outside of the church and Sunday School hymnals. This year the choir was larger than before, perhaps as many as forty voices—think of that in contrast with the three hundred now assembled in the choir-gallery of the Amphitheater! Some anthems had been attempted, but no oratorios, and no songs of the secular character. It was Professor C. C. Case who ventured with the doubtful permission of Dr. Vincent to introduce at a concert some selections from standard music outside the realm of religion. Nobody objected, perhaps because nobody recognized the significance of the step taken; and it was not long before the whole world of music was open to Chautauquans.

This writer remembers, however, that when at an evening lecture, Dr. Vincent announced as a prelude "Invitation to the Dance," sung by a quartette of ladies, he received next day a letter of protest against so immoral a song at a religious gathering. If it had been sung without announcement of its title, no one would have objected. On the following evening, Dr. Vincent actually offered a mild apology for the title. Since that time, the same title has been printed on the Chautauqua program, and the song encored by five thousand people. Surely, "the world do move!" *

Another step in the advancement of Chautauqua was the incorporation of the Assembly. Up to this year, 1876, the old charter of the Erie Conference Camp Meeting Association had constituted the legal organization. On April 28, 1876, new articles of incorporation were signed at Mayville, the county seat, providing for twenty-four trustees of the Chautauqua Lake Sunday School Assembly. In the charter the object was stated "to hold stated public meetings from year to year upon the grounds at Fair Point in the County of Chautauqua for the furtherance of Sunday School interests and any other moral and religious purpose not inconsistent therewith." We note that the old name Fair Point was still used to designate the place of the Assembly. But it was for the last time; with the next year's program a new name will appear.

One of the first acts of the new Board was to purchase a large addition to the camp-meeting ground on its eastern border, and to lay out streets upon it. This section included the campus and site of the buildings that now adorn the College Hill. Some readers may inquire how the streets of the Assembly received their names. During the Camp Meeting period, the streets were named after Bishops of the Methodist Episcoal Church—Simpson Avenue, Janes Avenue, Merrill Avenue, and so on. Under the Assembly régime a few more bishops were thus remembered; the road winding around from Palestine Park to the land-gate on the public highway was called Palestine Avenue; Vincent Avenue ran straight up the hill past the old Dining Hall, Miller Avenue parallel with it on the west; and other streets later were named after prominent Chautauqua leaders. Wythe the first Secretary, Root, the first Vice-President, Massey, a family from Canada making liberal contributions, Miss Kimball, the efficient Executive Secretary of the Reading Circle, and a few other names in Chautauqua's annals. The visitor to the present-day Chautauqua smiles as he reads one of the earliest enactments of the new Board, a resolution to instruct the Superintendent of Grounds "to warn the person selling tobacco on the grounds that he is engaged in an unlawful occupation." We hasten to add that this anti-tobacco regulation is no longer in operation.

The reader of this chapter perceives that the

centennial year marked notable advancements at Chautauqua: a lengthened and broadened program, the establishing of a newspaper, the beginning of the daily Children's Meeting with a course of Bible study for the young, the organizing of a definite course for the training of Sunday School teachers, the incorporation of the Assembly with a full Board of Trustees, with the transfer of the property from the former camp-meeting proprietorship, and a purchase of ground doubling the extent of its territory. Chautauqua, only three years old is already, in Scripture phrase, lengthening its cords and strengthening its stakes.

| Old Palace Hotel | Oriental Group | Lake-Shore |
|---|---|---|
| The Ark | Tent-Life | Old Dining Hall |
| N. E. Kitchen | Group of Workers | Woodland Path |

## CHAPTER VII

### A NEW NAME AND NEW FACES

THE fourth session of the Assembly opened in 1877 with a new name, *Chautauqua* taking the place of old Fair Point. The former title had caused some confusion. Fair Point was often misread "Fairport," and letters wandered to distant places of similar names. There was a Chautauqua Lake station on the Erie Railway, and a Chautauqua Point encampment across the lake from Fair Point, but the name "Chautauqua" had not been appropriated, and by vote of the trustees it was adopted; the government was requested to change the name of the Post Office, and the railroads and steamboats to place Chautauqua upon their announcements. Fair Point disappeared from the record, and is now remembered only by the decreasing group of the oldest Chautauquans.

Every season brings its own anxieties, and as the Assembly of 1877 drew near, a new fear came to the leaders of Chautauqua. A few will remember, and others have heard, that in 1877 took place the most extensive railway strike in the annals of the nation. The large station of the Pennsylvania Railroad in Pittsburgh was burned by a mob, and for weeks at a time, no trains ran either into or out of many important centers. Fortunately the strike was adjusted and called off before the Assembly opened, and on the first day four thousand people entered the gates, a far greater number than at any former opening.

On that year the menace of denominational rivalry threatened to confront Chautauqua. Across the lake, two miles from the Assembly, another point reaches westward, facing the Assembly ground. This tract was purchased by an enterprising company belonging to Baptist churches, and named Point Chautauqua. Its founders disclaimed any intention of becoming competitors with the Assembly. Their purpose, as announced, was to supply sites for summer homes, especially to members and friends of their own denomination. They began by building an expensive hotel at a time when the Assembly was contented with small boarding houses; and they soon followed the hotel with a large lecture-hall far more comfortable than either the out-door auditorium or the tent-pavilion at Chautauqua. To attract visitors they soon provided a program of speakers, with occasional concerts. Thus on opposite shores of the lake two institutions were rising, in danger of becoming rivals in the near future. Nor was Chautauqua Point the only rival in prospect. A year or two later a tent was erected near Lakewood for the holding of an assembly upon a "liberal" platform, where speakers of more advanced views of religion and the Bible could obtain a hearing. This gathering favored an open Sunday, and welcomed the steamers and railroad excursions on the day when the gates of Chautauqua were kept tightly closed. In those days the fear was expressed that Chautauqua Lake, instead of being a center for Christians of every name might furnish sites for separate conventions of different sects, and thus minister to dissension rather than to fellowship.

But these fears proved to be groundless. The "liberal" convocation down the lake held but one session, and left its promoters with debts to be paid. The founders of the Baptist institution made the mistake of beginning on too great a scale. The hotel and lecture-hall involved the corporation of Point Chautauqua in heavy debt, they were sold, and the place became a village, like other hamlets around the lake. The hotel was continued for some years, and the lecture-hall became a dancing pavilion, tempting the young people to cross the lake from Chautauqua where dancing was under a strict taboo. Perhaps it was an advantage to the thousands at the Assembly to find only two miles away a place where the rules were relaxed.

One story of a later season may be told in this connection, for it was without doubt typical. There are staid fathers and mothers attending lectures on sociology and civics in the Hall of Philosophy who could narrate similar experiences if only they would. A youth and two young lasses went out at the pier-gate for a sail across the lake. They landed at Point Chautauqua, refreshed their constrained bodies by a good dance, and then sailed home again. But it was late, the gate was closed, and it was of no avail to rattle the portals, for the gate-keepers were asleep in their homes far up the hill. The girls were somewhat alarmed, but the young man piloted them through the forest over a well-worn path to a place where some pickets of the fence were loose and could be shoved aside. They squeezed through and soon were safely at their homes.

But their troubles were not over. Their tickets had been punched to go out of the grounds, but not to come in again. Technically, in the eyes of the Chautauqua government they were still outside the camp. This young man, however, was not lacking in resources. He knew all the officials from His Whiskers, the supreme chief of police, down the list. Making choice of one gateman whose nature was somewhat social he called upon him in his box, talked in a free and easy way, picked up his punch and began making holes in paper and cards. When the gatekeeper's back was turned, he quickly brought out the three tickets, punched them for coming into the grounds, and then laid down the nippers. The girls, now officially within the grounds, were grateful to their friend, and to manifest their regard wrought for him a sofa-pillow which decorated his room in college.

Something should be said just here concerning the ticket-system of Chautauqua. It was devised by the genius of Lewis Miller, to whom invention was instinctive, and was improved to meet every possible attempt at evasion. There were one-day tickets, good for only one admission, three-day tickets, week-tickets, and season-tickets, all providing no admission on Sundays. They were not transferable, and all except the one-day variety bore the purchaser's name. Two or three times during the season officers visited every house and every lecture and class, even stopping everybody on the streets to see that no single-day tickets were kept for longer periods. Provision was made for exchanging at the office short-stop tickets for the longer time desired. If one wished to go outside the gate on an errand, or for a sail on the lake, he must leave his ticket, unless he was known to the gate-keeper, in order to prevent more than one person from using the same ticket. When one left the Assembly for good, he gave up his ticket. Every ticket had its number by which it could be identified if lost or found; and the bulletin-board contained plenty of notices of lost tickets.

It is said that one careful visitor carried his ticket everywhere for a day or two, at each lecture-hall and tent looking vainly for a window where it might be shown. As it did not seem to be needed, he left it in his room, only to find when he wished to take out a boat, that he must go home and get his ticket. When the day arrived for him to leave Chautauqua, he placed his ticket in the bottom of his trunk, as it would be needed no longer, intending to take it home as a souvenir for his memory-book. But, alas, at the gate, departing, he found that ticket an absolute necessity. Without it, apparently he must stay forever inside the walls of Chautauqua. So once more he overhauled his trunk, dug up his ticket from its lowest strata, and departed in peace.

One departure from camp-meeting customs at once wrought a change in the aspect of Chautauqua and greatly promoted its growth. We have noted the fact that in the earlier years no householder or tent-dweller was to receive boarders, and all except those who cooked at home ate in a common dining-hall. After the third Assembly, this restriction was removed and anyone could provide rooms and board upon paying a certain percentage of receipts to the management. The visitors who came in 1877 missed, but not in sorrow, the dingy old Dining-Hall, which had been torn down. But everywhere boarding houses had sprung up as by magic, and cottages had suddenly bulged out with new additions, while signs of "Rooms and Board" greeted the visitants everywhere. In fact, so eager were the landlords for their prey, that runners thronged the wharf to inform new arrivals of desirable homes, and one met these agents even at the station in Mayville. There was an announcement of the Palace Hotel, the abode of luxurious aristocracy. The seeker after its lordly accommodations found a frame building, tent-covered and tent-partitioned into small rooms for guests. But even this was an improvement upon the rows of cots in the big second story of the old lodging house, where fifty people slept in one room, sometimes with the rain dripping upon them through a leaky roof. Year by year the boarding cottages grew in number, in size, and in comfort. Fain would we name some of these hostelries, whose patrons return to them season after season, but we dare not begin the catalogue, lest by an omission we should offend some beloved landlady and her guests. In a few years the Palace Hotel, half-house and half-tent, gave place to the Hotel Athenæum, on the same site, whose wide balcony looks out upon the lake, and whose tower has been a home for some choice spirits. The writer knows this for he has dwelt beside them.

On the extreme southwestern limit of the old camp ground was a ravine, unoccupied until 1877. On the slopes of this valley the declivity was cleared and terraced, seats—this time with backs—were arranged upon its sides; toward the lake it was somewhat banked up to form a place for the speakers' platform. Over it was spread the tent, formerly known as "the pavilion," brought from the hill beside Vincent Avenue. This was the nucleus out of which grew in after years the famous

Old Hall of Philosophy

The Golden Gate

Prof. W. C. Wilkinson, Dr J. H Vincent, Lyman Abbott, Bishop H W. Warren

Chautauqua Amphitheater. At first it was used only on rainy days, but after a year or two gradually took the place of the out-of-doors Auditorium.

Near the book-store on the hill stands a small gothic, steep-roofed building, now a flower-shop. It was built just before the Assembly of 1877 as a church for the benefit of those who lived through the year at Chautauqua, numbering at that time about two hundred people. The old chapel was the first permanent public building erected at Chautauqua and still standing.

The program of '77 began with a council of Reform and Church Congress, from Saturday, August 4th to Tuesday, August 7th. Anthony Comstock, that fearless warrior in the cause of righteousness, whose face showed the scars of conflict, who arrested more corrupters of youth, and destroyed more vile books, papers, and pictures than any other social worker, was one of the leading speakers. He reported at that time the arrest of 257 dealers in obscene literature and the destruction of over twenty tons of their publications. There is evil enough in this generation, but there would have been more if Anthony Comstock had not lived in the last generation. Another reformer of that epoch was Francis Murphy, who had been a barkeeper, but became a worker for temperance.

His blue ribbon badge was worn by untold thousands of reformed drunkards. He had a power almost marvelous of freeing men from the chain of appetite. I was present once at a meeting in New York where from the platform I looked upon a churchful of men, more than three hundred in number, whose faces showed that the "pleasures of sin" are the merest mockery; and after his address a multitude came forward to sign Mr. Murphy's pledge and put on his blue ribbon. At Chautauqua Mr. Murphy made no appeal to victims of the drink habit, for they were not there to hear him, but he *did* appeal, and most powerfully, in their behalf, to the Christian assemblage before him. Another figure on the platform was that of John B. Gough,—we do not call him a voice, for not only his tongue, but face, hands, feet, even his coat-tails, were eloquent. No words can do justice to this peerless orator in the cause of reform. These were the three mighty men of the council, but the report shows twice as many names almost as distinguished.

On the evening of Tuesday, August 7th, came the regular opening of the Assembly proper, in the Auditorium on the Point. The report of attendance was far above that of any former opening day. Dr. Vincent presided and conducted the responsive service of former years—the same opening sentences and songs used every year since the first Assembly in 1874. We find fifteen names on the list of the speakers on that evening, representing many churches, many States, and at least two lands outside our own.

Is another story of Frank Beard on that evening beneath the dignity of history? When he came upon the platform, he found the chairs occupied, and sat down among the alto singers, where he insisted on remaining despite the expostulations of Mr. Sherwin. In the middle of the exercises, the steamboat whistle at the pier gave an unusually raucous scream. Mr. Sherwin came forward and told the audience that there was no cause for alarm; the sound was merely Mr. Beard tuning his voice to sing alto. Two or three speakers afterward incidentally referred to Mr. Beard as a singer, and hoped that he might favor the congregation with a solo. One of the speakers, an Englishman, prefaced his talk by singing an original song, set to Chautauqua music. That he might see his verses, Mr. Sherwin took down a locomotive headlight hanging on one of the trees, and held it by the side of the singer. The Englishman, short and fat, and Sherwin with dignity supporting the big lantern, formed a tableau.

Immediately afterward Dr. Vincent called on Mr. Beard to speak; and this was his opening, delivered in his peculiar drawl.

"I was a good mind to sing a song instead of making a speech, but I was sure that Professor Sherwin wouldn't hold the lantern for me to sing by. He knows that he can't hold a candle to me, anyhow!"

With Professor Sherwin, in charge of the music in 1877, was associated Philip Phillips, whose solos formed a prelude to many of the lectures. No one who listened to that silvery yet sympathetic voice ever forgot it. It will be remembered that President Lincoln in Washington, after hearing him sing *Your Mission*, sent up to the platform his written request to have it repeated before the close of the meeting. Mr. Phillips ever after cherished that scrap of paper with the noblest name in the history of America. Another musical event of the season of 1877 was the visit of the Young Apollo Club of New York, one of the largest and finest boy-choirs in the country. They gave three concerts at Chautauqua, which in the rank and rendering of their music were a revelation to the listening multitudes.

While we are speaking of the music we must make mention of songs written and composed especially for Chautauqua. In Dr. Vincent's many-sided nature was a strain of poetry, although I do not know that he ever wrote a verse. Yet he always looked at life and truth through poetic eyes. Who otherwise would have thought of songs for Chautauqua, and called upon a poet to write them? Dr. Vincent found in Miss Mary A. Lathbury another poet who could compose fitting verses for the expression of the Chautauqua spirit. If I remember rightly her first song was prepared for the opening in 1875, the second Assembly, and as the earliest, it is given in full. In it is a reference to some speakers at the first Assembly who went on a journey to the Holy Land, and to one, the Rev. F. A. Goodwin, whose cornet led the singing in 1874, who became a missionary in India.

### A HYMN OF GREETING

The flush of morn, the setting suns
  Have told their glories o'er and o'er
One rounded year, since, heart to heart
  We stood with Jesus by the shore.

We heard his wondrous voice; we touched
  His garment's hem with rev'rent hand,
Then at his word, went forth to preach
  His coming Kingdom in the land.

And following him, some willing feet
  The way to Emmaus have trod;
And some stand on the Orient plains,
  And some—upon the mount of God!

While over all, and under all,
  The Master's eye, the Master's arm,
Have led in paths we have not known,
  Yet kept us from the touch of harm.

One year of golden days and deeds,
  Of gracious growth, of service sweet;
And now beside the shore again
  We gather at the Master's feet.

"Blest be the tie that binds," we sing;
  Yet to the bending blue above
We look, beyond the face of friends,
  To mark the coming of the Dove.

Descend upon us as we wait
  With open heart—with open Word;
Breathe on us, mystic Paraclete
  Breathe on us, Spirit of the Lord!

Another song of the second Assembly, and sung through the years since at the services of the Chautauqua Circle, was written and set to music by Miss Lucy J. Rider of Chicago, afterward Mrs. Lucy Rider Meyer, one of the founders of the Deaconess movement in the Methodist Episcopal Church. It begins with the lines:

The winds are whispering to the trees,
  The hill-tops catch the strain,
The forest lifts her leafy gates
  To greet God's host again.

In the year of which we are writing, 1877, Mary A. Lathbury gave to Chautauqua two songs which have become famous, and are to be found in every hymnal published during the last generation. One is the Evening Song of Praise, "Day is dying in the West," written to be sung at the even-tide conferences beside the lake. The other, beginning, "Break thou the bread of life," was the study song for the Normal Classes. Another, less widely known abroad, but sung every year at Chautauqua is the Alumni Song, "Join, O friends, in a memory song." These were a few of the many songs written by Miss Lathbury at Dr. Vincent's request, and set to music by Professor Sherwin. Originally composed for the Normal Class, then the most prominent feature on the program, after the Chautauqua Circle arose to greatness in 1878, they were adopted as the songs of that widespread organization. For the C. L. S. C. a class song was written each year, until the Chautauqua songs grew into a book. Not all of these class songs have become popular, but quite a number are still sung at the Institution, especially at class-meetings and in the Recognition Day services.

At the Assembly of 1877 the Normal Class still stood in the foreground. Special courses of lessons were given to Primary Teachers, by Mrs. Emily

Huntington Miller, Mrs. Wilbur F. Crafts, and the every-popular "Pansy"—Mrs. G. R. Alden. The record informs us that the average attendance at the four normal tents was more than five hunred. Thorough reviews after the course were held from time to time, and this year two competitive examinations, one on August 14th for those unable to remain until the close, but received examination on the entire course,—fifty questions in number; the other on Tuesday, August 21st with three hundred candidates for the diploma.

From 1876 for a number of years it was the custom to hold an anniversary service on one evening, for the Normal Alumni. The graduates marched in procession, led by a band, a silken banner before each class, and every member wearing a badge, to the Pavilion in the ravine and afterward to its successor the Amphitheater, where Chautauqua songs were sung, and an address given by an orator, the President of the Normal Alumni introducing the speaker. It may have been in 1877, or maybe in a later year, that John B. Gough was the orator of the evening; and he began his address in this wise:

I don't know why I have been chosen to speak to the Alumni of Chautauqua, unless it is because I am an Alumni myself, if that is the right word for one of them. I am an alumni of Amherst College; M.A., Master of Arts. I have a diploma, all in Latin. I can't read a word of it, and don't know what it means, but those long Latin words look as if they must mean something great. When I was made an alumni I sat on the platform of the Commencement Day; the salutatorian—they told me that was his title—came up and began to speak in Latin. He said something to the President, and he bowed and smiled as if he understood it. He turned to the trustees, and spoke to them and they looked as wise as they could. He said something to the graduating class, and they seemed to enjoy it—all in Latin; and I hadn't the remotest idea what it was all about. I kept saying to myself, "I wish that he would speak just one word that I could understand." Finally, the orator turned straight in my direction and said, "Ignoramus!" I smiled, and bowed, just as the others had. There was one word that I could understand, and it exactly fitted my case!

On the lecture platform of 1877, the outstanding figure was the massive frame, the Jupiter-like head, and the resonant voice of Joseph Cook, one of the foremost men of that generation in the reconciliation of science with religion—if the twain ever needed a reconcilation. He gave six lectures, listened to by vast audiences. The one most notable was that entitled, "Does Death End All?" in which he assembled a host of evidences, outside of the Scriptures, pointing to the soul's immortality. Joseph Cook is well-nigh forgotten in this day, but in his generation he was an undoubted power as a defender of the faith.

If we were to name the Rev. James M. Buckley, D.D., in the account of each year when he spoke in the platform and the subjects of his addresses, there would be room in our record for few other lecturers. He was present at the opening session in 1874, and at almost every session afterward for more than forty years,—aggressive in debate, instantaneous in repartee, marvelous in memory of faces and facts, and ready to speak upon the widest range of subjects. Every year, Dr. Buckley held a question-drawer, and few were the queries that he could not answer; although in an emergency he might dodge a difficulty by telling a story. For many years he was the editor of the *Christian Advocate* in New York, known among Methodists as the "Great Official"; and he made his paper the champion of conservatism, for he was always ready to break a lance in behalf of orthodox belief or the Methodist system. Another speaker this year was Dr. P. S. Henson, a Baptist pastor successively in Philadelphia, in Chicago, and in Boston, but by no means limited tò one parish in his ministry. He spoke under many titles, but most popularly on

"Fools," and "The Golden Calf," and he knew how to mingle wisdom and wit in just proportions. Abundant as were his resources in the pulpit and on the platform, some of us who sat with him at the table or on a fallen tree in the forest, thought that he was even richer and more delightful, as well as sagacious in his conversation. Dr. Charles F. Deems, pastor of the Church of the Stranger in New York, also came to Chautauqua for the first time this year. He was at home equally in theology, in science, and on the questions of the day, with a remarkable power of making truth seemingly abstruse simple to common people. I recall a lecture on a scientific subject, at which he saw on the front seat two boys, and he made it his business to address those boys and simplify his message seemingly for them while in reality for his entire audience. But we cannot even name the speakers who gave interest to the program of 1877.

One event of that season, however, must not be omitted, for it became the origin of one noteworthy Chautauqua custom. Mr. S. L. Greene, from Ontario, Canada, a deaf-mute, gave an address before a great audience in the Auditorium under the trees. He spoke in the sign-language, telling several stories from the gospels; and so striking were his silent symbols that everyone could see the picture. We were especially struck with his vivid representation of Christ stilling the tempest. As he closed, the audience of at least two thousand burst into applause, clapping their hands. Dr. Vincent came forward, and said, "The speaker is unable to hear your applause; let us wave our handkerchiefs instead of clapping our hands."

In an instant the grove was transformed into a garden of white lilies dancing under the leaves of the trees, or as some said, "into a snow-covered field." The Superintendent of Instruction then and there adopted the Chautauqua Salute of the waving handkerchiefs as a token of special honor. It is sparingly given, only two or three times during the season, and never except when called for by the head of Chautauqua in person.

At the annual commemoration on "Old First Night" the Chautauqua salute is now given in a peculiar manner to the memory of Lewis Miller and other leaders who are no longer among us. At the call of the President, the handkerchiefs are slowly raised and held in absolute stillness for a moment; then as silently lowered. The Chautauqua salute is one of the traditions observed in minutest detail after the manner of the Founders.

Among the early issues of the *Assembly Herald* appear some verses worthy of a place in our history.

### THE CHAUTAUQUA SALUTE

BY MAY M. BISBEE

Have you heard of a wonderful lily
  That blooms in the fields of air?
With never a stem or a pale green leaf,
  Spotless, and white, and fair?
Unnamed in the books of wise men,
  Nor akin to the queenly rose;
But the white Chautauqua lily
  Is the fairest flower that grows.

Never in quiet meadows,
  By brookside cool and green,
In garden-plot, nor in forest glen,
  This wonderful flower is seen.
It grows in goodly companies,
  A theme for the poet's pen;
It loves not silence, nor cold nor dark,
  But it blooms in the haunts of men.

The nation trails its great men
  Of high and honored name,
With clapping of hands and roll of drums
  And trump that sings of fame;
But a sweet and silent greeting
  To the ones we love the best,
Are the white Chautauqua lilies
  In our summer home of rest.

When the beautiful vesper service
  Has died on the evening air,
And a thousand happy faces
  Are raised at the close of prayer,
The voice of our well-loved leader
  Rings out in its clear-toned might;
"We will give our salutation
  To an honored guest to-night."

Then out of the speaking silence
  The white wings rise to air,
Faintest of flutter and softest of sound,
  Hail to the lilies rare!
Thousands and tens of thousands,
  Swiftly the lilies grow,
Till the air is filled with the fluttering flowers,
  As the winter air with snow.

Hail to the fair white lilies!
  Sweetest of salutations!
The love of a thousand hearts they bear
  The greeting of the nations.
The fairest of earth-born flowers
  Must wither by-and-by;
But the lilies that live in the hearts they hail
  Will never, never die.

O cold blast, spare the lily-bed
  That bears the wonderful flower!
Give largely, O sky, of summer sun,
  Largely of summer shower,
Till the white flowers born in our summer home
  To earth's outermost rim be given;
And the lilies open their cups of snow
  In the garden beds of heaven.

At the final meeting of the Assembly in 1877, on Monday evening, August 20th, Dr. Vincent outlined some plans for the coming year,—a large hotel to replace the tented walls of the Pavilion Palace, a new meeting-place to be built with walls and roof over the natural amphitheater in the ravine, some further courses of study, and many improvements to the grounds. Then he added, "And I shall not be surprised if—well, I will not tell you—I have another dream I will not give you." (A voice: "Let's have it.") "No, I am going to hold that back, so you will want me to come next year. But I believe that something higher and larger is just out yonder in the near future. Next summer, if we all live, I will tell you about it." We shall see in the coming chapter what that new development of Chautauqua was to be,—the greatest in its history, and perhaps the greatest in the history of education through the land.

## CHAPTER VIII

### THE CHAUTAUQUA READING CIRCLE

THE "dream" of which Dr. Vincent gave a hint at the close of the 1877 Assembly was destined to become a reality in 1878. That year marks a golden milestone in the history of Chautauqua, for then was launched *The Chautauqua Literary and Scientific Circle,* that goodly vessel which has sailed around the world, has carried more than a half-million of passengers, and has brought inspiration and intelligence to multitudes unnumbered. The conception arose in its author's mind from the consciousness of his own intellectual needs. He had longed, but vainly, for the privilege of higher education in the college, but in his youth there were no Boards of Education with endowments extending a helping hand to needy students. His school-days ended in the academy, but not his education, for he was to the end of his life a student, reading the best books, even when their subjects and style demanded a trained mind. As one who knew him well and for more

Flower Girls on Recognition Day

Flower Girls of 1894

Elizabeth Vincent and Paul Harper leading

than a generation, I may say without hesitation that John Heyl Vincent possessed more knowledge and richer culture than nine out of ten men holding a college diploma.

But his heart went out in sympathy toward others who like himself had missed the opportunity of dwelling in college-cloisters, toward workers on the farm, at the forge, in the store, in the office, in the kitchen, and in the factory, whose longings were like his own. Many of these would read good books and drink at "the Pierian Spring," if only they knew where to find the fountain—in other words, if some intelligent, well-read person would direct them, and place the best books in their way. Gradually it dawned upon his mind that everyone has some margin of time, at least half an hour among the tweny-four, which might be made useful under wise counsel to win knowledge. He had not heard of that sentence spoken by the great President of Harvard, that "ten minutes a day, for ten years of a life, with the right books, will give any one an education." Indeed, that wise utterance came after the Chautauqua Circle had been established and was already giving guidance to many thousand people.

The conception came to Dr. Vincent of a course of reading, which might become to the diligent a course of study, to include the principal subjects of a college curriculum, all in the English language, omitting the mathematical and technical departments of science; a course that would give to its careful reader, not the mental discipline of four years in college, but something of the college outlook upon life and letters. It was to embrace the histories of the great nations that shaped the world—Israel, Greece, Rome, Great Britain, and America,—with shorter sketches of other important lands; a view over the literature of the ages, not in the original Greek, Latin, or German, but as translated into our own tongue, presented in a manner to give general understanding to the many, and also to awaken the aspiring reader by pointing out the path to thorough knowledge. There are tens of thousands who have studied the Bible only in the English version, yet could pass a better examination upon its contents than many graduates of the theological seminary. One might read such an account of Homer's *Odyssey*, or Virgil's *Æneid*, or Dante's *Paradiso*, or Goethe's *Faust*, as would inspire him to seek and study a complete translation of these masterpieces. Dr. Edward Everett Hale, from the beginning one of the counselors of the Chautauqua Course, said that it gives to its students "the language of the time"; not a full detailed knowledge, but such a general view as enables him to understand allusions and references, to be at home with the thinkers and writers of the age.

The Chautauqua Circle was not planned for specialists, seeking full knowledge upon one subject, but for general readers. Before it was inaugurated there was already established in Boston the Society for the Encouragement of Home Study. The student who desired aid through this useful organization was expected to select some one department of knowledge, and then a list of books or articles would be sent to him, with suggestions, questions, and an examination. If historical, it would not be history in general, but the history of one country, or one period in its annals. It might be the American, or French, or English Revolution—very thorough, but only for one seeking special knowledge. But the Chautauqua plan contemplated a general round of knowledge—history, literature, science, natural and social, art, and religion: and this broad conception was one great secret of its success. A story which is typical was told the writer of this volume as an absolute fact by one who claimed to know the persons referred to. A young lady called upon her pastor with this request;

"I wish that you would tell me of some good books to read. I'm tired of reading nothing but novels, and want to find some books that are worth while. Can't you give me the names of some such books?"

The minister thought a moment, and then said slowly, "Well, what kind of books do you want—religious books, for instance?"

"No," said the girl, "I do not know as I wish to read about religion. I get that in the church and the Sunday School. But there must be some good books of other kinds—can't you tell me of them?"

"What would you think of a course of reading in history?" asked the pastor. Her face brightened somewhat, and she answered, "Why, I think that I might like to read history. What would you recommend for me?"

The minister glanced at his own shelves, thought a moment, and then said, "Well, I can't all at once name a course on such an important subject as history. Come next Wednesday, and I'll have a list of good books for you."

She came, and he showed her a formidable catalogue of books, saying:

"I have done the best that I could do, but the list is longer than I had expected. It includes eighty volumes. I wrote down one hundred and twenty volumes at first, but cut it down to eighty, and it cannot be made shorter, not by a single volume. In fact, it is not as complete as it should be. You will begin with the greatest book of history in all literature—Gibbon's *Decline and Fall of the Roman Empire*, in nine volumes!"

The young lady was appalled, and never went through the first chapter of Gibbon's mighty work. This was before the Chautauqua Home Reading Course was evolved. After that had been launched any intelligent minister, or helpful librarian, would simply have said to the enquirer, "Send for a circular of the C. L. S. C.; that will give you exactly what you need."

There comes to my own mind a vivid remembrance of that evening when for the first time I heard those magic words—"The Chautauqua Literary and Scientific Circle." In the early spring of 1878, Dr. Vincent had just returned from an official visit to Europe, and I was no longer at Plainfield, five minutes' walk from his home, but by the revolution of the itinerant wheel a pastor, thirty miles distant. A message came asking me to spend an evening with him and talk over some new plans for Chautauqua. Of course, I obeyed the call, for I always gained more than I gave in any conversation with that fruitful mind.

We sat in front of the fireplace in his study, and I listened while for an hour he talked of a new organization which he proposed to launch in the coming season, to be named *The Chautauqua Literary and Scientific Circle;* with a course of study to be carried through four years, with forty minutes as each day's task, for nine or ten months of each year, in the various branches of knowledge, analogous to the four years of college study. He was so full of his theme and so eloquent upon it that I could only listen to the outpouring utterances. The general purpose was clear before him, but not the details of its operation. Dr. Vincent's eyes were ever set upward toward the mountain-tops glorious in the sunlight, and he did not always think of the thickets to be cut and the path to be made from the lower plain to the summit. I could see some of the difficulties in the way, some obstacles that must be overcome, and sagely shook my head in doubt of the scheme. It was a radical departure from the earlier ideals, for thus far everything on the Chautauqua program had been along the line of Sunday School training, and this was a forsaking of the well-trodden path for a new world of secular education. Why try to rival the high schools and arouse the criticism of the colleges? How would the regular constituency

Pioneer Hall: Class of 1882. C. L. S. C.

Old College Building

of Chautauqua feel at this innovation? No doubt under the spell of his enthusiasm, some would join the proposed class in literature and science—but how could science be studied by untrained people without laboratories, or apparatus, or teachers? And after the spell of the Chautauqua season would not the pledges be forgotten at home, and the numbers in the home classes soon dwindle away to nothing?

Dr. Vincent asked me a question as we sat in the glow of the fireplace. "How many do you think can be depended on to carry on such a course as is proposed?"

"Oh, perhaps a hundred!" I answered. "People who want to read will find books, and those who don't care for reading will soon tire of serious study."

The doctor sprang up from his chair and walked nervously across the room. "I tell you, Mr. Hurlbut, the time will come when you will see a thousand readers in the C. L. S. C."

I smiled, the smile of kindly unbelief! His impulse, his dream was noble, to be sure, but so utterly impracticable. I tell this little tale to show how far below the reality were the expectations of us both. Only a few years after this conversation the enrolled members of the

C. L. S. C. counted sixty thousand readers pursuing the course at one time, with probably as many more readers unregistered.

The opening evening of the Assembly was held on Tuesday evening, August 6th. The vesper service beginning, "The Day goeth away, The Shadows of evening are stretched out, Praise waiteth for Thee, O God, in Zion," etc., was read responsively in the Auditorium between the Miller Cottage and the Vincent tent, then not far from the Point, when a sudden shower fell and a general rush was made to the new Pavilion in the ravine on the west. That was the last opening service attempted out-of-doors. Since that evening, the Pavilion, soon to become the Amphitheater, has supplied the stage for the speakers, sedate or humorous, short or long,—some of them longer than the audience desired—on "Old First Night." A few lectures were given from time to time in the old Auditorium, but after the season of 1879 it was left for smaller meetings of couples in communion of soul on the seats here and there under the trees.

The inauguration of the Chautauqua Literary and Scientific Circle took place in the Pavilion on the afternoon of Saturday, August 10, 1878. On the platform, then lower than most of the seats, were a telescope, a microscope, a globe, some scientific apparatus, and a table filled with books, giving a scholastic setting to the exercises. Dr. Vincent presided, and with him were Bishop Randolph S. Foster of Boston, Dr. Henry W. Warren of Philadelphia, himself two years afterward to become a bishop, Professor William C. Wilkinson, whose pen in the following years wrote many books for the readers of the C. L. S. C., Professor James Strong of wide learning, and several other eminent men. The address of the day, unfolding the purpose and plan of the Circle, was given by Dr. Vincent. Many of us who heard him on that afternoon have thought since that this was the masterpiece of his lifetime, and it might worthily be so, for it launched a movement in education, the most influential and wide-reaching of any in the annals of the nation.

I wish that it were possible to reprint that great address as reported in full in the *Assembly Herald*, for never was the conception of Chautauqua at home for nine months of the year more clearly set forth, but a few quotations and outlines must suffice. He began by calling attention to four classes of people. First, those who inherit from their ancestors wealth, ease, and large intellectual opportunities, who find college doors opening almost of their own accord before them. Second, there are those born under the necessity of daily toil. For these the education of the public school is provided; but it is limited and rarely appreciated. Children go to school to get knowledge enough for bread-winning and no more. Third, there are those who, born under necessity, struggle into opportunity, fight their way up into power, and make themselves the intellectual heroes of their time. Fourth, there are many born under necessity, who lack the vision at the beginning, who enter upon a life of trade or labor which may bring them success, but who gradually awake to realize how much they have lost, without realizing that it is never too late to gain culture and that education ends only with life. This is the class in every community which our new organization aims to reach, to uplift, to inspire and stimulate. We propose to give to these people in every walk of life, both the rich, the middle class, and the poor—all in one class in their condition and their needs—the college student's outlook upon the world of thought, by short studies in literature and science, by the reading of books, by the preparation of synopses of books read, by written reports of books read, and by correspondence with experts in the several departments.

Here are some of the advantages of this organization: It will develop higher and nobler tastes, increase mental power, exalt home-life, giving authority and home-help in public school studies and organizing homes into reading circles. It will counteract the influence of our modern pernicious literature and sweeten and enrich the daily lives of poor and hard-working people. It will bring the more cultivated people into contact with the less scholarly, promote a true appreciation of science, and tend to increase the spiritual life and power of the church. All knowledge becomes glorified in the man whose heart is consecrated to God.

As I copy these words in the year 1920, more than forty years after they were spoken and printed, with each sentence there rise to my mind instances that have come to my own knowledge of every one of these prophecies fulfilled. Chautauqua through its home-reading course has accomplished far more than its founder even dreamed.

The speaker answered an objection to the plan of study based upon its superficiality.

Superficial it is, and so is any college course of study. The boy who stands at the close of his senior year, on Commencement Day, to receive his parchment and whatever honors belong to him, who does not feel that his whole course has been superficial, will not be likely to succeed in the after struggle of life. But superficiality is better than absolute ignorance. It is better for a man to take a general survey, to catch somewhere a point that arrests him; for the man who never takes a survey never catches the point in which dwell the possibilities of power for him. When you sow seed, it is not the weight of the seed put into the soil that tells, it is the weight of the harvest that comes after.

Here are some of the closing words of the address:

How glad I should be if I should find in the future years that more boys and girls are going to our high schools and universities because of the impulse received here at Chautauqua! And I say to you: with all your getting, get understanding. Look through microscopes, but find God. Look through telescopes, but find God. Look for Him revealed in the throbbing life about you, in the palpitating stars above, in the marvelous records of the earth beneath you, and in your own souls. Study the possibilities which God unfolds, and make of yourself all that you can. The harder the struggle, the brighter the crown. Have faith and holy purpose. Go on to *know* and to *will*, to *do* and *be*. When outward circumstances discourage, trample the circumstances under foot. Be master of circumstances, like the king that God has called you to be. God give you such hearts, such toil, such triumphs, and give you such masterhood as shall one day place you among the kings and priests of a redeemed and purified universe!

After the applause following this address subsided, a poem was read, written for the occasion by the ever-ready Mary A. Lathbury. It pictured the modern Chautauqua as representing the old Jerusalem which pilgrims sought for worship and inspiration. We can only quote its final stanzas:

The Life of God is shining
  Upon her where she stands;
And leaf by leaf unfolding
  Within her reverent hands,
The earth and seas and heavens
  Disclose her secrets old,
And every force of Nature
  Reveals its heart of gold!
Now knoweth she the answer
  That ends the schoolmen's strife,—
That knowledge bears no blossom
  Till quickened by the Life.

O holy, holy city!
  The life of God with men!
Descending out of heaven
  To ne'er ascend again.
O Light, O Life immortal!
  One sea above, below!
If unto us be given
  That blessed thing,—*to know*—
Hope's beatific vision,
  And Faith's prophetic sight
Shall die before the fullness
  Of that unclouded Light.

After the reading of the poem, Dr. Vincent said, "In the preparation for this important occasion, I have consulted some of the most experienced and practical educators of the country, and from a number of distinguished gentlemen I have received letters relating to this movement."

We can only quote a sentence or two from a few of these letters.

Dr. Lyman Abbott wrote:

> It seems to me if you can lay out such plans of study, particularly in the departments of practical science, as will fit our boys and young men in the mining, manufacturing, and agricultural districts to become, in a true though not ambitious sense of the term, scientific and intelligent miners, mechanics, and farmers, you will have done more to put down strikes and labor riots than an army could; and more to solve the labor problem than will be done by the Babel-builders of a hundred labor-reform conventions.

Professor Luther T. Townsend, of Boston University:

> Your plan for the promotion of Christian culture in art, science, and literature, among the masses of the American people, strikes me as one of the grandest conceptions of the nineteenth century.

Dr. A. A. Hodge, of Princeton:

> The scheme is a grand one, and only needs to insure its success that efficient administration which has so eminently characterized all your enterprises. History and nature are the spheres in which God exercises his perfections, through which they are

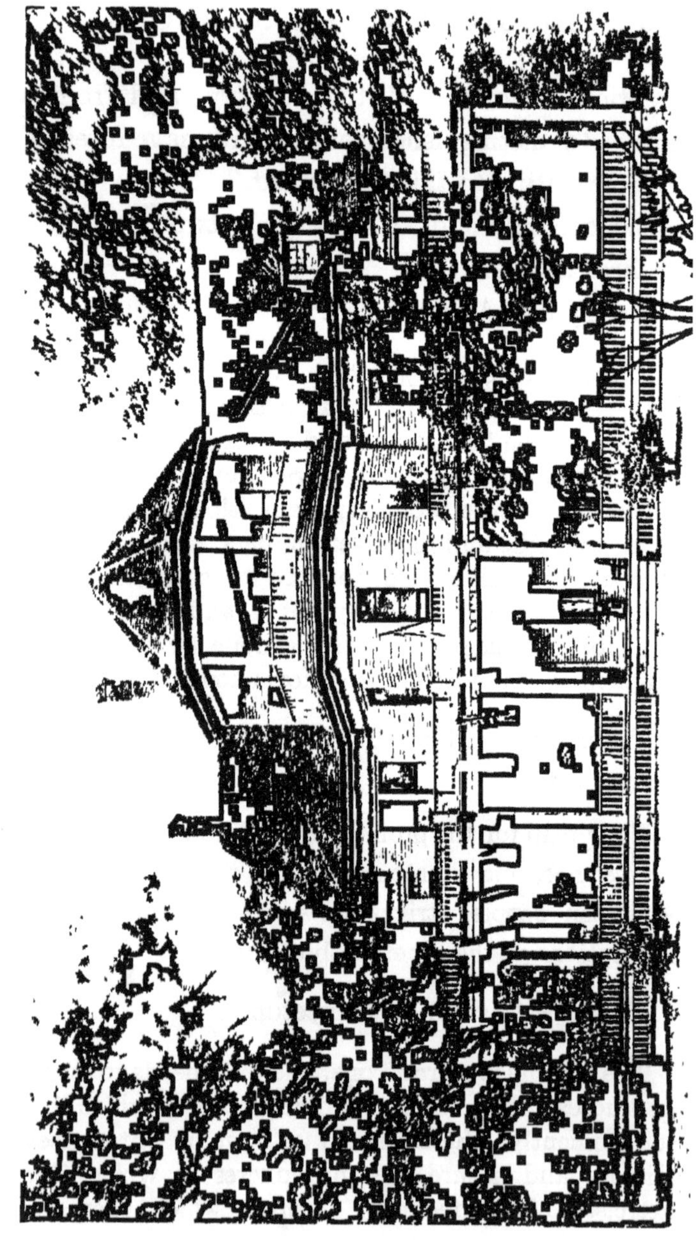

manifested to us. All human knowledge should be comprehended in the one system of which Christ is the center, and illuminated with the light of revelation.

Dr. Arthur Gilman:

Your fears of "superficiality" do not trouble me. For your course will probably aim rather to direct the mind toward the way in which you wish it to develop, than store it with the details of knowledge. You wish to awaken, rather than cultivate.

Dr. Howard Crosby, of New York:

Your scheme to induce business men and others to pursue useful courses of reading in science and history is worthy of all commendation. While we cannot expect to make such persons scientists or scholars, we may expect them to become appreciative of things scientific or scholarly, and to be able to discriminate between the false and the true.

He added some valuable suggestions regarding the kind of books that should be chosen; and the hope that the course, instead of becoming a substitute for the college, might lead to the college.

Dr. Charles F. Deems, of New York, gave his heartiest approval of the plan, and stated that he was holding in his own church classes in all the departments named, and would enroll them under the Chautauqua system, with examinations and the diploma at the completion of the course.

Dr. William F. Warren, President of Boston University, wrote a letter in which he said:

> You are aiming to secure that without which every system of education is weak, and with which any is strong; namely, interested personal home work the year round. And you seem to carry these home students to the point where they can go alone, if they cannot have the help of the schools.

One of these letters must be given in full, notwithstanding its length. Dr. Vincent introduced it with an account of his interview with its author, the venerable William Cullen Bryant, the oldest of his group—the American poets of the mid-century.

> I wrote him afterward a long letter [said Dr. Vincent], defining the scheme more fully. While in London a few weeks ago I received from him the following letter, written with his own hand,—written but a few weeks before his death. This letter has never been read in public and has never been in print.

> NEW YORK, May 18, 1878.
>
> MY DEAR SIR,
>
> I cannot be present at the meeting called to organize the Chautauqua Literary and Scientific Circle, but I am glad that such a movement is on foot, and wish it the fullest success. There is an attempt to make science, or a knowledge of the laws of the material universe, an ally of the school which denies a separate spiritual existence and a future life; in short, to borrow

of science weapons to be used against Christianity. The friends of religion, therefore, confident that one truth never contradicts another, are doing wisely when they seek to accustom the people at large to think and to weigh evidence as well as to believe. By giving a portion of their time to a vigorous training of the intellect, and a study of the best books, men gain the power to deal satisfactorily with questions with which the mind might otherwise have become bewildered. It is true that there is no branch of human knowledge so important as that which teaches the duties that we owe to God and to each other, and that there is no law of the universe, sublime and wonderful as it may be, so worthy of being made fully known as the law of love, which makes him who obeys it a blessing to his species, and the universal observance of which would put an end to a large proportion of the evils which affect mankind. Yet is a knowledge of the results of science, and such of its processes as lie most open to the popular mind, important for the purpose of showing the different spheres occupied by science and religion, and preventing the inquirer from mistaking their divergence from each other for opposition.

I perceive this important advantage in the proposed organization, namely, that those who engage in it will mutually encourage each other. It will give the members a common pursuit, which always begets a feeling of brotherhood; they will have a common topic of conversation and discussion, and the consequence will be, that many who, if they stood alone, might soon grow weary of the studies which are recommended to them, will be incited to perseverance by the interest which they see others taking in them. It may happen in rare instances that a person of eminent mental endowments, which otherwise might have remained uncultivated and unknown, will be stimulated in this manner to diligence, and put forth unexpected powers, and, passing rapidly beyond the rest, become greatly distinguished, and take a place among the luminaries of the age.

I shall be interested to watch, during the little space of life that may yet remain to me, the progress and results of the plan which has drawn from me this letter.

I am, Sir,
Very truly yours,
W. C. BRYANT.

The distinguished writer of this letter died only a month and four days after writing it, on June 12, 1878, as the result of a sunstroke while he was making an address at the unveiling of a statue in the Central Park. He was in the eighty-fifth year of his age.

After some short addresses by men on the platform, Bishop Foster, Professor Wilkinson, Dr. Strong, and others, Dr. Vincent announced as the first book of the course, Green's *Short History of the English People*, and invited all desirous of joining the C. L. S. C. to write their names and addresses upon slips of paper and hand them to anyone on the platform. It might have been supposed that a circular would be ready containing a statement of the course for the first year, regulations and requirements of the organization, the fee of membership, etc.; but in the enthusiasm of the time those desirable requisites had been forgotten. Everybody looked around for a slip of paper. Visiting cards were made useful, margins were torn off newspapers, and there was an overwhelming rush toward the platform to join the new circle. On that afternoon seven hundred names were received and the number grew hourly until the close of the Assembly. Nearly all the regular year-by-year visitors to Chautauqua became members of this "Pioneer Class," as it was afterwards named; and to this day its fellowship, after forty-two years, still continues one of the largest at its annual gatherings in Pioneer Hall, the building which it erected as its home.

The book-store was crowded with applicants for Green's History, and the few copies on hand, not more than half a dozen, were instantaneously disposed of. An order was telegraphed to the Harper Brothers in New York for fifty copies, on the next morning for fifty more, then for another hundred, day after day the demand increasing. The Harpers were astounded at the repeated calls, and telegraphed for particulars as to the reason why everybody at an almost unknown place called Chautauqua had gone wild in demand for this book. Their stock on hand was exhausted long before the Assembly was ended, and most of the members of this "Class of 1882" were compelled to wait a month or more for their books. Public libraries were by no means numerous in those days while Andrew Carnegie was making the millions to be spent later in establishing them, but wherever they were, Green's Short History was drawn out, and a waiting list made for it, to the amazement of librarians, who vainly proposed the substitution of other standard English histories. Whoever could buy, borrow, or beg a copy of Green, rejoiced—we hope that no Chautauquan, in his hunger for literature, *stole* one, but we are not sure. People otherwise honest have been known to retain borrowed umbrellas and books.

In the Class of 1882 eight thousand four hundred names were enrolled, for the members brought home from Chautauqua the good news, and families, neighbors, and friends everywhere sent in their applications. Later we shall learn what proportion of these followed the course through the four years and marched under the arches to their Recognition as graduates.

An addition had been made to the grounds on the west, and here Dr. Vincent chose a square shaded by abundant beech-trees, as the center and home of the C. L. S. C. He named it St. Paul's Grove, choosing the apostle who represented the combination of the fervent heart and the cultured mind, an ideal for all Chautauquans. Besides Dr. Vincent's address at this time, another was given by Governor A. H. Colquitt of Georgia, President of the International Sunday School Convention. The dedicatory prayer was offered by Bishop Foster and an appropriate hymn written by Dr. Hyde of Denver was sung by Professor Sherwin and his choir. St. Paul's Grove, and its pillared temple soon to rise, will appear often in our story as one of the sacred spots at Chautauqua.

We must not overlook the daily program during this epoch-making season of 1878. There were the daily classes studying Greek and Hebrew under Drs. Strong and Vail. There was a class in microscopy, with the Misses Lattimore; there was the normal class with a full number of students ending with the successful examination of more than one hundred and forty new members of the Normal Alumni Association. The annual reunion of the Normal Alumni was celebrated with the usual banners, procession, address, the illuminated fleet and fireworks.

The lecture platform of 1878 stood at as high a level as ever. If any one speaker bore off the honors of that year, it was Bishop Randolph S. Foster of the Methodist Episcopal Church, whose lectures on "Beyond the Grave" drew the largest audiences and aroused the deepest interest. They were afterward published in a volume which attracted wide attention, and brought some criticism from preachers of the conservative school. There were even some who talked of an impeachment and trial, but they did not venture to bring the greatest thinker and theologian in their church to the bar. Other lecturers who made their mark were Dr. Robert M. Hatfield of Chicago, President Charles H. Fowler, Dr. (soon after Bishop) John F. Hurst, Dr. John Lord, the historian-lecturer, Dr. Joseph Cook, Professor William North Rice, Dr. T. DeWitt Talmage, with his entertaining lecture on "Big Blunders," and Dr. Charles F. Deems on "The Superstitions of Science."

One remarkable meeting was held on the afternoon of the opening day, Tuesday, August 6th. In the Pavilion four men gave in turn the distinctive doctrines and usages of their several churches. These were the Rev. Mr. Seymour, Baptist, Rev. Mr. Williston, Congregationalist,

Rev. Dr. Hatfield, Methodist, and Rev. J. A. Worden, Presbyterian. Without attempt at controversy or criticism each speaker named the principles for which his branch of the Holy Catholic Church stood. There was the most cordial feeling. Each listener believed as strongly as before in his own denomination, but many felt a greater respect for the other branches of the true vine. At the close all the congregation sang together,

> Blest be the tie that binds
> Our hearts in Christian love.

A new building took its place upon the grounds, and speedily became the center of many activities. It was called "The Children's Temple," built through the generous gift of President Lewis Miller, in the general plan of his Sunday School Hall at Akron, Ohio, a central assembly room with folding doors opening or closing a number of classrooms around it. For many years it was the home of the Children's Class, under Rev. B. T. Vincent and Frank Beard, which grew to an attendance of three hundred daily. They wore badges of membership, passed examinations upon a systematic course, and received diplomas. Soon an Intermediate Department became necessary for those who had completed the children's course, and this also grew into a large body of members and graduates.

A host of events on this great Chautauqua season of 1878 must be omitted from this too long chapter in our story.

The Chautauqua Book-Store

## CHAPTER IX

### CHAUTAUQUA ALL THE YEAR

DURING those early years the Chautauqua sessions were strenuous weeks to both Miller and Vincent. Mr. Miller brought to Chautauqua for a number of seasons his normal class of young people from the Akron Sunday School, requiring them to attend the Chautauqua normal class and to take its examination. He acted also as Superintendent of the Assembly Sunday School, which was like organizing a new school of fifteen hundred members every Sunday, on account of the constant coming and going of students and teachers. But Mr. Miller's time and thoughts were so constantly taken up with secular details, leasing lots, cutting down trees, and setting up tents, settling disputes with lot holders and ticket holders, and a thousand and one business matters great and small —especially after successive purchases had more than doubled the territory of the Assembly,—that he was able to take part in but few of its exercises. One out of many perplexing situations may be taken as a specimen. In one purchase was included a small tract on the lake-shore outside the original camp ground, where some families from a distance had purchased holdings and built small cottages, being independent both of the camp-meeting and the Assembly. Some members of this colony claimed the right of way to go in and out of the Assembly at all times, Sundays as well as week-days, to attend lectures and classes without purchasing tickets. Others in the older parts of the ground under camp-meeting leases declared themselves beyond the jurisdiction of new rules made by the Assembly trustees. A strong party appeared demanding that the lot owners as a body should elect the trustees,—which meant that the future of a great and growing educational institution should be shaped not by a carefully selected Board under the guidance of two idealists,—one of whom was at the same time a practical business-man, a rare combination,—but by a gathering of lot-holders, not all of them intelligent, and the majority people who were keeping boarding-houses and were more eager for dollars than for culture. I remember a conversation with the proprietor of one of the largest boarding-houses who urged that the grounds be left open, with no gate-fees or tickets; but instead a ticket-booth at the entrance to each lecture-hall, so that people would be required to pay only for such lectures and entertainments as they chose to attend! I could name some Assemblies calling themselves chautauquas, where this policy was pursued; and almost invariably one season or at most two seasons terminated their history.

Added to these and other perplexities was the ever-present question of finance. The rapid growth of the movement caused a requirement of funds far beyond the revenue of the Association. Its income came mainly from the gate-fees, to which was added a small tax upon each lot, and the concessions to store-keepers; for the prices obtained by the leasing of new lots must be held as a sinking fund to pay off the mortgages incurred in their purchase. There came also an imperative demand for a water-supply through an aqueduct, a sewer-system, and other sanitary arrangements made absolutely necessary by the increase of population. In those years Mr. Miller's purse was constantly opened to meet pressing needs, and his credit enabled the trustees to obtain loans and mortgages. But despite his multitudinous cares and burdens, no one ever saw Mr. Miller harassed or nervous. He was always unruffled, always pleasant, even smiling under the most trying conditions. His head was always clear, his insight into the needs not only of the time but of the future also was always sure, and his spinal column was strong enough to stand firm against the heaviest pressure. He knew instinctively when it was wise to conciliate, and when it was essential to be positive. The present generation of Chautauquans can never realize how great is their debt of gratitude to Lewis Miller. The inventor and manufacturer of harvesting machines at Akron and Canton, Ohio, busy at his desk for eleven months, found the Swiss Cottage beside Chautauqua Lake by no means a place of rest during his brief vacation.

Nor were the burdens upon the other Founder lighter than those of his associate. The two men talked and corresponded during the year regarding the coming program, but the selection, engagement, and arrangement of the speakers was mainly Dr. Vincent's part. At the same hour, often half a dozen meetings would be held, and care must be taken not to have them in conflict in their location and their speakers. Changes in the program must often be made suddenly after a telegram from some lecturer that he could not arrive on the morrow. New features must be introduced as the demand and the opportunity arose,—the Baptists, or Methodists, or Congregationalists, or Disciples desired a meeting, for which an hour and a place must be found. The only one who kept the list of the diversified assemblages was Dr. Vincent. He had no secretary in those days to sit at a desk in an office and represent the Superintendent of Instruction. His tent at the foot of the grounds was a stage whereon entrances and exits were constant. Moreover, the audience was apt to measure the importance of a lecture by the presence of Dr. Vincent as presiding officer or a substitute in his place introducing the speaker. The Vincent temperament was less even and placid than the Miller; and the Assembly of those early years generally closed with its Superintendent in a worn-out physical condition.

And it must not be forgotten that Dr. Vincent like his Associate Founder was a busy working man all the year. He was in charge of the Sunday School work in a great church, supervising Sunday Schools in Buenos Ayres, and Kiu-kiang, and Calcutta, as well as in Bangor and Seattle. At his desk in New York and Plainfield he was the editor of nine periodicals, aided by a small number of assistants. Several months of every year were spent in a visitation of Methodist Conference setting forth the work, and stirring up a greater interest in it. He was lecturing and preaching and taking part in conventions and institutes everywhere in the land. Chautauqua was only one of the many activities occupying his mind, his heart, and his time.

The Assembly of 1878, with the inauguration of the C. L. S. C., had been especially exhausting to Dr. Vincent. Imagine, if you can, his feelings when he found his desks in the office and the home piled high with letters concerning the new movement for Chautauqua readings all the year. He was simply overwhelmed by the demands, for everybody must have an immediate answer. Walking out one day, he met one of the teachers of the High School, told her of his difficulties, and asked her if she could suggest anyone who might relieve him. She thought a moment, and then said:

"I think I know a girl of unusual ability who can help you,—Miss Kate Kimball, who was graduated from the High School last June, and I will send her to you."

She came, a tall young lady, only eighteen years old, with a pair of brown eyes peculiarly bright, and a manner retiring though self-possessed. Dr. Vincent mentioned some of the help that he required, but looked doubtfully at her, and said,

"I am afraid that you are too young to undertake this work."

She answered, "I would like to try it; but if you find that I am not equal to it, I will not be offended to have it given to some other person. Let me see if I can help you even a little."

That was the introduction of Miss Kate Fisher Kimball to the work and care of the Chautauqua Literary and Scientific Circle, of which she was the Executive Secretary until her death in 1917. She was born in 1860, at Orange, New Jersey, her father, Dr. Horace F. Kimball, being a dentist with office in New York. Young as she was, she at once showed rare abilities in administration. Under her vigorous and wise efforts, the C. L. S. C. was soon reduced to a system, the members were classified, the course was made orderly, circulars of various sorts were prepared and sent out to answer as many kinds of questions, and the calls from all over the nation, almost all over the world were met. Kate Kimball had a wonderful memory, as well as a systematic mind. Dr. Vincent would tell her in one sentence the answer to be sent to a letter, and twenty sentences in succession for twenty letters. She made no note, but remembered each one; would write to each correspondent a letter framed as it should be, with a clear statement, of just the right length, never getting the wrong answer on her pen. And if six months afterward, or six years, there came a letter requiring the same answer, she did not need to ask for information, but could send the right reply without consulting the letter-file. Thousands of correspondents who may never have met her will remember that signature, "K. F. Kimball," for they have been strengthened and inspired by letters signed with it.

I have heard more than one person say, "I want to go to Chautauqua, if it is only to become acquainted with K. F. Kimball."

Let me transcribe a few sentences written by Mr. Frank Chapin Bray, who as Editor of *The Chautauquan Magazine*, was for years in close relation with Miss Kimball.

> Many will always think of her as a kind of Chautauqua Mother Superior. The details of the work of an Executive Secretary are not transcribable for they were multifarious drudgeries year after year which defy analysis. During thirty-five years she made them the means of transmitting a great idea as a dynamic force vital to hundreds of thousands of men and women the world around.

Next to the originating genius of John H. Vincent, the influence which made the Chautauqua

Home Reading Course one of the mightiest educational forces of the nineteenth century was the tireless energy and the executive ability of Kate F. Kimball.

About 1912 she was suddenly taken with an illness, not deemed serious at the time, but later found to have been a slight paralytic shock. She was given a year's vacation from office work and spent most of it in England and on the continent. Some of her friends think that if she had absolutely abstained from work, she might have recovered her health; but while in England she visited nearly all its great cathedrals, and wrote a series of articles for *The Chautauquan* on "An English Cathedral Journey," afterward embodied in one of the best of the non-technical books on that subject. She returned to her desk, but not in her former vigor. Year by year her powers of thought and action declined, and she died June 17, 1917, in the fifty-seventh year of her age, leaving after her not only a precious memory but an abiding influence; for the plans initiated by her adaptive mind are still those effective in the shaping of the Chautauqua Circle.

The course of reading for the first year was as follows: Green's *Short History of the English People;* with it the little hand-book by Dr. Vincent—Chautauqua Text-Book No. 4, *Outline of English*

*History;* an arrangement by periods, enabling the reader to arrange the events in order; Chautauqua Text-Book No. 5, *Outline of Greek History;* Professor Mahaffy's *Old Greek Life;* Stopford Brooke's *Primer of English Literature;* Chautauqua Text-Book No. 2, *Studies of the Stars;* Dr. H. W. Warren's *Recreations in Astronomy;* J. Dorman Steele's *Human Psychology;* Dr. J. F. Hurst's, *Outlines of Bible History,* and *The Word of God Opened,* by Rev. Bradford K. Pierce. This included no less than eleven books, although four of them were the small Chautauqua textbooks, Nos. 2, 4, 5, and 6. All that was definitely required of the members was that they should sign a statement that these books had been read; but through the year a series of sheets was sent to each enrolled member, containing questions for examination, under the title "Outline Memoranda," in order not to alarm the unschooled reader by the terror of an examination. Moreover, the student was at liberty to search his books, consult any other works, and obtain assistance from all quarters in obtaining the answers to the questions. These questions were of two kinds, one requiring thought on the part of the reader, and not susceptible of answer at any given page of the book; such as: "Name the five persons whom you consider the greatest in

Hall of the Christ

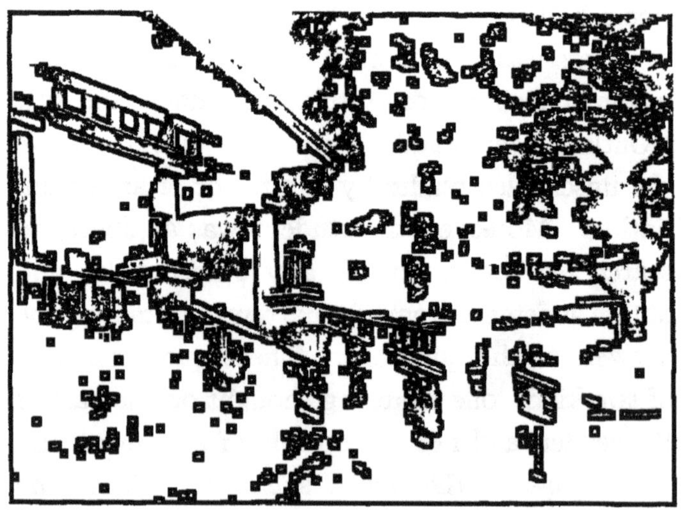

Entrance to the Hall of Philosophy

the history of England, and the reasons for your choice," "Name what you regard as five of the most important events in English history," etc. There were some other questions, of which the answer might or might not be found in any books of the books of the course, but questions to make the reader search and enquire; such as: "What did King John say when he signed Magna Charta?" "With what words did Oliver Cromwell dismiss the Long Parliament?" "What were the last words of Admiral Nelson?" These questions brought difficulty, not only to readers, but to school-teachers, pastors, and librarians, to whom they were propounded by puzzled students. At one time I was reading of a convention of librarians, where one of the subjects discussed was, how to satisfy the hordes of Chautauquans everywhere, asking all sorts of curious questions. The veterans of that premier class of 1882 still remember the sheet of the Outline Memoranda prepared by Dr. Warren, on his book *Recreations in Astronomy*. There may have been a member or two who succeeded in answering them all, but their names do not appear on any record.

Not all those, who in an hour of enthusiasm under the spell of Dr. Vincent's address on that opening day, wrote their names as members of the

C. L. S. C. persevered to the bitter end and won the diploma. Of the 8400 enrolled in the first class, only 1850 were "recognized" as graduates in 1882. Some of the delinquents afterward took heart of grace, and finished with later classes. But even those who fell out by the way gained something, perhaps gained an enduring impulse toward good reading. We frequently received word of those who had dropped the C. L. S. C. in order to obtain a preparation for college. Dr. Edward Everett Hale used to tell of a man whom he met on a railway train, who made a remark leading the doctor to say, "You talk like a Chautauquan—are you a member of the C. L. S. C.?" The man smiled and answered, "Well, I don't know whether I am or not. My wife is: she read the whole course, and has her diploma framed. I read only one book, and then gave up. But any institution that can lead a man to read Green's *Short History of the English People*, has done considerable for that man!"

As one by one the required books had been read by diligent members, there came urgent requests from many for the names of other books, on history, on sciences, and especially on the Bible. Dr. Vincent and his staff were compelled to look for the best books on special courses, supplementing the required course. By degrees almost a hundred of these courses were arranged, and have been pursued by multitudes. The one who read the regular course through four years was to receive a diploma; if he answered the questions of very simple "Outline Memoranda," his diploma was to bear one seal. If he took the stiffer "Outline Memoranda" described above, his diploma was to receive an additional seal for each year's work. Each special course was to have its own special seal. Any member who read the Bible through while pursuing the course, would have a gold crown seal upon his diploma. There were some elderly people who seemed to have nothing in the world to do, but to read special courses, fill out the memoranda, send for seals, and then demand another course on Crete or Kamchatka, or the Ten Lost Tribes of Israel, until Miss Kimball, her helpers, and her literary friends were kept on the jump to find books on these various subjects. Hanging on the walls of C. L. S. C. classrooms at Chautauqua are diplomas illuminated with a hundred seals or more, sent to the class headquarters as memorials of diligent readers who have passed away.

The readers of these seal-courses become members of various "orders" of different rank. Those whose diplomas show four seals belong to the "Order of the White Seal," those who have seven seals, to the "League of the Round Table," and if they have fourteen seals or more, the "Guild of the Seven Seals." Each of these societies holds its annual reunion at Chautauqua, wears its own badge, and marches behind its own banner in the procession.

The reference to seals brings us to another feature of Chautauqua, and especially of the C. L. S. C., which attracted universal attention and led many thousands into the charmed circle,—those touches of poetry and sentiment, which no one but Dr. Vincent could have originated. There were the three mottoes of the C. L. S. C. always made prominent in its prospectus and announcements, "We Study the Word and the Works of God"; "Let Us Keep Our Heavenly Father in the Midst"; and "Never be Discouraged." The second of these sentences was spoken by the venerable Hebraist, Dr. Stephen H. Vail, as with tears upon his face he parted with Dr. Vincent, at the session of 1877, a year before the announcement of the C. L. S. C. There was for each class a name. The first class to take a name was that of '84, established in 1880. They were continually calling for class-meetings until Dr. Vincent in his announcements spoke of them as "those irrepressible eighty-fours!" Whereupon they promptly adopted as their name, "The Irrepressibles," and their example was followed by the other classes. The class of 1882 took the name, "The Pioneers." Classes are known as "The Vincent Class," "The Lewis Miller Class"—others are named after Shakespeare, Tennyson, Sidney Lanier, etc. The class graduating in 1892 commemorated the discovery of America four hundred years before, by the name "Columbia." Then, too, each class has its own flower, which its members seek to wear on the great days of the C. L. S. C.; but only the Pioneer class of 1882 proudly bears before it in procession a hatchet, and its members wear little hatchets as badges. Dr. Hale said that the reason why the Pioneers carry hatchets is that "they axe the way!" Each class has its own officers and trustees, and though all its members are never assembled, and can never meet each other, they maintain a strong bond of union through correspondence. There is the great silk banner of the Chautauqua Circle leading the procession on Recognition Day, followed by the classes from 1882 until the present, each class marching behind its banner. In the early days, until the Chautauqua grounds became crowded, there was an annual "Camp Fire," all the members in a great circle standing around a great bonfire at night singing songs and listening to short speeches. These are only a few of the social influences which make the C. L. S. C. more than merely a list of readers. It is a brotherhood, a family bound together by a common interest.

The opening day of the Chautauqua readings is October first. On that day at noon, the members of the circle living at Chautauqua and others in the adjacent towns meet at the Miller bell tower on the Point. As the clock sounds out the hour of twelve all present grasp a long rope connected with the bells and together pull it, over and over again, sounding forth the signal that the Chautauqua year has begun. It is said that every true Chautauquan the world over, from Mayville to Hong-Kong, can hear the sound of that bell and at the summons open their books for the year's reading.

In one of the earlier years we received at the office a letter from the wife of an army officer stationed among the Indians, and far from any settlement. She wrote that she was a hundred and twenty-five miles from any other white woman, and felt keenly her loneliness. But on the day when her bundle of C. L. S. C. books arrived, she clasped it to her bosom and wept tears of joy over it, for she felt that she was no longer alone, but one in a great company who were reading the same books and thinking the same thoughts and enjoying one fellowship.

In one of the early classes was a young lady who, soon after sending in her name, sailed for South Africa to become a teacher in a girl's boarding-school. One day in the following June, when it was in the depth of winter in South Africa,—for in south latitude our seasons are reversed; they have a saying at the Cape "as hot as Christmas"—she came to her classes arrayed in her very best apparel. The girls looked at her in surprise and asked "Is this your birthday."

"No," she answered, "but it is the Commencement Day at Chautauqua in America, and everybody dresses up on that day!"

The thousands of readers in the Chautauqua fellowship naturally arranged themselves in two classes. About half of them were reading by themselves, individuals, each by himself or herself, —mostly herself, for at least three-fourths of the members were women, and their average age was about thirty years. The other half were united in groups, "local circles," as they were called. Some of these were community circles, people of one village or town, irrespective of church relations; other circles were connected with the churches. In those days before the Christian Endeavor Society, the Epworth League, and other nation-wide organizations had appropriated the interest of the young people, the Chautauqua Circle was the literary society in many churches.

I recall the testimony of a Methodist minister of those days, given to me when I met him at his conference in the Middle West.

> When I was sent to my last church, I learned that there was a reading circle among its members, and I heard the news with some dismay, for in more than one place I had started a literary society and found that it was necessary for me to supply all the thought and labor to keep it in operation, to plan the course, to select people to write papers and persuade them to do it, to be ready to fill vacancies on the program. And as soon as I stopped supplying steam, the society was sure to come to a stand-still. But at this church I found a Chautauqua Circle that was taking care of itself. Its programs were provided, the members were reading a regular course and making their reports; they presided in turn at the meetings, and I was not called upon to take any part unless I desired it. Also in the prayer-meetings, I could soon recognize the members of the Circle by a touch of intelligence in their testimonies.

It is the opinion of the writer that if one could ascertain the history of the woman's clubs that now cover the country, and ascertain their origin, it would be found that nearly all of the older woman's clubs arose out of Chautauqua Circles whose members, after completing the prescribed course, took up civics or politics, or literature. It would be an interesting study to ascertain how far the General Federation of Women's Clubs of America was an outgrowth of the Chautauqua movement.

## CHAPTER X

### THE SCHOOL OF LANGUAGES

THE year 1879 marked an extension in more than one direction of Chautauqua's plans and program. The season was lengthened to forty-three days, more than double the length of the earlier sessions. On July 17th began the classes in The Chautauqua Normal School of Languages, held in a rough board-walled, white-washed building, which had formerly been used as a lodging-house, but was no longer needed since cottages had opened their doors to guests. This may be regarded as the formal opening of the Chautauqua Summer Schools, although already classes had been held, some of them three years, others four years, in Greek, Hebrew, and kindergarten instruction. We will name the faculty of this year. Greek was taught by a native of Greece, Dr. T. T. Timayenis, of New York; Latin by Miss Emma M. Hall, of the Detroit High School, afterward a missionary-teacher in Rome, Italy; Prof. J. H. Worman, of Brooklyn, N. Y., taught German, never speaking one word of English in his classes, although a fluent speaker and

Congregational House

Fenton Memorial, Deaconess' House

author in English. Prof. A. Lalande was the teacher of the French language; Dr. Stephen M. Vail continued his classes in Hebrew, and Dr. James Strong in Greek; Prof. Bernhard Maimon of Chicago, taught Oriental languages; and Prof. A. S. Cook, then of Johns Hopkins, but soon afterward of Yale, conducted a class in the study of Anglo-Saxon language and literature. These studies were pursued from a fortnight before the formal opening of the Assembly until its close, making courses of six weeks, carried on in an intensive manner. Each professor pushed his department as though it were the only one in the school, and his students could scarcely find time to rest themselves by rowing on the lake or walking in the woods with their classmates.

Allied to the School of Languages was the Teachers' Retreat, opening at the same time but closing just before the Assembly proper. This was outside the realm of Sunday School instruction, being intended for secular teachers and presenting the principles and best methods of education. One of its leaders was Prof. J. W. Dickinson, Secretary of the Massachusetts State Board of Education, an enthusiast as well as a master. He had at his command a fund of witticisms and stories, always in the direct line of his teaching, which added not a little to the interest of his lectures. I was with him at the table for a fortnight, and his juicy talk made even a tough steak enjoyable. Associated with Dr. Dickinson were Prof. William F. Phelps of Minnesota, Dr. Joseph Alden of the State Normal School, Albany, N. Y., and Dr. John Hancock, President of the National Teachers' Association. In the following year, 1880, the School of Languages and Teachers' Retreat were united, and the Summer School program was again enlarged. Year by year new departments were added, until Chautauqua became a summer university, and such it continues to this day, offering more than two hundred courses, taught by nearly one hundred and fifty instructors. Perhaps the most popular courses have always been those in physical culture, pursued by teachers in public and private schools, enabled by Chautauqua to make their work in their home schools more efficient and extensive. One might spend weeks at Chautauqua, attending the lectures and concerts in the Amphitheater and the Hall, and enjoying the bathing and boating opportunities of the Lake, yet never realizing that on College Hill, and down at the Gymnasium, are nearly five thousand young men and young women diligently seeking the higher education.

A third sideline during this season of 1879 was the Foreign Mission Institute, held by missionary leaders of the Congregational, Methodist, Presbyterian, and Baptist organizations, and addressed by missionaries at home from many lands. Chautauqua was a pioneer in bringing together representatives of different churches for conference upon their work of winning the world to Christ. This series of missionary councils has been continued without the omission of a year through all the history of Chautauqua since 1879.

The Sixth Chautauqua Assembly opened on its regular evening, the first Tuesday in August, 1879. The ravine which had been the seat of the Pavilion and birthplace of the C. L. S. C. had been transformed into a great auditorium of permanent materials and fairly comfortable seats for five thousand people. It was a great advance upon any of the earlier meeting places, and made it no longer necessary to carry one's umbrella to the lectures. But a heavy rain on the extensive roof would make even the largest-lunged orator inaudible, and the many wooden pillars supporting the roof had a fashion of getting themselves between the speaker and the hearers. Notwithstanding these minor drawbacks, it proved to be one of the best audience-halls in the land for large assemblies, for its acoustic properties were almost perfect. No speaker ever heard his words flung back to him by an echo, and the orator who knew how to use his voice could be heard almost equally well in every corner of the building. When Dr. Buckley stood for the first time upon its platform, and looked at its radiating and ascending seats, he said to Dr. Vincent, "This is a genuine *amphitheater*." The name was adopted, and the Amphitheater became the meeting place for all the popular lectures and the great Sunday services. Many were the distinguished speakers, men and women, who stood upon its platform, and as many singers whose voices enraptured throngs. At a popular concert almost as many seemed to be standing, crowded under the eaves, as were seated beneath the roof.

The old Amphitheater stood until 1897. In that year the building of the Massey Memorial Organ made some changes necessary. The old building was taken down, and a new Amphitheater arose in its place, having above it a trussed roof and supported from the sides, and no pillars obstructing the view. It has been said that the Chautauqua Amphitheater will seat ten thousand people, but a careful computation shows that fifty-five hundred, or at the utmost fifty-six hundred are its limit upon the benches, without chairs in the aisles. But another thousand, or even fifteen hundred may sometimes be seen standing back of its seats at a popular lecture or concert.

In the season of 1879, one of the leading speakers was an Englishman, the Rev. W. O. Simpson of the Wesleyan Church, who had been for some years a missionary in India. His graphic pictures of village life in that land were a revelation, for Kipling and his followers had not yet thrown the light of their genius upon the great peninsula and its people. Mr. Simpson was over six feet in height and large in every way, in voice as well as in girth. We all hoped to meet him yet many years at Chautauqua, for he seemed to be abounding in health. But a few months later we learned of his sudden death. In those years it was the Chautauqua custom to hold a memorial service for men prominent in the class-room or on the platform, and it fell to my lot to speak in 1880 upon the Rev. W. O. Simpson. I sent to England for printed matter relating to his life, and among the appreciative articles found one story which is worthy of remembrance.

When Mr. Simpson was a student of theology at the Wesleyan Theological School, he chanced one day to read the announcement of a lecture upon the Bible, and went to hear it. To his amazement he found himself at an infidel meeting, listening to a virulent attack upon the Holy Scriptures. In the middle of his lecture, the speaker said:

> There are undoubtedly good things in the Bible, but anyone who is familiar with the ancient writers of Greece, and especially those of India, knows well, if he would tell the truth, that all the good things in the Bible were stolen from earlier scholars and sages, and were originally better spoken or written than by the so-called authors of the Bible, who took them at second-hand. If anybody here is prepared to deny that statement, let him stand up and say so!

Instantly this young student of theology stood up, six feet high, and at that time in his life very slim in his figure. That he might be seen readily he stood on the seat, and a fellow-student said that he loomed up apparently ten feet high. He held a little red-covered book, and stretching his long arm toward the speaker, said something like this:

> I hold in my hand a copy of the New Testament, and I wish to say that in this little book, only a quarter of the Bible, you will find a clearer light on man's nature, and character, and destiny than may be read in all the ancient books of the world taken together.

He paused, seized the little volume with both hands, tore it in two parts, flung one part down to the floor, and still holding the rest of it, went on:

I have thrown aside one-half of this book, but this half contains the four gospels of our Lord, which will tell more what man may be here and will be hereafter than can be found in all the books of ancient Rome, or Greece, or Chaldea, or India, or China.

Then he tore out three leaves from the fragment, flung all the rest on the floor, and fluttering the torn pages, said:

These six pages contain Christ's Sermon on the Mount, setting forth a higher standard of righteousness, a clearer view of God, and a better knowledge of man's nature than all the other ancient books on earth. That is my answer to the speaker!

And leaving the torn book on the floor, he walked out of the room.

Other speakers in the new Amphitheater in the summer of 1879 were Dr. Henry W. Warren, in the next year a Bishop; Frank Beard, with his caricatures and stories; Dr. C. H. Fowler, Dr. Joseph Cook, Bishop Foster, Dr. Alexander A. Hodge, the Princeton theologian, Dr. John Lord, the historian, Hon. J. W. Wendling of Kentucky, who brought brilliant oratory to the service of Christianity in an eloquent lecture on "The Man of Galilee"; Prof. J. W. Churchill, one of the finest readers of his time; Dr. George Dana Boardman of Philadelphia; and Dr. Vincent himself, always greeted by the largest audiences. Let us say, once for all, that Dr. Buckley was a perennial visitor, with new lectures every year, and his ever-popular answers to the question-drawer. If there was a problem which he could not solve, he could always turn the tables on the questioner with a story or a retort.

One event of 1879 not to be passed over was the dedication of the Hall of Philosophy in St. Paul's Grove. Dr. Vincent suggested the plan of the building, to be set apart for the uses of the C. L. S. C. and the interests of general culture. As everybody who has been to Chautauqua knows, it was in the form of a Greek temple, an open building surrounded by plain columns, which may have resembled marble, but were made of wood. The dedication was held on August 5th, and addresses were given by Dr. Vincent, Rev. W. O. Simpson, and Dr. Ellinwood. There are thousands of Chautauquans, some of them dwelling in distant lands, who are ready to declare that in all the week, the most precious hour was that of the five o'clock Vesper Service on Sunday afternoon, when the long rays of the setting sun fell upon the assemblage, as they sang "Day is dying in the West," and they united in that prayer of Thomas à Kempis, beginning, "In all things, O my soul, thou shalt rest in the Lord always, for He is the everlasting rest of the saints."

In the fall and winter of 1891 this writer was the traveling companion of Bishop Vincent in Europe. Every Sunday afternoon at five o'clock, whether on the Atlantic, or in London, Lucerne, Florence, or Naples, we brought out our copies of the vesper service and read it together, feeling that in spirit we were within the columns of that Hall in the Grove.

This year, 1879, the second year of the C. L. S. C., brought to its Founder a problem which threatened the ruin of the circle, but in its happy solution proved to be a powerful element in its success. This was to be the Roman Year of the course, and in the original conception the Pioneer Class of 1882 would take up Roman history, while the new class of 1883 would begin as its predecessor had begun, with English history. If this plan had been carried out, as announced in the early circulars for that year's study, then in every church and community two classes must be organized and conducted with different readings. Another year would require three circles, and still another four circles. Could members and leaders be found for four separate clubs in one locality? Would not the circle break up into fragments from the weight of the machinery needed to keep the wheel in motion? Just then came the suggestion—made by President Lewis Miller, as Dr. Vincent told me at the time—that *both* the classes should read the books together, making the same course the second year for the Pioneers, and the first year's reading of "the Vincents," as the members of '83 named themselves. In a college there is a progression of studies, for one science must follow another; but in the Chautauqua Circle, it makes no difference whether the reader begins with the history of Greece or of Rome, or of England, or of America. New members can enter any year and read with those already reading. The Circle is a railroad train on a track with four stations. You can board the train in England, America, or Greece or Rome, and when you have gone the round and reached the station where you began, you have completed the course and receive your certificate ornamented with all the seals that you have won by additional reading and study. The present four-year cycle of the C. L. S. C. consists of the English, American, Classical, and Modern European years.

One more event of 1879 must not be forgotten. The Park of Palestine had fallen into decrepitude. Some of its mountains had sunk down, and the

Baptist Headquarters and Mission House

course of the River Jordan had become clogged up, so there was danger of a lake at a spot where none was on the map, and of a dry bed below, long after the Israelites had finished their crossing. Moreover, some mischievous boys had mixed up its geography by moving a few of the cities. Bethel was found where Kirjath-jearim should be; Joppa had been swept by the ice in the breaking up of winter into the Mediterranean Sea, and Megiddo was missing. The task of reconstructing the Park was given to Dr. W. H. Perrine of Michigan, a scholar and an artist, who had traveled in the Holy Land, had painted a panorama of it, and had constructed a model in plaster. He rebuilt the Park from more permanent materials, and succeeded in making it more accurate in some details, as well as more presentable in appearance. But man-made mountains are by no means "the ever-lasting hills," and the Park of Palestine needs to be made over at least once in ten years if it is to be kept worthy of Chautauqua.

## CHAPTER XI

### HOTELS, HEADQUARTERS, AND HAND-SHAKING

### (1880)

THE seventh session of the Assembly opened in 1880 with another addition to the Chautauqua territory. Fifty acres along the Lake shore had been acquired, and the Assembly-ground was now three times as large as that of the old Fair Point Camp Meeting.

This season saw also the foundation laid for a large hotel. It is worthy of record that the Hotel Athenæum was built not by the Assembly Board, but by a stock company of people friendly to the movement and willing to risk considerable capital in its establishment. More than one promising Assembly had already been wrecked and many more were destined to bankruptcy by building large hotels before they were assured of guests to fill them. It must be kept in mind that everywhere the Chautauqua constituency was not, and is not now, the wealthy class who frequent summer hotels and are willing to pay high prices for their entertainment. A Chautauqua Assembly, whether in the east or the west, is mainly composed of people possessing only moderate means, but eager for intellectual culture. Whenever a Chautauqua has been established in connection with the conventional summer hotel, either it has become bankrupt from lack of patronage, or the hotel has swallowed up the Assembly. The Hotel Athenæum at Chautauqua was not the property of the Assembly, and might have failed—as many, perhaps most, of the summer hotels at watering-places have failed once or more than once in their history—without endangering the Assembly itself. The men who built the Athenæum, led by Lewis Miller and his business partners, risked their money, and might have lost it, for there were seasons when it paid no dividends to the stockholders, and other seasons when the profits were small. Yet this hotel drew by degrees an increasing number of visitors who were able and willing to enjoy its advantages over those of the earlier cottage boarding houses, and it led to better accommodations and a more liberal table in the cottages, until now the Hotel Athenæum is only one of a number of really good houses of entertainment at Chautauqua. It is given prominence in our story because it was first in its field. By the way, the name "Hotel Athenæum" was given by Dr. Vincent, who liked to impart a classical tone to buildings in an educational institution.

The building was begun in 1880 and opened in the following year, though even then not fully completed. It occupied the site of a three-story edifice bearing the high-sounding name "Palace Hotel," a structure of tent-cloth over a wooden frame, divided by muslin partitions, and three stories in height. When rooms for the ever-increasing multitudes at Chautauqua were few, the Palace Hotel was a blessing to many visitors. Some distinguished men slept in those tented rooms, and inasmuch as a sheet partition is not entirely sound-proof, their snores at night could be heard almost as far as their speeches by day. Some there were in the early eighties who shook their heads as the walls of the new hotel rose, and dreaded the tide of worldliness which would follow; but the Hotel Athenæum has become a genuine helper to the Chautauqua spirit, for its great parlor has opened its doors to many receptions, and the witty after-dinner speeches at banquets in its dining-hall would fill more than one volume.

Another building which deserves mention is the Congregational House, opened in 1880; the first church headquarters established at Chautauqua.

We have seen how the denominations were recognized from the earliest years, and meeting places provided for their prayer meetings and conferences. The need was felt by a number of the larger churches of a place where their members could find a welcome on arrival, could form an acquaintance with fellow-members, could meet each other in social gatherings and prayer meetings, and could promote the fraternal spirit. The example of the Congregationalists was soon followed. The Presbyterian headquarters, aided by a liberal donation of Mr. Elliott F. Shepard of New York, was the earliest brick building on the ground, solid and substantial, befitting the church which it represented. After a few years its size was doubled to make a Mission House, where missionaries of that church, home and foreign, could enjoy a vacation at Chautauqua. The Methodist House is one of the largest, for its chapel is the home of the Community Church at Chautauqua through the entire year, the church home of the resident population of every denomination. The Disciples of Christ, or Christian Church, purchased a large boarding-house, built before it a pillared porch, giving it a noble frontage and furnishing rooms for guests in the upper stories. The United Presbyterians built a chapel, serving also as a social room. The Protestant Episcopalians also erected a chapel consecrated to worship, but later established also a Church Home. The Unitarians purchased and improved a property fronting on St. Paul's Grove. The Baptists built a large headquarters on Clark Avenue, the street extending from the Amphitheater to the Hall of Philosophy, and the Lutherans obtained a large building near it. In all these Denominational Houses there is an absence of clannish feeling. No church uses its headquarters as a propaganda of its peculiar views; and in the receptions fellow Christians of every branch are always welcome. When some eminent man comes to Chautauqua, his church holds a reception in his honor, and everybody who would like to take his hand flocks to the meeting at his church headquarters. Speaking of receptions, I must tell of one wherein I was supposed to take a leading part, but found myself left in the rear. Dr. Vincent announced that at four o'clock, in the Hall of Philosophy, a reception would be given to Dr. Edward Everett Hale. He said to me:

Now, Dr. Hurlbut, I place this reception in your hands to manage. Dr. Hale comes from Boston and is accustomed to the formalities of the best society. Be sure to have this reception held in the proper manner. Let the Doctor stand in front of the platform, have ushers ready to introduce the people, and let there be no indiscriminate handshaking.

I promised to see that everything should be done decently and in order, and a few minutes before the hour appointed, walked over to the Hall. I was amazed to see a crowd of people, all pressing toward the center, where the tall form of Dr. Hale loomed above the throng, shaking hands apparently in every direction. I rushed upon the scene and vainly endeavored to bring about some semblance of order. The reception was a tumultuous, almost a rough-and-tumble, affair, everybody reaching out for the guest in his own way. It came about in this manner, as I learned.

Everybody at Chautauqua knows that the bell invariably rings five minutes before the hour, giving notice that the exercises may begin promptly on the stroke of the clock. But Dr. Hale did not know this, and when the five-minute bell rang, he rose and said:

"The time for the meeting has come, but nobody seems to be in charge. Let us begin the reception ourselves without waiting."

He stood up, and began shaking hands right and left, without waiting for introduction, and when the four o'clock bell sounded, the reception was in full sweep, everybody crowding around at once and grasping his hand. Before the first throng had satisfied its desires, another stream poured in and the general tumult continued until the five o'clock hour compelled an adjournment, the Hall being required for another meeting.

At the close, Dr. Hale remarked to me, "I especially like the informality of such gatherings here at Chautauqua. This has been one of the most satisfactory receptions that I have ever attended!"

Chautauqua was already coming to the front as a convention-city. Its central location between New York and Chicago, with ready transportation north and south, its Amphitheater for great meetings, with numerous halls and tents for smaller gatherings and committees, the constant improvement in its lodging and commissary departments, its attractive program of lectures and entertainments, and not the least, its romantic out-of-door life, began to draw to the ground different organizations. The Woman's Christian Temperance Union, led by Frances E. Willard, returned to its birthplace for its sixth annual convention, and the National Educational Association brought members from every State, presided over by Dr. J. Ormond Wilson. This Association embraced educators of widely diverging views, and some entertaining scraps occurred in its discussions. For example, the kindergarten instruction at Chautauqua was under the direction of Madame Kraus-Boelte, and her husband, a learned but rather obstinate German, Professor Kraus. There was an Americanized kindergarten, whose representative came, hired a cottage, and hung out her sign, but much to her displeasure was not allowed to conduct classes. It would never answer to let anybody hold classes unauthorized by the management, for who could tell what educational heresies might enter through the gate? But this aggressive lady paid her fee, joined the N. E. A., and in the kindergarten section proceeded to exploit her "improvements" upon the Froebel system. This aroused the ire of Professor Kraus, and in vigorous language he interrupted her address, declaring, at first in English, then half in German as his anger rose:

"Dat iss not kindergarten! Dere is but one kindergarten! You can call dat whatever you please, but not kindergarten! You can call it joss-house, if you choose, but you must not say dat mix-up is a kindergarten!"

The audience enjoyed the discussion all the more because of this scramble between opposing schools.

There was another, and more dignified, controversy on the Chautauqua platform in 1880. On its program was the honored name of Washington Gladden, of Columbus, Ohio, to speak upon the Standard Oil Company and its misdeeds. A friend of Dr. Vincent, who was an officer of the Standard Oil, said that it would only be fair to hear the other side, and proposed Mr. George Gunton of New York as a speaker. So it came to pass that two able men spoke on opposite sides of the mooted question. Each gave an address and afterward had an opportunity of answering the other's arguments. So far as I know, this was the first debate on public questions at Chautauqua, and it was succeeded by many others. An effort is made to have the burning questions of the time discussed by representative speakers. Some exceedingly radical utterances on capital and labor have been made on the Chautauqua platform, but it must not be inferred, because the audience listened to them respectfully, or even applauded a particularly sharp sentence, that Chautauqua was in accord with the speaker's sentiments.

On the list of speakers at this season may be read the following, a few among many names: Prof. J. H. Gilmore of Rochester University gave a series of brilliant lectures upon English literature.

Methodist Headquarters

Ram Chandra Bose of India gave several lectures, philosophic and popular. Dr. Sheldon Jackson of Alaska thrilled a great audience with an appeal for that outlying but unknown land of ours. Schuyler Colfax, Vice-President of Grant's first administration, gave a great lecture on "Abraham Lincoln." Professor Borden P. Bowne of Boston University made the deep things of philosophy plain even to unphilosophic listeners. Other orators in the new Amphitheater were Dr. Robert R. Meredith of Boston, Dr. J. O. Means of the American Board of Commissioners for Foreign Missions, and Dr. W. W. Keen of Philadelphia. The Fisk Jubilee Singers made their first visit this year; and with the Northwestern Band and the Assembly Chorus, already counted by the hundreds, under Professors Sherwin and Case, made music one of the most popular features of the program.

This year was also notable for the first appearance of the *Chautauquan Magazine*, containing a part of the required readings of the C. L. S. C. It was launched and made successful by the financial, business, and editorial ability of Dr. Flood, who ventured his capital boldly and won deserved success. The ever-welcome "Pansy," Mrs. G. R. Alden, this season read a new story, published soon afterward. With Mrs. Alden in those early years was a serious small boy, ever at his mother's side, rarely entering into the sports of childhood. If we could have looked forward a quarter-century, we might have seen in him the coming Professor Raymond M. Alden of the Leland Stanford faculty, one of the most eminent scholars and critics in the Department of English Literature, and an authority quoted in all lands where the English language is spoken or read.

A visitor came to Chautauqua at the session of 1880, whose presence brought the place and the Assembly into notice throughout the nation. General James A. Garfield was at that time the candidate of his party for President of the United States. He came to Chautauqua on Saturday, August 7th, for a week-end rest in a strenuous campaign, expressing a wish not to be called upon for any public address or reception. He worshiped with the great congregation on Sunday morning, his entrance with a group of his friends being received in respectful silence. In the afternoon he mentioned to Dr. Vincent that he had heard of Palestine Park and would like to visit it. As the lectures in the Park were generally given by me, I was detailed to walk through the model and point out its localities. As we went out of Dr. Vincent's tent a small company was standing around, waiting for a sight of the candidate. They followed us, and as we walked on toward the Park, people came flocking forth from every house and tent. By the time we reached the Land of Palestine, it was well-nigh covered with the crowds, extending from Dan to Beer-sheba. No former Palestine lecture of mine had ever drawn together such a multitude! It became impossible to find the cities covered by the multitudes. But I was somewhat surprised to perceive that the General knew where at least the important localities belonged even though they were not visible. He pointed out half a dozen of the cities named in the Bible, and gave their names without hesitation or suggestion. We desired to make a sort of pilgrimage through the land, but found an army obstructing our journey.

On the next morning, as General Garfield was about to leave, Dr. Vincent asked him, not to make a political speech, but to give in a few words his impressions of Chautauqua. He consented, and standing upon a stump, in the presence of a hastily assembled gathering, gave a ten-minute address, of which the following is a part.

You are struggling with one of the two great problems of civilization. The first one is a very old struggle: It is, how shall we get any leisure? That is the problem of every hammer stroke, of every blow that labor has struck since the foundation of the world. The fight for bread is the first great primal fight, and it is so absorbing a struggle that until one conquers it somewhat he can have no leisure whatever. So that we may divide the whole struggle of the human race into two chapters; first, the fight to get leisure; and then the second fight of civilization—what shall we do with our leisure when we get it? And I take it that Chautuaqua has assailed the second problem. Now, leisure is a dreadfully bad thing unless it is well used. A man with a fortune ready made and with leisure on his hands, is likely to get sick of the world, sick of himself, tired of life, and become a useless, wasted man. What shall you do with your leisure? I understand Chautauqua is trying to answer that question and to open out fields of thought, to open out energies, a largeness of mind, a culture in the better senses, with the varnish scratched off. We are getting over the process of painting our native woods and varnishing them. We are getting down to the real grain, and finding whatever is best in it and truest in it. And if Chautuaqua is helping garnish our people with the native stuff that is in them, rather than with the paint and varnish and gew-gaws·of culture, they are doing well.

As we looked upon that stately figure, the form of one born to command, and listened to that mellow, ringing voice, no one dreamed that within a year that frame would be laid low, that voice hushed, and that life fraught with such promise ended by an assassin's bullet!

The Assembly of 1880 came to its close on August 19th, after a session of thirty-eight days. Although the C. L. S. C. had come to the foreground and held the center of the stage, the normal work and Bible study had not been neglected. The teacher-training classes were now under the charge of Dr. Richard S. Holmes and Rev. J. L. Hurlbut. The Children's Class was maintained with a daily attendance approaching three hundred, the lessons taught by Rev. B. T. Vincent and pictures drawn by Frank Beard; also Mr. Vincent conducted an Intermediate Class in Bible Study. In all these classes for older and younger students, more than two hundred and fifty passed the examination and were enrolled as graduates.

On the last evening of the Assembly, after the closing exercises, there was seen a weird, ghostly procession, in white raiment, emerging from the Ark and parading solemnly through the grounds, pausing before the Miller Cottage and the Vincent Tent for a mournful, melancholy musical strain. This was the "ghost walk" of the guests in the Ark. Some eminent Doctors of Divinity and Ph.D.'s. were in that sheeted procession, led by Professors Sherwin and Case, engineered, as such functions were apt to be, by Frank and Helen Beard. The ghost walk grew into an annual march, until it was succeeded by a more elaborate performance, of which the story will be told later.

## CHAPTER XII

### DEMOCRACY AND ARISTOCRACY AT CHAUTAUQUA (1881)

THE eighth session opened on Thursday, July 7th, and continued forty-seven days to August 22d. A glance over the program shows that among the lecturers of that year was Signor Alessandro Gavazzi, the founder of the Free Italian Church, whose lectures, spiced with his quaint accent, and emphasized by expressive shoulders, head, glance of eye, held the interest of his auditors from the opening sentence to the end. No verbal report, however accurate, can portray the charm of this wonderful Italian. Professor W. D. McClintock of the University of Chicago, gave a course on literature, analytic, critical, and suggestive. Dr. William Hayes Ward, Dr. Daniel A. Goodsell, afterward a Methodist Bishop, Professor Charles F. Richardson, Dr. Edward Everett Hale, Dr. A. E. Dunning, Editor of *The Congregationalist;* General O. O. Howard, who told war stories in a simple, charming manner; Dr. Philip

Schaff, one of the most learned yet most simple-hearted scholars of the age; Dr. A. A. Willetts, with his many times repeated, yet always welcome lecture on "Sunshine," were among the men whose voices filled the Amphitheater during the season. The Fisk Jubilee Singers were with us again and Signor Giuseppe Vitale made the birds sing through his wonderful violin.

The success of the C. L. S. C., which was widening its area every month, inspired Dr. Vincent to look for new fields to conquer. He established this year the C. Y. F. R. U., initials standing for The Chautauqua Young Folks Reading Union, which proposed to do for the boys and girls what the Reading Circle was accomplishing for men and women. But it was found after a few years of trial that the school-age seeks its own reading and is not responsive to direction in literature on a vast scale, for the C. Y. F. R. U. was not successful in winning the young readers.

Another scheme launched this year met with the same fate;—The Chautauqua School of Theology. It was thought that many ministers who had not received a theological education would avail themselves of an opportunity to obtain it while in the pastorate. This was to be not a course of reading, but of close study, under qualified instruction in each department, with examinations, a diploma, and a degree. But it required more thorough study and much larger fees than a mere course of reading, and those who needed it most were often the poorest paid in their profession. It did not receive the support needful for its success, it had no endowment, and after an experiment extending through a number of years, it was reluctantly abandoned. Some of us have believed that if the Chautauqua Correspondence School of Theology could have found friends to give it even a moderate endowment, it might have supplied an education needed by a multitude of ministers.

The Hotel Athenæum was opened in 1881 and speedily filled with guests. It aided in bringing to Chautauqua a new constituency and also spurred the cottage boarding-houses to improve their accommodations and their fare. From the beginning the waiters and other helpers at the Hotel, and also in the cottages, have been mostly young people seeking to obtain higher education, and paying their way at Chautauqua by service. I remember one morning finding a Hebrew book on my breakfast table. One meets unaccustomed things at Chautauqua, but I was quite sure the *menu* was not in that language. I called the attention of the young man who brought in the breakfast to the book. He told me that he was studying Hebrew with Dr. Harper, and from time to time we had some conversation concerning his college work. Twenty years afterward I met a prominent Methodist minister at a Conference, who said to me, "Don't you remember me, Dr. Hurlbut? I used to wait on your table at Chautauqua and we talked together about Hebrew." That minister was a member of several General Conferences and some years ago was made one of the Bishops in his church.

Mrs. Ida B. Cole, the Executive Secretary of the C. L. S. C., is responsible for the following: A woman once said, "Chautauqua cured me of being a snob, for I found that my waitress was a senior in a college, the chambermaid had specialized in Greek, the porter taught languages in a high school, and the bell-boy, to whom I had been giving nickel tips, was the son of a wealthy family in my own State who wanted a job to prove his prowess."

There are a few, however, who do not take kindly to the democratic life of Chautauqua. I was seated at one of the hotel tables with a well-known clergyman from England, whose sermons of a highly spiritual type are widely read in America; and I remarked:

Unitarian Headquarters

"Perhaps it may interest you to know that all the waiters in this hotel are college-students."

"What do you mean?" he said, "surely no college student would demean himself by such a servile occupation! But it may be a lark, just for fun."

"No," I answered, "they are men who are earning money to enable them to go on with their college work, a common occurrence in summer hotels in America."

Said this minister, "Well, I don't like it; and it would not be allowed in my country. No man after it could hold up his head in an English University or College. I don't enjoy being waited on by a man who considers himself my social equal!"

Other eminent Englishmen did not agree with this clergyman. When I mentioned this incident a year later to Principal Fairbairn of Oxford, he expressed his hearty sympathy with the democracy shown at Chautauqua, and said that whatever might be the ideas of class-distinction in English colleges, they were unknown in Scotland, where some of the most distinguished scholars rose from the humblest homes and regardless of their poverty were respected and honored in their colleges.

Dr. Vincent, ever fertile in sentimental touches,

added two features to the usages of the C. L. S. C. One was the "Camp fire." In an open place a great bonfire was prepared; all the members stood around in a circle, clasping hands; the fire was kindled, and while the flames soared up and lit the faces of the crowd, songs were sung and speeches were made. This service was maintained annually until the ground at Chautauqua became too closely occupied by cottages for a bonfire to be safe. It is noteworthy that on the day after the camp fire, there was always a large enrollment of members for the C. L. S. C. Of course, the camp fire was introduced at other Assemblies, by this time becoming numerous, and it attracted not only spectators, but students to the reading-course. At our first camp fire in the Ottawa Assembly, Kansas, an old farmer from the country rushed up to Dr. Milner, the President, and said:

"I don't know much about this ere circle you were talking about, but I'm going to jine, and here's my fifty cents for membership and another for my wife."

There were only twenty members around the fire that night, but on the next day, there were forty or more on the registry at the Chautauqua tent.

The camp fire died down after a number of

years, but the Vigil, also introduced in 1881, became a permanent institution. In the days of chivalry, when a youth was to receive the honor of knighthood, he spent his last night in the chapel of the castle, watching beside his armor, to be worn for the first time on the following day. Dr. Vincent called upon the members of the Pioneer class of the C. L. S. C., destined to graduate on the following year, to meet him in the Hall of Philosophy late on Sunday night, after the conclusion of the evening service. All except members of the class were requested not to come. The hall was dimly lighted, left almost in darkness. They sang a few songs from memory, listened to a Psalm, and to an earnest, deeply religious address, were led in prayer, and were dismissed, to go home in silence through the empty avenues. After a few years the Vigil was changed from a Sunday evening of the year before graduation to the Sunday immediately preceding Recognition Day, for the reason that on the graduation year, the attendance of any class is far greater than on the year before. The Vigil is still one of the time-honored and highly appreciated services of the season. Now, however, the Hall is no longer left in shadow, for around it the Athenian Watch Fires lighten up St. Paul's Grove with their flaring tongues. Generally more people are standing outside the pillars of the Hall, watching the ceremonials, than are seated before the platform, for none are permitted to enter except members of the class about to graduate.

I am not sure whether it was in this year, 1881, or the following that Dr. Vincent inaugurated the Society of Christian Ethics. This was not an organization with a roll of membership, dues, and duties, but simply a meeting on Sunday afternoon in the Children's Temple, at which an address on character was given, in the first years by Dr. Vincent. It was especially for young people of the 'teen age. No one was admitted under the age of twelve or over that of twenty. The young people were quite proud of having Dr. Vincent all to themselves, and strongly resented the efforts of their elders to obtain admittance. No person of adult years was allowed without a card signed by Dr. Vincent. These addresses by the Founder, if they had been taken down and preserved, would have formed a valuable book for young people on the building up of true character. They were continued during the years of Dr. Vincent's active association with Chautauqua and for some time afterward; addresses being given by eminent men of the Chautauqua program. But very few speakers could meet the needs of that adolescent age. By degrees the attendance decreased and after some years the meeting gave place to other interests.

The regular features of the season went on as in other years. The schools were growing in students, in the number of instructors, and in the breadth of their courses. The Sunday School Normal Department was still prominent, and on August 17, 1881, one hundred and ninety diplomas were conferred upon the adults, intermediates, and children who had passed the examination.

# CHAPTER XIII

## THE FIRST RECOGNITION DAY

(1882)

THE opening service of the ninth session was begun, as all the opening sessions of previous years, in the out-of-doors Auditorium in front of the Miller Cottage. But a sudden dash of rain came down and a hasty adjournment was made to the new Amphitheater. From 1882 onward, "Old First Night" has been observed in that building. A few lectures during the season of '82 were given in the old Auditorium, but at the close of the season the seats were removed, save a few left here and there under the trees for social enjoyment; and the Auditorium was henceforth known as Miller Park.

The crowning event of the 1882 season was the graduation of the first class in the Chautauqua Literary and Scientific Circle. Taking into account the fact that it was the first class, for which no advertising had been given and no announcement made in advance, the number graduated at the end of the four years was remarkably large, over eighteen hundred, of which eight hundred received their diplomas at Chautauqua and a thousand more at their homes, some in distant places. Years afterward I met a minister in a small town in Texas who had seen the report of the inauguration of the C. L. S. C., had read Dr. Vincent's address on that occasion, and joined the Class of 1882, its only member, as far as he knew, in his State. One member was a teacher in South Africa, others were missionaries in India and China. Most of the regular visitors to Chautauqua in those early days were members of this class, so that even now, after nearly forty years, the Pioneer Class can always muster at its annual gatherings a larger number of its members than almost any other of the classes. For many years Mrs. B. T. Vincent was the President of the Class, and strongly interested in its social and religious life. She instituted at Chautauqua the "Quiet Hour," held every Saturday evening during the Assembly season, at Pioneer Hall, by this class, a meeting for conversation on subjects of culture and the Christian life. It is a touching sight to look upon that group of old men and women, at their annual farewell meeting, on the evening before the Recognition Day, standing in a circle with joined hands, singing together their class song written for them by Mary A. Lathbury, and then sounding forth their class yell:

Hear! Hear! Pioneers!
Height to height, fight for right,
Pioneers!
Who are you? Who are you?
We are the class of eighty-two!
Pioneers—Ah!

No college class was ever graduated with half the state and splendor of ceremony that was observed on that first Recognition Day, in a ritual prepared by Dr. Vincent, and observed to the letter every year since 1882. He chose to call it not a Commencement, but a Recognition, the members of the Circle being *recognized* on that day as having completed the course and entitled to membership in the Society of the Hall in the Grove, the Alumni Association of the C. L. S. C.

A procession was formed, its divisions meeting in different places. The graduating class met before the Golden Gate at St. Paul's Grove, a gate which is opened but once in the year and through which none may pass except those who have completed the course of reading and study of the C. L. S. C. Over the gate hung a silk flag which had been carried by the Rev. Albert D. Vail of New York to many of the famous places in the world of literature, art, and religion. It had been waved from the summit of the Great Pyramid, of Mount Sinai in the Desert, and Mount Tabor in the Holy Land. It had been laid in the Manger at Bethlehem, and in the traditional tomb of Jesus in Holy Sepulcher Church. It had fluttered upon the Sea of Galilee, upon Mount Lebanon, in the house where Paul was converted at Damascus, and under the dome of St. Sophia in Constantinople. It had been at the Acropolis and Mars' Hill in Athens, to Westminster Abbey, and to Shakespeare's tomb at Stratford, to the graves of Walter Scott and Robert Burns. Upon its stripes were inscribed the names of forty-eight places to which that flag had been carried. The class stood before the Golden Gate, still kept closed until the moment should come for it to be opened, and in two sections the members read a responsive service from the Bible, having wisdom and especially the highest wisdom of all, the knowledge of God, as its subject.

At the same time one section of the parade was meeting in Miller Park, in front of the Lewis Miller Cottage. Another was at the tent where lived Dr. Vincent, and still another division, the most interesting of all, on the hill, in front of the Children's Temple. This was an array of fifty little girls in white dresses, with wreaths in their hair and baskets of flowers in their hands. At the signal, the procession moved from its different stations, and marched past the Vincent Tent, led by the band and the flower girls, and including every department of Chautauqua, officials, trustees, schools, and Sunday School Normal Class. In the later years each class of graduates marched, led by its banner, the Class of 1882, the Pioneers, bearing in front their symbol, the hatchet. Before all was the great banner of the C. L. S. C. presented to the Circle by Miss Jennie Miller, Lewis Miller's eldest daughter, bearing upon one side a painting of the Hall of Philosophy and the three mottoes of the Circle; on the other a silk handkerchief which had accompanied the flag on its journey to the sacred places. The pole holding up the banner was surmounted by a fragment of Plymouth Rock.

The march was to the Hall of Philosophy, where the orator, officers, and guests occupied the platform, the little flower girls were grouped on opposite sides of the path from the Golden Gate up to the Hall; the graduating class still standing outside the entrance protected by the Guard of the Gate. A messenger came from the Gate to announce that the class was now prepared to enter, having fulfilled all of the conditions, and the order was given, "Let the Golden Gate now be opened."

Lutheran Headquarters

United Presbyterian Chapel

The portals were swung apart, and the class entered, passing under the historic flag and successively under four arches dedicated respectively to Faith, Science, Literature, and Art, while the little girls strewed flowers in their path. As they marched up the hill they were greeted by Miss Lathbury's song:

### THE SONG OF TO-DAY

Sing pæans over the Past!
  We bury the dead years tenderly,
  To find them again in eternity,
Safe in its circle vast.
Sing pæans over the Past!

Farewell, farewell to the Old!
  Beneath the arches, and one by one,
  From sun to shade, and from shade to sun,
We pass, and the years are told.
Farewell, farewell to the Old!

Arise and possess the land!
  Not one shall fail in the march of life,
  Not one shall fail in the hour of strife,
Who trusts in the Lord's right hand.
Arise and possess the land!

And hail, all hail to the New!
  The future lies like a world new-born,
  All steeped in sunshine and dews of morn,
And arched with a cloudless blue
All hail, all hail to the New!

All things, all things are yours!
  The spoil of nations, the arts sublime
  That arch the ages from oldest time,
The word that for aye endures—
All things, all things are yours!

The Lord shall sever the sea,
  And open a way in the wilderness
  To faith that follows, to feet that pass
Forth into the great TO BE
The Lord shall sever the sea!

The inspiring music of this inspiring hymn was composed, like most of the best Chautauqua songs, by Prof. William F. Sherwin. The class entered, and while taking their seats were welcomed in the strains of another melody:

A song is thrilling through the trees,
  And vibrant through the air,
Ten thousand hearts turn hitherward,
  And greet us from afar.
And through the happy tide of song
  That blends our hearts in one,
The voices of the absent flow
  In tender undertone.

CHORUS

Then bear along, O wings of song,
  Our happy greeting glee,
From center to the golden verge,
  Chautauqua to the sea.

Fair Wisdom builds her temple here,
  Her seven-pillared dome;
Toward all lands she spreads her hands,
  And greets her children home;
Not all may gather at her shrine
  To sing of victories won;
Their names are graven on her walls—
  God bless them every one! *Chorus.*

O happy circle, ever wide
  And wider be thy sweep,
Till peace and knowledge fill the earth
  As waters fill the deep;
Till hearts and homes are touched to life,
  And happier heights are won;
Till that fair day, clasp hands, and say
  God bless us, every one! *Chorus.*

Another responsive service followed, read in turn by the Superintendent and the class, and then Dr. Vincent gave the formal Recognition in words used at every similar service since that day:

*Fellow-Students of the Chautauqua Literary and Scientific Circle.*

DEARLY BELOVED:

You have finished the appointed and accepted course of reading; you have been admitted to this sacred Grove; you have passed the arches dedicated to Faith, Science, Literature, and Art; you have entered in due form this Hall, the center of the Chautauqua Literary and Scientific Circle. And now as Superintendent of

Instruction,[1] with these my associates, the counsellors of our Fraternity, I greet you; and hereby announce that you, and your brethren and sisters absent from us to-day, who have completed with you the prescribed course of reading, are accepted and approved graduates of the Chautauqua Literary and Scientific Circle, and that you are entitled to membership in the Society of the Hall in the Grove. "The Lord bless thee and keep thee; the Lord make his face shine upon thee, and be gracious unto thee; the Lord lift up his countenance upon thee and give thee peace."

After another song, the Marshal of the procession took charge, and the order of march was renewed, the newly graduated class in the rear, followed by the Superintendent, Counsellors, and officers. The company marched to the Amphitheater, on the way the procession dividing and forming on both sides of the street, while the officers and the graduating class passed through the open files, thus bringing the graduating class at the head of the line into the Amphitheater. Here more songs were sung and other responsive readings were rendered before an audience that thronged the building. The oration on the first graduation service was given by Dr. Henry W.

[1] After Dr. Vincent's title was changed to "Chancellor of the Chautauqua University" that form was used; and in his absence the President said instead "as representing the Chancellor of the Chautauqua University."

Warren, who had been elevated to the episcopate two years before. After the oration a recess was taken, and in the afternoon the concluding service was held and the diplomas were conferred upon the eight hundred graduates present by the hand of Dr. Vincent.

In most college commencements that I have attended, the President takes the diplomas at random from a table and hands them to the class as they come, not giving to each graduate his own diploma, and afterward there is a general looking up one another and sorting out the diplomas until at last each one obtains his own. But Miss Kimball, the Secretary, devised a plan by which all the diplomas were numbered and each graduate was furnished with a card showing his number. These numbers were called out ten at a time, and each graduate was able to receive his own (mostly *her* own) diploma, while the audience heard the name upon it and the number of seals it bore for special reading and study.

It should be mentioned that some members of the class arrived on the ground too late to pass with their classmates through the Golden Gate and under the arches. For their benefit the Gate was opened a second time before the afternoon meeting, and a special Recognition service was held, so that they might enjoy all the privileges of the class. This is another custom continued every year, for always it is needed.

After a year or two it entered the facetious minds of Mr. and Mrs. Beard to originate a comic travesty on the Recognition service, which was presented on the evening after the formal exercises, when everybody was weary and was ready to descend from the serious heights. This grew into quite an institution and was continued for a number of years—a sort of mock-commencement, making fun of the prominent figures and features of the day. Almost as large an audience was wont to assemble for this evening of mirth and jollity, as was seen at the stately service of the morning. This in turn had its day and finally grew into the Chautauqua Circus, an amateur performance which is still continued every year under one name or another.

We have given much space to the story of the first Recognition Day, as a sample of the similar services held every year afterward, growing with the growth of the C. L. S. C. But there were other events of '82 scarcely less noteworthy. On that year a great organ was installed in the Amphitheater, and its effect was soon seen in the enlargement of the choir and the improvement in the music. We can mention only in the briefest manner some of the speakers on the platform for that year: such as Dr. W. T. Harris of Concord, Mass., afterward U. S. Commissioner of Education; Professor William H. Niles of Boston; Mr. Wallace Bruce; Dr. T. DeWitt Talmage; Dr. Wm. M. Blackburn of Cincinnati, the church historian; Dr. A. D. Vail of New York, who told in an interesting manner the story of the banner and the flag; Dr. Mark Hopkins, the great college President; Bishop R. S. Foster; Anthony Comstock and John B. Gough, with others equally distinguished whose names we must omit. One new name appeared upon the program of this season which will be read often in the coming years, that of Mr. Leon H. Vincent, the son of Rev. B. T. Vincent. He gave a course of lectures on English literature, mingling biographical, social, and critical views of the great writers, attracting large audiences. We shall find him among the leading lights of Chautauqua in the successive chapters of our story.

An institution which began that year and has been perpetuated must not be omitted—the Devotional Conference. Both of the Founders of Chautauqua were strong in their purpose to hold the Christian religion ever in the forefront at the

Assembly. Various plans were tried during the early years, but none seemed to reach the constituency of Chautauqua until Dr. Benjamin M. Adams, at Dr. Vincent's request, began holding a daily service of an hour. This attracted a large attendance and was continued for a number of years, as long as Dr. Adams could conduct it. Afterward an arrangement was made which has become permanent. Every season a series of eminent clergymen are engaged, each to serve for one week as chaplain. He preaches the Sunday morning sermon in the Amphitheater, and on the following five days at ten o'clock conducts the Devotional Hour in the same place, giving a series of discourses, Bible readings, or addresses. The speaker of each week is a man of national or international fame. The greatest preachers in the American pulpit have spoken at this service, and the audience is surpassed in numbers only by the most popular lectures or concerts. Many there are who deem this the most precious hour in the day.

# CHAPTER XIV

## SOME STORIES OF THE C. L. S. C.

## (1883, 1884)

WE must hasten our steps through the passing years at Chautauqua. Our readers may take for granted that the regular departments were continued; that the Summer Schools were adding new courses and calling new professors; that the Normal Class for the training of Sunday School workers was still held, no longer in the section-tents nor in the Children's Temple, but under a large tent on an elevation where two years later was to stand the Normal Hall, built for the class, but after some years transferred first to the Musical Department, later to the Summer Schools and partitioned into class-rooms. The Children's Class was still held by Dr. B. T. Vincent and Professor Frank Beard, for our friend with the crayon was now in the faculty of the School of Art in Syracuse University.

In 1883 the session was forty-five days long, from July 14th to August 27th. A new feature of the program was an "Ideal Foreign Tour through Europe," with illustrated lectures on various cities by C. E. Bolton, and "Tourists' Conferences" conducted by his wife, the cultured Mrs. Sarah K. Bolton. Mrs. Emma P. Ewing of Chicago taught classes in the important art of cookery. Professor Charles J. Little gave a course of lectures. Hon. Albion W. Tourgee, residing at Mayville, who had achieved fame soon after the Civil War by his story, *A Fool's Errand*, gave lectures in the Amphitheater. Professor William C. Richards showed brilliant illustrations in physical science. Dr. P. S. Henson entertained while he instructed; President Julius H. Seelye, Dr. W. F. Mallalien, later a Bishop, President Joseph Cummings of Northwestern University, Hon. Will Cumback of Indiana, and many others, gave lectures.

A new instructor entered the School of Languages in 1883, in the person of William Rainey Harper, then Professor in the Baptist School of Theology at Morgan Park, Illinois, afterward to be the first President of the University of Chicago. No man ever lived who could inspire a class with the enthusiasm that he could awaken over the study of Hebrew, could lead his students so far in that language in a six weeks' course, or could impart such broad and sane views of the Biblical literature. From this year Dr. Harper was one of the leaders at Chautauqua, and soon was advanced to the principalship of the Summer Schools. In the after years, while Dr. Harper was President of the University of Chicago, and holding classes all the year, in summer as well as winter, he was wont to take the train every Friday afternoon, in order to spend Saturday and Sunday at Chautauqua. Chautauquans of those days will also remember the recitals by Professor Robert L. Cumnock of Northwestern University, a reader who was a scholar in the best literature.

The class of 1883, though not as large as its predecessor, the Pioneers, was graduated with the same ceremonies, the address on Recognition Day given by Dr. Lyman Abbott of New York, one of the Counsellors of the Circle. Five years had now passed since the inauguration of this movement, and from every quarter testimonials of its power and incidents showing its influence were received. Let me mention a few of these which came under my own notice.

I met a lady who mentioned that she and her husband were reading the course together and they found the only available hour between six and seven in the morning, before breakfast. For the study of the course they both had risen at half past five for a year or more. One result of this early morning reading was, she said, that at the breakfast table they told the children stories of history and science, which she thought turned their minds toward knowledge. Among the books was one on Human Physiology—a book, which, by the way, I did not rate very highly and objected to as being so elementary as to become almost juvenile; yet that book awakened such an interest that the lady began to read more widely and deeply on the subject, after a few months entered the Woman's Medical College in New York, during her course took several prizes, and graduated with high honors. It may have been that she foresaw what came, the failure of her husband's health, so that of necessity she became the bread-winner for her family. She was a successful physician, honored in the community, the Chautauqua Circle having opened to her wider opportunities of knowledge and usefulness.

Two college professors of high standing have told me that they were first awakened to a desire and determination for higher education through their early readings in the C. L. S. C.

One rather amusing yet suggestive incident came to my notice. Visiting a city in the Middle West, I met a lady who told me that she belonged to a club of young people who met weekly in a card party. One member told the rest about the C. L. S. C. which she had joined and showed them the books, whereupon they all sent in their names as members, and the card club was transformed into a Chautauqua Reading Circle.

I was seated with Dr. Edward E. Hale at a C. L. S. C. banquet in New England, when he pointed out a middle-aged gentleman at the head of one of the tables and told me this story about him.

While a boy he came to his father and said, "I don't want to go to school any longer, I want to go to work and earn my own living, and there's a place in Boston that is open to me." "Well," said his father, "perhaps you would better take the place, I've noticed that you are not paying much attention to your studies of late. I'm very sorry for I have set my heart on giving you a good education. You don't know now, but you'll find out later that the difference between the man who gives orders and the man who takes them is that generally one of the two men knows more than the other, and knowledge brings a man up in the world." The boy went to Boston and took a job in a big store, and he found that he was taking a good many orders from those above him and giving none to others. He realized that for success in life he needed an education. Ashamed to give up and go home, he began to attend an evening school which some of us had established. There I met him and was able to give him some encouragement and some help. He became a well-read and, in the end, a successful business man. As soon as he heard of the Chautauqua Circle, he began to read its books and was made President of a local circle. That table is filled with the members of his circle and he sits at the head of it.

I wish that I could write down a story as it was told me by Dr. Duryea, at Chautauqua. It was of a man who sat at his table in the Hotel and was always in a hurry, never finishing his meals in his haste to get to lectures and classes. The Doctor got him to talking and he forgot to drink his coffee while telling his story. He said that he kept a country store in a village in Arkansas, where the young men used to come in the evenings and tell stories together. He felt that he was leading a rather narrow life and needed intelligence, but did not know where to obtain it. There were books enough in the world, but how could he choose the right ones? A newspaper fell under his notice containing some mention of the C. L. S. C.; he sent his fee to the office, obtained the books for the year, and began to read in the intervals of time between customers in his store. For retirement he fixed up a desk and shelf of books in the rear of the shop. Some of his evening callers said, "What have you got back there?" and he showed his books, telling them of the C. L. S. C. A number of them at once decided to join, and soon he found himself the conductor of a Chautauqua Circle with twenty members. They fixed up a meeting place in a store-room in a garret under the eaves, talked over the topics, and read papers. When the text-book on electricity was before them, they made experiments with home-made batteries and ran wires all around the room. The man said, "Those fellows look to me to answer all sorts of questions, and I find that I am getting beyond my depth. I have come to Chautauqua to fill up and I'm doing it. But the difficulty is that too many things come at the same time; here's a lecture on American authors and one on biology, and one on history, all at once, and I never know which to attend. But Chautauqua is a great place, isn't it?"

A servant in a family, while waiting at the table, heard the lady and her daughters talking of the Circle which was being formed. The girl asked her mistress if she would be permitted to join. With some hesitation, the lady said, "Why, yes, if you really wish to read the books, you can be a member." This serving-maid soon showed herself as the brightest scholar in the group, far superior in her thirst for knowledge to her young mistresses. She was encouraged and aided to seek a higher education, entered a Normal School, and became a successful teacher.

One letter received at the office contained, in brief, the following: "I am a working-man with six children and I work hard to keep them in school. Since I found out about your Circle, I have begun to read, getting up early in the morning to do it. I am trying hard to keep up, so that my boys will see what father does—just as an example to them."

A letter from a night watchman said, "I read as I come on my rounds to the lights, and think it over between times."

A steamboat captain on one of the western rivers wrote that he enjoyed reading the books and found the recollection of their contents a great benefit, "for when I stand on the deck at night I have something good to think about; and you know that when one has not taken care of his thoughts they will run away with him and he will think about things he ought not."

I was well acquainted with a gentleman and his wife, both of unspotted character, but unfortunately living apart from some incompatibility. He was accustomed to call upon her every fortnight, in a formal manner, professedly to meet their children, and on one of his visits he mentioned that he was beginning the C. L. S. C. readings. She was desirous of knowing what those letters meant; he explained and gave her a circular of information. She, too, joined the Circle, and next time at his call they spent an evening pleasantly discussing the subjects of reading that both were pursuing. From a fortnightly they dropped into a weekly interview, and after a time spent nearly all their evenings together. One day I met them together, and being aware of their former relations, I perhaps showed surprise. The husband took me aside and said that they were now living together very happily, thanks to the C. L. S. C. They had forgotten their differences in a common object of interest.

In the early years of the C. L. S. C. one book of the course was on the subject of practical Christianity. At one time, the religious book was *The Philosophy of the Plan of Salvation*, by Dr. Walker, a work widely read two generations ago and regarded as a standard. We received at the office a letter from a high-school teacher who said that he was an agnostic and did not wish to read such a book—could he not read some scientific work by Tyndall or Huxley in place of it? Miss Kimball referred his letter to me, and I took it to Dr. Vincent. He considered the question, and then wrote in substance this answer:

If you were a Unitarian, you could read a volume by James Martineau; if you were a Roman Catholic, you could read one of many good Catholic religious books; if you were a Jew you might take some book upon your own religion. But you call yourself an agnostic, that is, one who does not know God and has no religion, and therefore, to meet the requirements of your course it will be necessary for you to read some candid, sane work on the Christian religion; and such is Walker's "Plan of Salvation."

The letter closed with a friendly request that he would read the book without a strong prejudice against it, and some hearty sympathetic sentences which Dr. Vincent knew how to write. For a year we heard nothing of the man; we concluded that he had been offended at the requirement and had left the Circle. We were surprised when at last another letter came from him stating that he had read the book, at first unwillingly, but later with deep interest; also that association with believers in the Circle had shown them, not as he had supposed, narrow and bigoted, but broad in their views. He had seen in them a mystic something which he desired; he had sought and found it. "To-day," he wrote, "I have united with the Presbyterian Church, and this evening I led the Christian Endeavor meeting."

Dr. Hale told of a man who had been formerly a

pupil and youth in his church, who was suffering from nervous prostration, and lay down in a shack in an out-of-the-way place in Florida, almost ready to die. His eyes were drawn to the orange-colored cover of a magazine which he had never seen before, *The Chautauquan*. He opened it at random and began to read. "Are you a child of God? Are you a partaker of the divine nature? If you are, work with God! Don't give up working with God!" It seemed to him like a voice from heaven. On that moment he said to himself, "I will not die, but live!" He began to read the magazine and followed it by reading the books to which the magazine made reference. They opened before him a new field of thought and made of him a new man. He told this story to Dr. Hale in his own church and said: "I am here because of that orange-covered *Chautauquan* which I found lying under the bench in that old cabin."

It is possible, nay, it is certain, that the Chautauqua Circle, by being not a church society, but a secular organization permeated by the Christian spirit, has exercised an influence all the stronger to promote an intelligent, broad-minded Christianity.

Everyone active in Chautauqua work through a series of years could narrate many stories like the above, and doubtless some more remarkable;

but I have given only a few out of many that could be recalled out of an experience with the C. L. S. C. through more than forty years. As I have looked upon the representatives of the graduating class in the Hall of Philosophy, I have often wished that I might know some of the life-stories of those who, often through difficulties unknown, have carried the course through to completion.

An eminent minister wrote to me recently as follows:

At a place where I became pastor I found two sisters who were living in dark seclusion, brooding in melancholia as the effect of a great sorrow. They attended church, but took no part in our work, and none at all in society. I did my best to comfort those young women and bring them out of their monasticism. But it was all in vain. Their broken spirits revolted from a religion of happiness. A few years after my pastorate was ended there, and I was preaching elsewhere, I visited the town and was surprised to find both those women among the most active women in the church, happy, gifted, and universally esteemed. What had wrought the change? They chanced to hear of the Chautauqua Reading Course and sent for the books and magazines. They pursued the course, graduated, and visited Chautauqua. It awakened their entire being and brought them into a new world. They were literally born anew. I have witnessed wonderful changes in people, but never any that was more thorough, real, and permanent than in those young women.

South Ravine, Near Children's Playground

Muscallonge

Bathhouse and Jacob Bolin Gymnasium

Let us name also some of the leading events of the Assembly of 1884. As the organ of the C. Y. F. R. U. Dr. Flood established *The Youth's C. L. S. C. Paper* for boys and girls. It was an illustrated magazine, but only twelve numbers were published, as the field for periodical literature for young people was already well covered. "The Chautauqua Foreign Tour," a series of illustrated lectures on the British Isles, was conducted this year by Rev. Jesse Bowman Young, Professor H. H. Ragan, and Mr. George Makepeace Towle. Music was abundant and varied this season, the choir being led by Professors Sherwin and Case in turn; concerts by a remarkable quartet, the Meigs Sisters; the delightful singers of southern plantation and revival songs, the Tennesseans; the Yale College Glee Club; Miss Belle McClintock, Mrs. J. C. Hull, Mr. E. O. Excell, and Miss Tuthill, soloists. Dr. Charles J. Little gave a course of lectures on English literature; Dr. Henson, Miss Susan Hayes Ward, Dr. J. W. Butler of Mexico, and Dr. S. S. Smith of Minnesota were among the lecturers. We heard Ram Chandra Bose and Dennis Osborne of India, and Sau Aubrah of Burmah, a most interesting speaker on the customs of his country and his impressions of ours. Principal Fairbairn of Oxford made the history of philosophy interesting, and the Rev. A. J. Palmer of New York won instant fame by his great war lecture, "Company D, the Die-no-more's," given on Grand Army Day to a great concourse of old soldiers.

On Saturday, August 23d, a reception was given to the Governor of Pennsylvania, Hon. Robert E. Pattison. Friday, August 15th, was observed as the decennial anniversary of the Woman's Christian Temperance Union. I find on the program of that year a series of colloquies named "The Socratic Academy," conducted by Dr. H. H. Moore. I know not what subjects they discussed, nor how they discussed them, but I remember Dr. Moore as one able to shed light on any subject that he chose to present. As I read the program of any one of those years at Chautauqua, I realize how utterly inadequate must be any sketch like the above to bring it before a reader.

By this time three classes of the C. L. S. C. had been graduated, '82, '83, and '84. Four more classes were pursuing the course, so that C. L. S. C. members present at Chautauqua might now be counted by the thousand. There was a strong class-spirit. Each class had its name, its motto, its badge, and its banner, and ribbon badges were fluttering everywhere. Every day came announcements from the platform of class-meetings, and it was sometimes difficult to provide for them all. During the season of 1884 two classes united their interests, raised money, and purchased a small octagonal building near the Hall of Philosophy. These were the classes of '83 and '85. The movement for class headquarters was growing; all the other classes began the raising of building funds, and those who looked into the future saw all around St. Paul's Grove the prospect of small buildings rising. How would the grounds appear when forty classes should have little headquarters —a C. L. S. C. village? The plan began to be mooted of a Union Class Building, to be realized later.

## CHAPTER XV

### THE CHAPLAIN'S LEG AND OTHER TRUE TALES

(1885–1888)

THE twelfth year of the Assembly, 1885, opened with a preliminary week, beginning July 7th, for the Teachers' Retreat and the School of Languages, and closed with "After-week," making the entire session fifty-three days long, ending on August 28th. But the official "opening" did not take place until the traditional date, Tuesday, August 7th. For years, indeed from the beginning, Dr. Vincent had set his heart on having a chime of bells at Chautauqua. The practically minded trustees urged for some needed improvement, and buildings for the growing schools, but the poetic conception carried the day, and in 1885 the Meneely chime of ten bells was heard at the opening in July. Some common souls in cottages around complained of their frequency, awaking folks early in the morning and breaking their naps in the afternoon, but to most their mellow music was a welcome sound.

It has always been the rule that quiet must reign on the grounds after the night bells at 10:00 P.M., and watchmen have been wont to knock at doors where the rule was honored in the breach instead of the observance. A parlor full of young people enjoying themselves does not always come to silence in a minute. I remember one house near the Point where dwelt an elderly lady with abundant gray hair but a young heart, and also with an attractive daughter. That home was exceedingly popular among the younger set, and their meetings—doubtless held for the discussion of serious subjects, for the voices were sometimes loud—were often prolonged beyond the time of the bells. One night an unusually imperative rap of the watchman's stick on the front door startled the group. The door was opened a little and the matron put forth her head with the words loudly spoken, "Shoot, if you must, this old gray head!" whereupon the watchman departed without a word.

In the revolution of the Chautauqua Circle, 1885 was known as the Roman year, having as its major subject Latin history and literature. The studies of the "Foreign Tour" in the Assembly program embraced lectures, with illustrations on Italian cities and scenery. Dr. Vincent's fertile mind conceived a plan to aid the students of the course, and incidentally to advertise it, by a series of object-lessons. He divided Pratt Avenue, the path leading up to the college on the hill, into sections corresponding by their relative lengths to the periods of Roman history, and erected at the proper points along the road, posts to commemorate the leading events, with dates and names of the great men of the several periods. These milestones were black, with inscriptions in white. As people passed by they would be reminded of the leading facts in the story of the Eternal City. Often might be seen members of the C. L. S. C., notebook in hand, storing their minds with the dates and events in the annals of Rome. The coal-black pillars had a somewhat sepulchral look and suggested a graveyard. One lady who was a stranger at Chautauqua, and evidently not a member of the C. L. S. C., asked Dr. R. S. Holmes, one of the leading workers, "Can you tell me why all these tombstones have been set up here. Surely all the men named on them cannot be buried along this street!" The question was also asked if it was proposed each year to set up a row of trophies on other streets for the American year, the English year, the Greek year, and by degrees to turn all Chautauqua into a memorial grove for great men and great deeds of all the ages; but at the close of the season the monuments were gathered up and carried away, leaving no successors.

The lecture platform of 1885 was as strong as ever. Dr. Charles F. Deems of New York delivered the baccalaureate sermon on Sunday, August 16th, an unique discourse on the short text, "One New Man" (Eph. 2:15), and the Recognition Address on the following Wednesday was by Dr. E. E. Hale of Boston. A special series of "Yale University Historical Lectures" was given by Professor Arthur M. Wheeler. Bishop Cyrus D. Foss of the Methodist Episcopal Church preached on Sunday, August 23d. Dr. John P. Newman delivered a lecture on August 25th in memory of President U. S. Grant, of whom he had been a friend and pastor. This year a young man made his first appearance upon the Chautauqua platform, not yet as a lecturer, but introducing speakers in felicitous sentences and presiding with the ease of an experienced chairman. This was Mr. George Edgar Vincent, just graduated from Yale University, from whom Chautauqua and the world in general was to hear before many years.

In 1885, the institution received a new charter from the Legislature of New York, giving it the name "Chautauqua University" and the power to confer degrees. By vote of the Board, the title "Chancellor of the Chautauqua University" was given to Dr. Vincent. It was hoped to establish a college for study by correspondence, with reviews of the subjects taught in the summer meeting. But the expense of a professional staff was great and the number of students was not large enough to support it without an endowment. The Chautauqua University might have won a place in the world of education, if friends had been found to bestow upon it a liberal endowment, but among the varied gifts of Dr. Vincent was not that peculiar talent for raising money. The University did not prosper, and in 1898 the Trustees voluntarily surrendered to the Regents of the University of the State of New York the examination of candidates and the conferring of degrees. Again the title was changed and the University became "The Chautauqua System of Education."

The year 1886 ushered in some improvements. In place of the old wharf stood a new pier building, three stories high, with stores on the upper balcony, for the steamboat still brought most of the Chautauqua crowds and at their arrival a throng was always present to greet them. Above the building rose a tower, from which sounded forth over the lake and through the Grove the melody of the Chautauqua chimes. On the hill was the new Jewett House, given by Mrs. A. H. Jewett as a home for self-supporting young women, teachers and others, while at Chautauqua.

The program of that year shows that a faculty of sixteen conducted the work in the Chautauqua Teachers' Retreat, and fifteen others gave courses in the School of Languages. Lessons in Harmony, Organ and Piano, Drawing and Painting were also added. The Chautauqua School of Physical Education was established under the direction of Dr. W. G. Anderson. All these were signs that the system of summer schools at Chautauqua was increasing its range of study, as well as growing in the number of its students.

One of the lecturers at this season was Professor Caleb T. Winchester of Wesleyan University. It was a privilege to listen to his scholarly yet delightful account of a ramble in the English lake country, with estimates of the literary lights who made that region famous. Dr. Wm. H. Milburn, the blind chaplain of the United States Senate, Dr. Russell H. Conwell, with his lecture of "Acres of Diamonds," Dr. Edward E. Hale and Mrs. Mary A. Livermore also gave lectures. Dr. Hale read his story, *In His Name;* and at the close of his reading came a general rush for his autograph. I happened to be in charge of the platform, and tried to excuse the speaker from adding to his burdens, but he declared his willingness to meet the demands of the people and wrote in every album offered. In the crowd was a little girl, shabbily dressed, who had no album, but brought a scrap of brown paper which she had picked up. Dr. Hale looked at the torn fragment, then took the copy of his story from which he had been reading, wrote on its fly-leaf his name, and handed it to the little girl.

Two lecturers from the South attracted attention. One was the Rev. J. W. Lee, an able, broad-minded man; the other was the unique evangelist, Rev. Sam P. Jones, whose utterances were sometimes eloquent, sometimes jocose, sometimes shocking, but always interesting. Dr. Willis J. Beecher of the Auburn Theological Seminary, Dr. John Hall of New York, and President William F. Warren of Boston University were also among the speakers.

Readings were given by Will M. Carleton, George W. Cable, and General Lew Wallace, from their own writings. An immense crowd packed the Amphitheater to hear General Wallace read from his *Ben Hur* the story of the Chariot Race. But candor compels us to say that it was not very

Athletic Club

Boys' Club Headed for Camp

thrillingly rendered. One who listened said, "He never got his horses off the walk." Other readers were George Riddle of Boston and Professor R. L. Cumnock of Northwestern University. This summer Mrs. Frank Beard collected and conducted an Oriental Exhibition.

Almost every year Frank Beard was at Chautauqua, teaching a class in art, making pictures in the children's class, giving one or two crayon lectures, and occasionally on Sunday evenings an illustrated Bible reading. As already intimated, that was the age when there was a craze for autographs, and everybody carried around an autograph album, seeking signatures from the celebrities. After a popular lecture a crowd hastened to the platform and a hundred hands, each holding an album, would be stretched out toward the speaker, demanding his autograph. Of course every child, and nearly every grown-up, must have Frank Beard's autograph, and with it a picture drawn by his hand. Frank said once in a religious meeting that his idea of heaven was a place where there were no autograph albums.

Every year at Chautauqua is held a National Army Day, when the Civil War veterans from near and far assemble, wear their G. A. R. uniforms and badges, and listen to an address in the

Amphitheater. One year, I think it was 1886, but I am not sure, the orator was late in coming, and Mr. Beard, himself a veteran of the war, was called upon to fill the vacancy. He told the story of "The Chaplain's Leg," of which some incredulous people have doubted the authenticity. As I remember it was somewhat as follows. He would come forward, slapping his right leg, and saying:

That is a good leg, but it isn't mine. It belonged once to the chaplain of our regiment; I was in a battle and happened to have a tree between myself and the whole rebel army. There was a change in the front, and I started to make a detour to another tree. Just in the middle of my march I ran against the chaplain, who was also making a detour, and at that moment came along a rebel shell, which took off one of his legs and also one of mine. We lay on the ground only a minute or two, and then an ambulance took us and the two legs on board. They carried us to the field hospital, and put on our legs, which grew just as they should, so that after a few weeks I was dismissed as cured. Well, I had been a long time, for me, without liquid refreshment, and I knew that out in the woods near the camp was an extemporized bar, in the shape of a board laid on two stumps of trees. I found it hard to walk in that direction, and had to pull my right leg along; but I thought that it needed only a little practice to be as good as ever. I got to the bar and ordered a glass of something; it might have been ginger-pop or it might have been something else. Just after it was poured out and before I could take hold of it, that right leg of mine lifted itself up and kicked over the whole contraption—glass, and jug, and bar, and then in spite of all I could do, stumped me back to camp! And on the way I passed the chaplain who was being dragged out *to* the bar, while I was being pulled away from it. Then I knew what had happened in the hospital; they had put each leg on the wrong man, and I must carry around the chaplain's leg as long as I lived. The leg took me to church; at first it was pretty tough, but I got used to it. That leg brought me to Chautauqua, and here I am to-day, brought by the chaplain's leg. Some time ago I gave by request a lecture with pictures in the Sing Sing prison, and there among the convicts sat my old friend the chaplain, wearing a striped suit. What brought him there I can't imagine, unless—well, I don't know what it was.

The Assembly of 1887 was fifty-eight days in length, from July 2d to August 28th. The schools were still growing in the number of students and enlarging their courses. Some of the new departments were the Arabic and Assyrian languages, mathematics, chemistry, oratory and expression, stenography, mineralogy, and geology. To house these classes and the army of students, buildings were urgently needed, and this year a College Building arose overlooking the lake. It stood until two years ago, when on account of its dilapidation as well as its incongruity with the modern plans of the schools, it was taken down.

During the season of 1887, the Fourth of July Address was given by Hon. Roswell G. Horr, member of Congress from Michigan. Dr. Fairbairn from Oxford was with us again, also the Rev. Mark Guy Pearse of England, Dr. Charles J. Little, Dr. John A. Broadus of Louisville, one of those scholars who know how to present great truths in a simple manner, Chaplain McCabe, Dr. Charles R. Henderson, on social questions of the time, and Mrs. Mary A. Livermore. Rev. Sam P. Jones was also on the platform for the second season. He gave his powerful sermon on "Conscience" with not a sentence to provoke a smile, but a strong call to righteousness. Another address, however, contained an application which called forth a smile all over the audience. It was known that Dr. Vincent was being strongly talked of as a candidate for Bishop in the Methodist Episcopal Church, and in the following May, 1888, he was elected to that office. Dr. Vincent was presiding at Mr. Jones' lecture. In the address Jones managed to bring in an allusion to bishops. Then turning halfway round toward the chairman, he said, "Doctor Vincent, I shouldn't wonder if they made you and me bishops before long. You see the thing's coming down."

The class graduating this year in the C. L. S. C.

was the largest in the history of the Circle. It included in its membership the Rev. G. R. Alden and his wife, and was named in her honor, the Pansy class. At this time the enrolled members of the C. L. S. C. were more than eighty thousand in number.

The Assembly of 1888 opened on July 3d and closed on August 29th, fifty-eight days in length. The summer school was now announced as the College of Liberal Arts. I notice in the list of subjects taught: Old French, Scandinavian languages and literature, Sanskrit, Zend and Gothic, Hebrew and Semitic languages, and philology. It is not to be supposed that all of these classes were overcrowded with students, but those in physical culture and arts and crafts were very popular. The annual exhibition of the gymnastic classes has been for years one of the most thronged events on the program, and in anticipation the Amphitheater is filled long in advance of the hour for beginning the exercises.

Among the lecturers of this season were Mrs. Alden, "Pansy," who read a new story, *The Hall in the Grove;* Dr. William R. Harper, Dr. Frank W. Gunsaulus, Dr. Joseph Cook, Dr. Talmage, Dr. Hale, General Russell A. Alger, and George W. Bain. Dr. Phillips Brooks, giant in body and in soul, preached one of his sermons, sweeping in swift utterances like a tidal wave. One hardly dared draw a breath for fear of losing his mighty periods. Bishop William Taylor of Africa, was also present, and thrilled his hearers, yet in a calm, quiet manner, absolutely free from any oratorical display. There was a charm in his address and the most critical hearers felt it, yet could not analyze it. I met, not at Chautauqua but elsewhere, a lawyer who admitted that he rarely attended church because he could not endure the dull sermons; but after listening to Bishop Taylor, said that if he could hear that man he would go to church twice, even three times, on a Sunday. And yet in all his discourse there was not a rhetorical sentence nor a rounded period.

Mr. Leon H. Vincent was again at Chautauqua, with his literary lectures. Either during this season or the one when he came next—for he was generally present every alternate year—it became necessary to move Leon Vincent's lectures from the Hall of Philosophy to the Amphitheater, on account of the number who were eager to hear them. Among those who gave readings were Mr. Charles F. Underhill of New York, Mr. George Riddle, and Professor R. L. Cumnock.

The Methodists, both of the North and the South, have always formed a large element in the

Chautauqua constituency, partly because of their number throughout the continent, but also because both the Founders of the Assembly were members of that church. This year, 1888, the Methodist House was opened, in the center of the ground, and at once became the social rallying place of the denomination. Its chapel, connected with the House, was built afterward by the all-year residents at Chautauqua as the home of the community church, which is open to all and attended by all, the only church having a resident pastor and holding services through the year, nominally under the Methodist system, but practically undenominational.

In May, 1888, Dr. John H. Vincent, after twenty years in charge of the Sunday School work as Secretary and Editor, was elected and consecrated a Bishop in the Methodist Episcopal Church. For some years his episcopal residence was at Buffalo, within easy distance of Chautauqua, but his new duties required him to travel even more widely than before, and he needed an assistant to care for the work of the Assembly. Mr. George E. Vincent, able son of distinguished father, was this year appointed Vice-Principal of Instruction, and assumed a closer supervision of the program of Chautauqua.

In this year, also, Dr. William Rainey Harper was made Principal of the College of Liberal Arts, all the departments of the Summer School being under his direction. Another name appears on the record of 1888, the name of Alonzo A. Stagg, haloed in the estimate of young Chautauqua with a glory even surpassing that of the two Founders. For Stagg, just graduated from Yale, could curve a baseball more marvelously than any other man in America. He was one of the instructors in the gymnasium, and organized a team that played with most of the baseball clubs for miles around Chautauqua, almost invariably winning the game. It was said that the athletic field rivaled the Amphitheater in its crowds when Stagg played.

# CHAPTER XVI

## A NEW LEAF IN LUKE'S GOSPEL

(1889–1892)

THE Assembly of 1889 opened on July 3d and continued fifty-five days, to August 26th. Several new buildings had arisen since the last session. One was the Anne M. Kellogg Memorial Hall, built by Mr. James H. Kellogg of Rochester, New York, in honor of his mother. In it were rooms for kindergarten, clay modeling, china painting, and a meeting place for the Chautauqua W. C. T. U. It stood originally on the site of the present Colonnade Building, the business block, and was moved to its present location to make room for that building. Mr. Kellogg was an active worker in the Sunday School movement and from the beginning a regular visitor at Chautauqua. Another building of this year was the one formerly known as the Administration Office, on Clark Avenue in front of the book-store and the old Museum, now the Information Bureau and the School of Expression. When the offices of the Institution were removed to the Colonnade, the old Administration Building was given up to business, and it is now known as a lunch-room. The School of Physical Culture, under Dr. W. G. Anderson, had grown to such an extent that a new gymnasium had become a necessity, and one had been erected on the lake-front. In the newer part of the grounds many private cottages arose, of more tasteful architecture than the older houses.

A notable event of this season was the visit of former President Rutherford B. Hayes of Ohio. Among the lecturers of 1889 we find the name of Mr. Donald G. Mitchell, whose *Reveries of a Bachelor* and *Dream-Life*, published under the pseudonym of Ik Marvel, are recognized classics in American literature. Other eminent men on the platform were Professor Hjalmar H. Boyesen of Columbia University, Professor J. P. Mahaffy of Dublin University, Dr. Lyman Abbott, Dr. Frank W. Gunsaulus, Dr. Washington Gladden, Dr. John Henry Barrows, Professor Frederick Starr, who could make anthropology interesting to those who had never studied it, Professor Herbert B. Adams, and Corporal Tanner, the U. S. Commissioner of Pensions, a veteran who walked on two cork legs, but was able to stand up and give a heart-warming address to the old soldiers. Dr.

Chautauqua Woman's Club House

Rustic Bridge

W. R. Harper, who was teaching in the School of Theology, gave a course of lectures on the Hebrew prophets. Bishop Cyrus D. Foss, one of the great preachers of the Methodist Episcopal Church, delivered a sermon on one of the Sundays. The South sent us an able lecturer in Richard Malcolm Johnson. The orator on Recognition Day, of the Class of '89, was Dr. David Swing of Chicago, who spoke on "The Beautiful and the Useful." Dr. Russell H. Conwell gave some lectures, abundant in their illustrative stories.

I think that this was the year, but am not certain, when Dr. Conwell preached one Sunday in the Amphitheater a sermon of remarkable originality, listened to with the closest attention by his hearers, because he kept them guessing as to his subject until he was more than half-way through. He said in opening, "I will give my text at the end of the sermon, if I don't forget it; but I will tell you my subject. I am going to speak of a man whom our Lord called the Model Church Member." We all began wondering who that man was, but nobody could recall him. He said that this model man lived among the mountains, and spoke of the influence of surroundings upon character; then that where he lived there were two churches, one large, the other small, one aristocratic and popular, the other of the lower classes, despised; and that this man was a member of the church looked down upon; but these facts gave us no hint as to the model man's identity. He puzzled us once more by saying that this was a business man who had good credit, and we were still in the fog;—when did Jesus ever talk about credit? Then he told in graphic manner, making it seem as if it had happened the day before, the story of the Good Samaritan, and the problem was solved. But he astonished us again by saying, "There was one part of this story which for some reason St. Luke left out of his gospel, and I am going to tell it now";—and of course everybody was eager to hear a brand-new Bible story not found in the Scriptures. He told that this man who had been robbed and beaten on the Jericho road, after his recovery at the inn, went home to Jerusalem, met his family, and then took his two boys up to the Temple to return thanks for his restoration. The service in all its splendor was described. One boy said, "Father, see that priest waving a censer! What a good man he must be!" But the man said, "My boy, don't look at that hypocrite! That is the very priest who left me to die beside the road!" After a few minutes, the younger boy said, "See that Levite blowing a trumpet! He looks like a good man, doesn't he?" And the father said, "My boys, that is the very Levite that passed me by when I was lying wounded! Let us go away from this place." And then one of the boys said, "Let us find the church of the Good Samaritan, and worship there." And Dr. Conwell added, "My text is, 'Go thou and do likewise!'" No one who heard that sermon, so full of surprises, could ever forget it.

The elocutionary readers who entertained us during that season were Professor Cumnock, A. P. Burbank, George Riddle, George W. Cable, reading his own stories, and Mr. Leland Powers of Boston, with his rendering of *David Copperfield*, several other stories, and a play or two. Without the aid of costume or "making up," it was wonderful how he could change facial expression, and voice, and manner instantaneously with his successive characters. We saw Mr. Micawber transformed in an instant into Uriah Heep. From 1889, Mr. Powers was a frequent visitor, and his rendering of novels and plays enraptured the throngs in the Amphitheater. For many seasons he was wont to appear on alternate years. On Old First Night, when the call was made for those present on the successive years, while the regulars stood up and remained standing as each year was named, it was interesting to watch the down-sittings and uprisings of Leland Powers. But we shall hear his voice no more, for even while we are writing the news of his death comes to us.

In this year, 1889, the musical classes were organized as the Chautauqua School of Music, with instructors in all departments. Inasmuch as all people do not enjoy the sound of a piano, practicing all day scales and exercises, a place was found in the rear of the grounds for a village of small cottages, some might call them "huts," each housing a piano for lessons and practice. I am told that forty-eight pianos may be heard there all sending out music at once, and each a different tune.

The year 1889 brought another man to Chautauqua who was well-beloved and will be long remembered, the pianist and teacher, William H. Sherwood, who showed himself a true Chautauquan by his willing, helpful spirit, no less than by his power on the piano. When death stilled those wondrous fingers, Mr. Sherwood's memory was honored by the Sherwood Memorial Studios, dedicated in 1912.

When we realize that Chautauqua is a city of frame-buildings, packed closely together on narrow streets, in the early years having exceedingly inadequate protection against fires, we almost wonder that it has never been overswept by a conflagration. From time to time there have been fires, most of them a benefit in clearing away old shacks of the camp-meeting strata; and one took place on a night during the season of 1889. It swept away a row of small houses along the southwestern border of Miller Park, toward the Land of Palestine. Their site was kept unoccupied, leaving a clear view of the lake, except on one corner where a handsome building was erected, the Arcade. While the main entrance to the grounds was at the Pier, this was a prosperous place of business, but after the back door became the front door, through the coming of the Chautauqua Traction Company, giving railroad connection with the outside world, the business center of Chautauqua shifted to streets up the hill.

The year 1890 came, bringing the seventeenth session of the Assembly. This was the year when the Presbyterian House was opened, and also the C. L. S. C. building, erected by Flood and Vincent, for Mr. George E. Vincent was now a partner with Dr. Flood in publishing *The Chautauquan Magazine* and the books of the C. L. S. C. Subsequently the business of publication was assumed by the Institution, and the building has been for many years the book-store, with rooms on the floor above for classes in the School of Expression.

An announcement in the program of the College of Liberal Arts was that a School of Journalism would be conducted by Hamilton Wright Mabie, essayist, and one of the editors of *The Outlook.* Leon H. Vincent gave another course of literary lectures. Dr. Henry L. Wayland of Philadelphia was one of the speakers. John Habberton, author of the "best seller" some years before, *Helen's Babies*, lectured, read, joined the C. L. S. C. Class of 1894, and was made its President. Dr. Francis E. Clark, father of the Christian Endeavor Society, came and was greeted by a host of young Endeavorers. Dr. Alexander McKenzie of Cambridge, Mass., preached a great sermon. Mr. Robert J. Burdette, at that time an editor, but afterwards a famous Baptist preacher, gave one of his wisely-witty lectures. The Hon. John Jay, worthy son of one of New York's most distinguished families, gave an address. Dr. Fairbairn of Oxford was again among us, with his deep lectures, yet clear as the waters of Lake Tahoe. The orator on Recognition Day was Mrs. Alice Freeman Palmer, whose term as President made Wellesley great. Mr. Thomas Nelson Page gave readings from his own stories of southern life before the Civil War. A young man appeared on the platform for the first time, but not the last, who was destined to stand forth in a few years as one of the foremost of Americans. This was Theodore Roosevelt, whose lectures at Chautauqua were later expanded into the volumes on *The Winning of the West.* Colonel Thomas Wentworth Higginson, soldier and historian, also gave lectures.

At the opening of the season in 1891, the members of the Chautauqua Circle counted more than a hundred thousand. Nine classes had been graduated, another large class was to receive its diplomas during that summer, and there were three undergraduate classes each of nearly twenty thousand members, with another class as large in prospect. Only a small section of each class could be present at Chautauqua, the vast majority of its members being far away, some in distant lands. But among those who came to the Assembly, the social spirit was strong. They loved to meet each other, held social reunions and business meetings constantly. Each of the four oldest classes, from '82 to '85, had its own building as headquarters, but all the later classes were homeless and in need of homes. It was a great boon to these classes when at last, in 1891, the C. L. S. C. Alumni Hall was completed and opened. Its eight classrooms were distributed by lot and furnished by the gifts of the members. As new classes were organized year after year, they were welcomed by the classes already occupying the rooms. It was not many years before each room became the home of two classes, then after eight years more of three classes, meeting on different days, but united in the general reception on the evening before the Recognition Day. Beside the eight class-rooms on the second floor of the Alumni Building there is a large hall which is used before the Recognition Day by the graduating class, and during the rest of the season by the new entering class. In 1916, after the death of Miss Kate F. Kimball, Secretary of the C. L. S. C., this hall was named "The Kimball Room." The Alumni Building with its wide porches became at Chautauqua a social center for the members of the Circle and many have been the friendships formed there. On this season of 1891 the United Presbyterian House was opened.

The section of the Summer Schools formerly known as The Teachers' Retreat, but now beginning to be called "The School of Pedagogy," was this year (1891) under the direction of that master-teacher and inspiring leader, Colonel Francis W. Parker of Chicago. He gave several lectures on the principles of teaching, but many besides the teachers listened to them with equal interest and profit. One of these lectures was entitled, "The Artisan and the Artist"; the artisan representing those in every vocation of life who do their work by rule; the artist, those who pay little attention to regulations, but teach, or preach, or design buildings, or paint pictures out of their hearts; and these are the Pestalozzis, the Michael Angelos, the Beechers of their several professions. We had a course of delightful essay-lectures in the Hall of Philosophy by Miss Agnes Repplier. The Rabbi of the Temple Emanuel in New York, Dr. Gustave Gottheil, gave some enlightening lectures upon the principles of the Jewish faith. At that time a prominent Roman Catholic priest, the Rev. Edward McGlynn, was in rebellion against the hierarchy of his church, and maintaining a vigorous controversy in behalf of religious freedom. He had been dismissed from one of the largest churches in New York, and with voice and pen was denouncing the Pope, Cardinals, and Bishops. Father McGlynn came to Chautauqua and delivered a powerful address in the Amphitheater, pouring forth a torrent of language, shot as from a rapid-firing cannon. While at Chautauqua he was entertained at a dinner in one of the cottages with a number of invited guests. From the moment of meeting at the table, he began to talk in his forceful manner, never stopping to take breath. Dr. Buckley was present and several times opened his mouth but found no chance to interject a word, which was an unusual state of affairs for one who generally led the conversation.

Another speaker who was heard with interest was Jacob A. Riis, with his illustrated lecture on "How the Other Half Lives." Mr. Riis was only a newspaper reporter, not occupying an editorial chair, but Theodore Roosevelt spoke of him as "New York's most useful citizen." The cause of woman suffrage and reform had a splendid showing this season, for Frances E. Willard, Anna Howard Shaw, Susan B. Anthony, and Mary A. Livermore, all spoke upon the Amphitheater platform. A visitor who made many friends was Rev. Dr. Percival, headmaster of Rugby School. Julia Ward Howe gave interesting reminiscences of Longfellow, Emerson, and other literary lights whom she had known intimately. John Fiske, one of America's greatest historians, gave a course of lectures on the discovery and settlement of this continent. Another historian whom we heard was John Bach McMaster, whose lectures were like a series of dissolving views, picture succeed-

Post-Office Building

ing picture, each showing the great events and the great men of their period. In this year Dr. Horatio R. Palmer assumed charge of the musical department, and for the first time waved his baton before the great chorus in the Amphitheater gallery.

As everybody knows, the four hundredth anniversary of the discovery of America was observed everywhere in 1892. Chautauqua commemorated it in lectures on Columbus and his fellow-voyagers, and by a pageant presenting scenes from the history. The Chautauqua class graduating that year was named the Columbia Class, and as its members, several hundred strong, marched in the procession, Chancellor Vincent was astonished to see in the line his wife, wearing the graduating badge of cardinal ribbon. She had read the course through four years and kept it a secret from him, revealed for the first time at that Recognition service. The address on that day was delivered by Dr. Frank W. Gunsaulus on "The Ideal of Culture."

Among the chief speakers in 1892 we find the names of two Presidents of Cornell University, Dr. Andrew D. White and Dr. James G. Schurman; Dr. J. Monro Gibson, a London pastor and one of the Board of Counsel of the C. L. S. C. was with us; also Ballington Booth, Henry Watterson, the journalist, and President Merrill E. Gates of Amherst College. At this session also the Girls' Club was organized and conducted by Miss Mary H. Mather of Wilmington, Del.

In the announcements of this year, the title of Chautauqua University was allowed to lapse, and in place of it appeared "The Chautauqua System of Education."

## CHAPTER XVII

### CLUB LIFE AT CHAUTAUQUA

(1893–1896)

WHEN the Chautauquans gathered for the twentieth Assembly on July 1, 1893, they found some changes had taken place. The old Amphitheater, which had faithfully served its generation, but had fallen into decrepitude, no longer lifted its forest of wooden pillars over the ravine. In its place stood a new Amphitheater, more roomy and far more suitable to the needs of the new day. It was covered by a trussed roof supported by steel columns standing around the building, so that from every seat was an unobstructed view of the platform. The choir-gallery was enlarged to provide seats for five hundred. The platform was brought further into the hall, making room for an orchestra. The seats were more comfortable, and could now hold without crowding fifty-six hundred people. A few years later, the old organ gave place to a greater and better one, the gift of the Massey family of Toronto, a memorial of their father, the late Hart A. Massey, one of the early Trustees of the Assembly. Under the choir-loft and on either side of the organ, rooms were arranged for offices and classes in the Department of Music.

During the previous season, 1892, a Men's Club had been organized and had found temporary quarters. It now possessed a home on the shore of the Lake, beside Palestine Park. In its rooms were games of various sorts, cards, however, being still under the ban at Chautauqua.[1] Newspapers and periodicals, shower-baths, and an out-of-door parlor on the roof, very pleasant except on the days when the lake flies invaded it. The Men's Club building had formerly been the power house of the electrical plant, but one who had known it of

[1] From the *Handbook of Information* published by the Chautauqua Institution (1918) we give the following extract. "The Chautauqua tradition which taboos card playing and social dancing, and the rule which forbids the sale or importation of alcoholic beverages, disclose the influence which dominated the early life of the Assembly. As to card playing and dancing, the tradition is preserved not because all agree in condemning these things in themselves, but because they are deemed unsuitable to Chautauqua conditions and even hostile to its life. It is believed that they would prove divisive and distracting, and that they suggest a very different type of society from that which Chautauqua seeks to set up for a few summer weeks. Chautauqua, therefore, disapproves these diversions as not only unnecessary, but as involving disintegrating influences. The fact that many who indulge in these amusements at home express gratification that they are not permitted at Chautauqua is significant."

old would scarcely recognize it as reconstructed, enlarged, and decorated. To make a place for the dynamo of the electric system, an encroachment had been made upon Palestine Park; a cave had been dug under Mount Lebanon, and the dynamo installed within its walls. The age of King Hiram of Tyre, who cut the cedars of Lebanon for Solomon's Temple, and the age of Edison, inventor of the electric light, were thus brought into incongruous juxtaposition. A chimney funnel on the summit of Mount Lebanon, it must be confessed, seemed out of place, and the Valley of Coele-Syria, between Lebanon and Hermon, was entirely obliterated. Bible students might shake their heads disapprovingly, but even sacred archæology must give way to the demands of civilization.

An improvement less obvious to the eye, but more essential to health, was the installation of a complete sewer system. As the sewage is not allowed to taint the water of the lake, it is carried by pipes to a disposal plant at the lower end of the ground and chemically purified. The water rendered as clear as crystal is then permitted to run into the lake, while the sludge is pressed by machinery into cakes used as fertilizer. An artesian well on high ground supplies pure water in abundance, with taps at convenient places for families.

Originally the water in use came from wells. These were carefully tested by scientific experts, and most of them were condemned, but a few were found to give forth pure water and are still in use, though frequently and carefully tested. Near the Men's Club is a spring of mineral water containing sulphur and iron. It has the approval of chemists and physicians, and many drink it for its healthful effect.

One who looks over the programs of Chautauqua through successive years will notice the number of the clubs for various classes and ages. Largest of all is the Woman's Club, of which Mrs. Emily Huntington Miller was the first President, succeeded by Mrs. B. T. Vincent, and carried on under her leadership for many years. When on account of failing health Mrs. Vincent felt compelled to resign her office, her place was taken by Mrs. Percy V. Pennybacker of Texas, who had been President of the General Federation of Woman's Clubs in the United States. This Club includes more than two thousand members, and its daily meeting in the Hall of Philosophy brings together a throng, often too large for the building. In 1918 the Club purchased a cottage fronting on the lake, near the Hotel Athenæum, as a headquarters, a place for social gatherings and rest rooms for women.

Besides the Women's Clubs and the Men's Club, there are at least a dozen other associations of people having tastes and interests bringing them together. We will name the most important of these without regard to their chronological order.

There is the Athletic Club for men and boys over sixteen, directing the organized sports and providing all forms of out-of-door recreation. It has a club house on the lake with bowling alleys and boat room, shower baths and lockers, and a reading room.

The Golf Club has a nine-hole course, situated on the rising ground of eighty acres opposite the traction station. The money has been contributed for a Country Club House, soon to be built at the entrance. The donors, it is understood, are Mr. Stephen J. Munger of Dallas, Texas, one of the Trustees, his wife, and Mrs. Frank B. Wilcox of St. Petersburg, Florida, in memory of her husband.

Chautauquans of some years' standing will remember the old croquet ground, where now stands the Colonnade, and the group of solemn graybeards who used to frequent it and knock the balls through the big arches all day. No matter what popular lecturer was speaking in the Amphitheater, the passer-by would find that same serious company. I used to pass them while going to my home and coming from it several times each day. On one occasion I stopped and struck up an acquaintance with a tall old gentleman who always wore a high hat and a long double-breasted coat. I learned that he was the President of a Bank among the mountains of Pennsylvania, and that he had come to Chautauqua suffering from nervous prostration, making him utterly unable to do business and scarcely desiring to live. He passed the croquet court, sat down, and was invited to play. He began and found himself, for the first time in many months, actually interested in doing something. He began to enjoy his meals and to sleep at night. All that summer he played croquet, never listening to a lecture, and at the end of the season went home almost well. From that time croquet became more than his recreation, almost his business. He told me that there were others like himself who found health and a new enjoyment of life in the game. When the ground was needed for the new business block, the courts were removed to the ravine on the other side of the grounds, near the gymnasium. About that time croquet was developed into a more scientific game, a sort of billiardized croquet, with walls from which a ball would rebound, and arches a quarter of an inch—or is it only an eighth of an inch?—wider than the ball. To find a name for the new game they struck off the first and last letters, so that croquet became Roque, and in due time the Roque Club arose, with a group of players who live and breathe and have their being for this game. People come from far, and I am told, to attend its tournaments at every season.

There is also a Quoit Club meeting on the ground near Higgins Hall, beside the road leading up College Hill.

The Young Woman's Club is for those over fifteen years of age, while the Girl's Club has its membership between eight and fifteen, meets in its own Club House near the roque courts, and is enthusiastically sought by those no longer little girls, yet not quite young women.

Wherever one walks around Chautauqua he is sure to see plenty of boys in blue sweaters bearing on their bosoms the monogram in big letters C. B. C., initials of the Chautauqua Boys' Club. They too have their headquarters near the athletic field and find something doing there all day long.

For the little ones, there is the kindergarten at Kellogg Hall, and out of doors beside it the playground, where the tots make cities out of sand and find other pleasures. And we must not forget the Children's Paradise, the completely equipped playground in the ravine at the northwestern part of the grounds. I remember hearing Jacob A. Riis, the father of the city playgrounds, say in one of his lectures: "They tell me that the boys play ball in the streets of New York and break windows when the ball goes out of the way. Good! I hope they will break more windows until the city fixes up playgrounds for them!" Jacob Riis lived long enough to see at Chautauqua one of the finest playgrounds, and to find in it one of the happiest crowds of children on the continent. One blessing for tired mothers at Chautauqua is that their children are in safekeeping. They may be turned loose, for they can't get outside the fence, and in the clubs and playgrounds they are under the wisest and most friendly care.

There are Modern Language Clubs in French and Spanish, with conversations, recitations, and songs in these languages. "No English Spoken Here," might be written over their doors, although nearly all their members elsewhere do their talking in the American patois. There was a German Club, but it was suspended during the war, when German was an unpopular language and has not yet been reëstablished.

Sherwood Memorial Studios

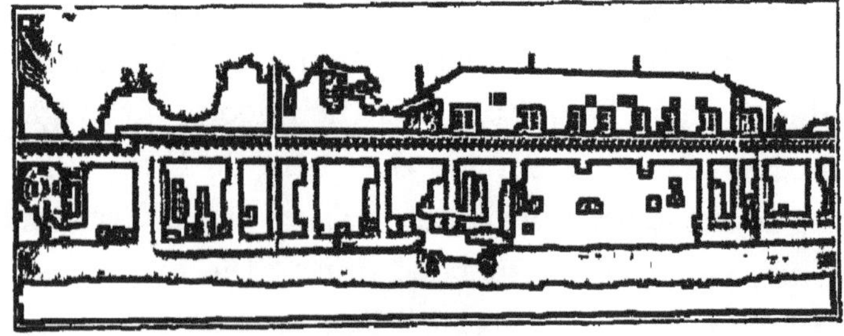

Traction Station

The Music Club holds gatherings, in the Sherwood Music Studios on College Hill.

There is a Press Club, composed of men and women who write books and articles for publication. They hold social receptions for acquaintance among wielders of the quill; perhaps it would be more accurate, though less classic, to say, "pounders of the typewriter." Several times each season they have an "Author's Night," when well-known writers, some of them famous, read their own productions.

There is a Lawyers' Club, a Masonic Club, and a Grange Club, the latter having its own building of Greek architecture; also a College Fraternity Club of the wearers of sundry pins and keys.

The Bird and Tree Club has a large and representative membership of those interested in identifying and protecting the fauna, flora, and bird life of Chautauqua and its vicinity. On the Overlook, beyond the Athletic Field, they have established a herbarium for the preservation of the different forms of trees found on the ground.

We must group together, begging pardon of the members, many other organizations, such as the W. C. T. U. All Americans know, some of them to their cost, what those four letters stand for; the Y. W. C. A., which has opened a Hospitality

House of Welcome and Rest on Pratt Avenue; the Daughters of the American Revolution, coming from every part of the land for gatherings at Chautauqua; the Order of the Eastern Star, whose secrets none but the initiated know; the College Men's Club, the College Women's Club, the Ministers' Club, and there used to be, perhaps is still, an Octogenarians' Club, whose members must swear to eighty years of life. The King's Daughters and King's Sons meet weekly at the Pier Buildings, and the Chautauqua Education Council, made up of Superintendents, principals and teachers, holds two regular sessions each week. If there are any more clubs, and their titles are sent to the author of this book, they will appear in the new edition, after the first hundred thousand copies are disposed of.

But we are forgetting the title of this chapter and must name some of those who helped to make Chautauqua successful during the quadrennium between '92 and '96. In 1893 Henry Drummond repeated at Chautauqua his Lowell lectures in Boston on "The Ascent of Man." There were still some old-fashioned "kiver to kiver" believers in the verbal inspiration of the Bible who were alarmed to find an eminent Christian leader accept so fully the conclusions of science; but the overwhelming sentiment of Chautauqua was of rejoicing at his harmonizing the most evangelical religion with the most advanced scholarship. Jane Addams gave some lectures on modern problems of family and social life; Edward Eggleston, long before a leader of the Sunday School Army, by turns preacher, story-writer (his *Hoosier School-Master* marked an epoch in American literature, say the critics) and historian, was with us once more after many years of absence. He said in an introduction, "I am glad to be again among Sunday School workers, real crazy people, for I believe that nobody can be a first-class Sunday School man unless he has a little crack in his head on that subject." Frank G. Carpenter, who had traveled in almost every land of earth, told us stories of his experiences and observations; Kate Douglas Wiggin read charmingly some of her own stories; Mr. John Temple Graves spoke in his fine rounded periods on some topics of the time; Hon. Roswell G. Horr of Michigan instructed while he entertained us. Dr. A. J. Palmer, who had thrilled the old soldiers with his "Company D," now gave another lecture to them on "Comrades." Besides these we heard on the platform Dr. Philip S. Moxom, Professor George H. Palmer of Harvard, and his wife, Alice Freeman Palmer; President Harper, Dr. Von Holst; Dr. Conwell, and Dr. Joseph Cook, returning to the platform with restored vigor after some years of nervous breakdown. Miss Willard was with us again, and with her Lady Henry Somerset of England, the head of the W. C. T. U. in that land.

In 1894 the Department of Elocution took a new title, "The School of Expression," and enlarged its sphere under Professor S. H. Clark of the University of Chicago, and Mrs. Emily M. Bishop. The program of the years shows the school of Political Science to be remarkably strong, with such teachers as Dr. Herman Von Holst, Herbert B. Adams of Johns Hopkins, and another Dr. Adams of Yale. Professor Graham Taylor of Chicago spoke on social questions, capital and labor. Hon. Theodore Roosevelt, already rising to fame, was again on the platform. General James A. Beaver, ex-governor of Pennsylvania; Professor Richard G. Moulton; Hon. Carroll D. Wright, United States Commissioner of Labor; Mr. Anthony Comstock, and Dr. E. E. Hale, Chautauqua's strong friend, were some of the speakers. Dr. Hale, always original in his methods, said that he had only thirty minutes to speak on "Poverty and Pauperism." He began by saying, "I will stand on one side of this desk and speak fifteen minutes on poverty." He showed in seven points that every one of us belonged to the class named "poverty" and each one should help the others. Then he walked over to the other side and gave seven points on "pauperism," for which there were reasons but no excuses. Poverty was a blessing; most of the world's greatest benefactors have been poor men; but pauperism is an unmitigated evil and should be stamped out of existence. General O. O. Howard, U. S. A., was again on the platform in 1894, also President William H. Crawford of Allegheny College, whose lecture on "Savonarola" made a deep impression. There was great interest to see and hear Miss Helen Keller, the wonderful girl, blind, deaf, and dumb, who had learned to speak without hearing a voice, and had been graduated from Radcliffe College of Harvard University with the highest honor. Another of the lecturers was Mr. Jahu DeWitt Miller, whose private talk was as good as his public lectures, which is high praise. The Recognition Day address this year was by Dr. E. E. Hale, on "The Education of a Prince," the prince being the poorest child living in America. It is worth remembering that a photograph of the procession on that day shows at the head of the flower-girl division—which now included boys, although the girls were still in the majority—two mites of children, one Paul Vincent Harper, son of President Harper, the other Isabel Vincent, the daughter of Professor George E. Vincent. Those same children are now Mr. and Mrs. Paul Vincent Harper of Chicago, still walking together.

In 1895, the season extended through fifty-nine days, from June 29th to August 26th. Two new buildings, besides many new cottages, were now upon the ground. One was the Baptist headquarters on Clark Street, the other Higgins Hall on College Hill, built by the gift of Governor Higgins of New York State. In the Schools during this season strong emphasis was laid on the Department of English, with such instructors as Professor C. T. Winchester of Wesleyan, Professor A. S. Cook of Yale, Professor Sherman of the University of Nebraska, and Professor Lewis of the University of Chicago. The last named gentleman bore a striking resemblance to the portraits of Shakespeare; so that as he walked around (habitually without a hat on his head) everybody was struck with the likeness. I was told that when he sat down at Shakespeare's traditional school-desk in Stratford, a crowd gathered before the windows and the word was passed around "Shakespeare has come to life again!"

Other speakers in 1895 were Professor Richard G. Moulton, Dr. Josiah Strong, President G. Stanley Hall, Professor Francis G. Peabody of Harvard, Major J. B. Pond, Dr. John Henry Barrows, Dr. Edward Everett Hale, President Harper, Prof. John Fiske, Principal Fairbairn, and the distinguished General of the Confederate Army, John B. Gordon, Senator from Georgia. His lecture on "The Last Days of the Confederacy," was one of the great occasions of the season, and it was noteworthy that many veterans of the G. A. R. were among the loudest in their applause when their foe of thirty years before came upon the platform. Another event of the summer was the visit of Governor William McKinley of Ohio, a year before his nomination and election to the Presidency. During this season also we were entertained with readings by Professor S. H. Clark, Mr. Will M. Carleton, and Miss Ida Benfey.

In the year 1895 another movement was begun at Chautauqua, which like the W. C. T. U. has swept over the entire continent and wrought mightily for the public welfare. At a Kindergarten Mothers' Meeting during the session, Mrs. Theodore W. Birney of Georgia, gave an address urging a National Congress of Mothers, and her appeal awakened a prompt response. Many of those who had listened to her carried her message to their own home-towns; Mrs. Birney at women's clubs and gatherings gave her plea over and over; and when the General Federation of Women's clubs held its convention in her native State of Georgia she presented the proposition to the members. From that convention in 1896, a call was issued for a National Congress of Mothers, to be held in the National Capital. Mrs. Birney gave a year of tireless and wise preparation for the meeting, which began on February 17, 1897. She was called to be President of the National Congress, with Miss Mary Louisa Butler as Organizing Secretary. The work was aided by the wide-reaching influence and liberal gifts of Mrs. Phebe A. Hearst, who has been rightly called the Lady Bountiful of the movement. Out of this National Congress grew the holding of State-congresses in every part of the country and the organization of local branches in almost every city. The Congress of Mothers now has its central office in Washington, D. C. It is divided into twenty-five departments of work—such as Americanization, Child Hygiene, Child Labor, Education, Mothers' Circles, Thrift, and many others, each having its chairman and plan of effective work. Out of a meeting at Chautauqua, in 1895, has grown a nation-wide movement in aid of mothers and teachers.

In 1896 the schools were again reorganized under Dr. Harper's supervision. The School of Fine Arts and the New York Summer Institute for Teachers were new departments, the latter under the direction of the Regents of the New York State University. The School of Sacred Literature was increased in its faculty, having among them President Harper, Professor Shailer Mathews, and Professor D. A. McClenahan of the United Presbyterian Theological School. Prominent among the lecturers this year were Dr. George Adam Smith of Scotland, Dr. Gunsaulus, Rev. S. Parkes Cadman, Dr. Booker T. Washington, Rev. Dr. George A. Gordon, Dr. Charles F. Aked, then of England, but soon to become an American, Professor F. G. Peabody, Dr. Nicholas Murray Butler, soon afterward the President of Columbia University, and Dr. Russell H. Conwell. A lady appeared on the platform whose experience had been unlike that of any other woman in the land. This was Mrs. Robert E. Peary, who accompanied her husband on one of his North Pole explorations and had a daughter born within the polar circle—"The snow baby," as she was called. She gave a lecture with stereopticon views descriptive of the life in the frozen North. Another woman gave a lecture this year upon her travels in Equatorial Africa, Miss Jessie T. Ackerman. President Charles W. Eliot of Harvard University gave the oration on Recognition Day, his subject being "America's Contribution to Civilization." In looking through the list of the speakers on Recognition Day, I find the names of no less than ten college presidents, and also that of the Hon. William T. Harris, United States Commissioner of Education, who might be regarded as standing at the head of the nation's educational system. The value of Chautauqua as a force in education has been fully recognized by the highest authorities.

Arts and Crafts Building

Miller Bell Tower

# CHAPTER XVIII

## ROUNDING OUT THE OLD CENTURY

(1897–1900)

THE Chautauqua session of 1897 was fifty-nine days long, from June 26th to August 23rd. This year the School of Domestic Science, directed by Mrs. Emma P. Ewing, attracted attention. Almost as many ladies whose cookery was accomplished by servants, as those who broiled their own steaks and baked their own puddings, met in Mrs. Ewing's model kitchen, learning to make bread, to prepare appetizing sauces and dressings, and to learn how to serve tables with refinement. I remember hearing one lady remark that until she had received Mrs. Ewing's instruction she had never really known how to make good bread.

Among those who gave lectures in 1897, we find the names of Anna Howard Shaw, Ballington and Maud Booth, Bishop (better known as Chaplain) McCabe; quite a list of college presidents—Goucher of Baltimore, Hyde of Bowdoin, Harper of Chicago, John Finley of New York, and G. Stanley

Hall of Clark; also Professor Graham Taylor, Mr. Percy Alden of England, and Mr. Jacob Riis. A new reader of noble presence, rich voice, and rare dramatic power, recited on the platform of the Amphitheater and assisted in the School of Expression—Mrs. Bertha Kunz Baker, who was to entertain us through many years. Professor Clark gave readings; Mr. George W. Cable rendered a number of his own stories; Mrs. Jessie Eldridge Southwick and Miss Katherine Oliver also gave recitals.

After Dr. Vincent's election as Bishop in 1888, he found it increasingly difficult to supervise the ever-increasing work of Chautauqua. Often during the Assembly season he would be compelled to hold conferences in the far west, and one year in South America. In 1896, his episcopal residence was changed from Buffalo to Topeka, Kansas, and in 1900 he was removed to Zurich, Switzerland, to take charge of Methodist missions in Europe. More and more he delegated the care of Chautauqua to his son, who, one of the most popular of lecturers, was supreme in his ability as administrator. In 1898 Professor George E. Vincent was formally appointed Principal of Instruction, and very soon every department of Chautauqua, both in its lecture platform and its educational work, felt the touch of a master hand. Some of us oldsters who had loved Chautauqua from its earliest years, had felt anxious for its future as we saw one of its Founders called aside into other fields, and the other failing in strength, although we knew not how near was his earthly end. But we all had a sense of relief and confidence that the future of Chautauqua was assured when we found "George" taking his father's place as executive in the Department of Instruction. The Bishop retained the title of Chancellor, however, as long as he lived.

In 1898 a new building was erected on College Hill—The Hall of Pedagogy. The report of the season's work showed that attendance had increased in the schools twenty-five per cent. over the last year, the advance being distributed quite evenly among the departments. By this time nearly all the universities and many of the colleges were holding summer schools, yet Chautauqua, first in the field, was still leading in its membership. This year Chautauqua received a visit from Lord Aberdeen, the Governor-General of the Dominion of Canada, and his wife, the Countess. Americans are apt to look for a freezing dignity on the part of the higher nobility, and some were a little surprised to find the Governor-General and his Lady unreservedly approachable, and unaffectedly democratic in manner.

Some of those who gave lectures in 1898 were Dr. Richard T. Ely of the University of Wisconsin, President Thirkield of Atlanta, afterward Bishop, Dr. Moulton, Miss Jane Addams, Hon. Murat Halstead, General John B. Eaton, Mr. Leon H. Vincent, Bishop Daniel A. Goodsell, Dr. J. H. Barrows, President of Oberlin, President Faunce of Brown, Dr. Robert McIntyre, also to become a Bishop in due time, Dr. Charles E. Jefferson of New York, Dr. Amory H. Bradford of Montclair, N. J., and Mr. John Kendrick Bangs. Mr. Leland Powers was with us on his biennial visit, and recitals were also rendered by Mr. C. F. Underhill, Mr. John Fox, Miss Isabel Garghill, Mr. Will Carleton, and Miss Ida Benfey. Up to that date, the season of 1898 was one of the most successful in Chautauqua history.

At this time, the *Chautauquan Magazine*, the organ of the C. L. S. C., and the *Daily Assembly Herald*, were taken over by the trustees, and the *Chautauqua Press* was established as the publishing agency for the periodicals and books of the C. L. S. C. Mr. Frank Chapin Bray was appointed Editor. By birth and education he was a thorough Chautauquan, having, as it were, grown up on the ground from early childhood and gone through all the courses from the Children's Class to the C. L. S. C. As a small boy he had sold the *Assembly Herald;* as a young man had written for its columns, and he is not the only journalist who took these steps upward to a literary career.

The season of 1899 opened with a cloud hanging over Chautauqua, bringing sorrow to one family and deepest sympathy from many.

On February 17, 1899, Lewis Miller died in a hospital in New York where he had been taken to undergo an operation from which he failed to rally. He was seventy years of age and had given his whole heart and the best of his life to Chautauqua. But for Lewis Miller there would have been no Chautauqua, though there might have been an Assembly under some other name. He had chosen the place, had urged the location, and in its inception had aided in its plans, had supervised its business interests, and had contributed generously to its needs. At the opening of the "Old First Night" service in August, 1899, the white lilies bloomed in his honor, but instead of being waved, were held in solemn stillness for a full minute, and then slowly lowered, and this memorial has been observed on every "Old First Night" since.

The names of Lewis Miller and John H. Vincent stand together in equal honor as the two Founders of Chautauqua. Next to these Founders we remember on "Old First Night" two of the Vice-Presidents of the Board of Trustees, the late Francis H. Root of Buffalo, and Clem. Studebaker of South Bend, Indiana, both wise counsellors and generous givers to Chautauqua.

During the session of 1899, Theodore Roosevelt was for the third time the guest of Chautauqua. The war with Spain had come and gone; he had been Colonel of the Rough Riders, and was now Governor of New York. One of those Rough Riders was young Theodore Miller, the son of the Founder of Chautauqua, and the only Yale student to lay down his life in that campaign. His memory is preserved by the Miller Gate on the University campus. Another Governor was with us that summer, Robert L. Taylor of Tennessee. The two brothers Taylor were the heads respectively of the two political parties in their State, were candidates opposed to each other, stumped the State together, slept together every night, played the violin together at their meetings, and then after the concert, made their speeches against one another. The writer of these pages may claim a humble part in their careers, for both of them as boys, and also an older brother, were students under his teaching in 1864 and '65 in Pennington Seminary, New Jersey. We could tell some stories about those three Taylor boys, but we refrain. I think that the Republican Taylor, Alfred, is even now (1920) the Governor of Tennessee, as his brother was its Democratic Governor in 1899.

Another visitor of about this date, though we are not certain of the precise year, was Mr. Horace Fletcher, whose name is in the dictionary in the word "Fletcherize," which means to count the chewing of each mouthful thirty times before swallowing it. We have tried some steaks in the early Chautauquan days when fifty chews would hardly make an impression. He spoke on the platform, and the few who could hear him said that his talk was not about dietetics, but foreign politics, though the two words are somewhat alike and they may have misunderstood him. His fiftieth birthday came while he was at Chautauqua, and he celebrated it by doing some amazing stunts, double somersaults, etc., into the lake at the diving place. I sat at the table next to his at the Athenæum and noticed that he ate very slowly, but I could not count the chews on each mouthful. A lady at the same table told me that Mr. Fletcher eschewed coffee but put seven lumps of sugar in his tea, calmly observing that his "system needed sugar." I know some young people who have the same opinion concerning their own systems, if one may judge by the fate of a box of chocolates in their hands.

In this year the School of Religious Teaching was reorganized, the Department of Sacred Literature being conducted by Chancellor Wallace of Toronto, and that of Religious Pedagogy, by Dr. J. R. Street. We may as well insert here the fact that for many years before, and during the seasons since that year, Sunday School lessons were taught in the morning and a lecture given at the Park of Palestine in the afternoon by the author of this volume. The plan with the lessons has been to give every morning a preview of a coming Sunday School topic, so that by the close of the season all the lessons for six months to come have been taught, and at Palestine Park to treat the geography of the land historically in a series of lectures. Also, it should be remembered that every Sunday of the Chautauqua season, from the first year, a Sunday School has been held in the morning, for all ages from youngest to oldest, the grades being taught in different places on the grounds by specialists in their several departments. For some years, if one strayed on Sunday morning over Palestine Park, he might find a class of boys seated on the hills around Nazareth listening to a lesson on the boyhood of Jesus, and a group of girls looking down on the Sea of Galilee, while a teacher was telling stories of the tempest stilled and the five thousand fed.

Prominent upon the lecture platform in 1899 were Prof. C. T. Winchester, Dr. Charles E. Jefferson, Prof. John Fiske, Prof. A. B. Hart, Bishop C. B. Galloway of the Methodist Episcopal Church, South, President Faunce, Dr. George Adam Smith, Dr. E. E. Hale, and Governor G. W. Atkinson of West Virginia. Mr. John Kendrick Bangs was also on the platform with readings.

The year 1900 rounded out a century, and one of its outstanding events at Chautauqua was a course of lectures by Principal Fairbairn of Oxford on "The Nineteenth Century." He asserted that in the ages to come, this hundred years will be looked upon as perhaps the greatest of all the centuries in the world's progress made during that period. He spoke in turn upon the historical, the political, the inventive, the literary, the religious, and the philosophic progress, giving without a written reminder names, dates, facts, processes of thought in the widest range. Many regarded it as one of the ablest and most enlightening series of addresses that they had ever heard.

Among the new faces on the platform we saw Dr. Lincoln Hulley, the new President of the John B. Stetson University of Florida, an exceedingly interesting speaker and a charming personality. We heard also Mr. Edward Howard Griggs in a series of lectures in the Amphitheater, and an appreciative class also met him in the school. From 1900 until the present, Mr. Griggs has given us biennial courses, and on "Old First Night" his tall form rises and sits down as the record is made up for every alternate year. No lecturer on thoughtful subjects has more engagements or brings together larger audiences than Mr. Griggs. Dean Charles D. Williams of Trinity Cathedral, and in a few years Bishop (Protestant Episcopal) of Detroit, an independent thinker and powerful preacher, welcomed both on the platform and in the pulpit many times since that appearance, his first among us. I think also that Professor Bliss Perry of Harvard spoke for the first time this season, also President Benjamin Ide Wheeler. Others who came as old friends were Prof. Moses Coit Tyler, President Henry Churchill King, Dr. Graham Taylor, Dr. Cadman, Mr. Edward Howard Griggs, Mrs. Carrie Chapman Catt, Miss Susan B. An-

South Gymnasium

thony, and Miss Jane Addams. I must not forget that this summer Mr. Francis Wilson was with us again, and gave a lecture upon Eugene Field and his poetry, an appreciation inspired by friendship as well as literary insight. On a former visit to Chautauqua Francis Wilson not only joined the C. L. S. C., but formed a reading circle in his dramatic company, directing their studies and holding their literary meetings in railroad stations, in hotel parlors, and in the green rooms of theaters, wherever they chanced to be when the meeting day arrived.

On August 7, 1900, the corner stone of the Hall of Christ, "Aula Christi," was laid. The address on that occasion was given by Bishop James M. Thoburn of India. Bishop Vincent was now living overseas in Zurich, Switzerland, and could not be present. The stone was laid by Principal George E. Vincent and a telegram from his father was read. This Hall was one of the creations of Bishop Vincent's poetic mind. He aimed to make it a building not large, but beautiful, a sort of shrine, a chapel for meditation and prayer, a place of quiet, spiritual fellowship, not of class teaching, but of thoughtful addresses on themes directly relating to our Lord. Bishop Vincent did not possess the genius for raising large sums of money for his conceptions; he shrank from pressing them upon rich men. Another projector would have ventured boldly, demanded contributions and obtained them, to build the Hall at once; but Dr. Vincent was delicate in speaking of it, though all knew his ardent desires for this ideal. The building grew slowly as gifts were received. Begun in 1899, it was not dedicated until 1912. Although no thought of his own honor in this building was in the Founder's mind, yet to many it stands as his monument at Chautauqua. Most appropriately it is used as the center for the Department of Religious Work, and daily lectures are given within its walls on Biblical themes.

As Dr. George Vincent was now an associate professor in the University of Chicago, it became necessary for him to have some assistance in the management of the Chautauqua program and platform. Mr. Scott Brown was this year appointed General Director and Vice-Principal of Instruction.

## CHAPTER XIX

### OPENING THE NEW CENTURY

### (1901–1904)

THE season of 1901 was the longest of any thus far, sixty days, from July 1st to August 29th. In the schools Manual Training was introduced under the direction of Mr. Henry J. Baker, also a school of Library Training under the general guidance of Mr. Melvil Dewey, at that time New York State Librarian, and soon after made one of the Chautauqua trustees. The resident director of this school was at first Miss Mary E. Hazeltine of Jamestown; later, and up to the present time, Miss Mary E. Downey, of the Utah State Library. The growth of public libraries throughout the country has made this school very popular among young women seeking the profession of librarian.

Some voices new to Chautauqua were heard from the Amphitheater platform in 1901, such as Dr. O. P. Gifford of the Baptist Church, Captain Richmond Pearson Hobson, Mrs. L. Ormiston Chant of England, a descendant of the great

Edmund Burke, we were informed, and the Governor of New York, Hon. Benjamin B. Odell. Mr. Joseph Jefferson, whom all the world of that generation knew as "Rip Van Winkle," gave a lecture showing the relations of the lecture platform and the stage. Rev. John McNeill, whose speech showed that he came from the north of the Tweed, preached a powerful and searching sermon. Dr. Robert Stuart McArthur gave a lecture on "Mountain Peaks in Russian History." Dr. Hale, President Crawford, Mr. Leland Powers, Dr. S. H. Clark, Dr. Moulton, and Mr. George W. Bain were among the old Chautauqua favorites of that season. As the C. L. S. C. Class of 1900 had taken the name "The Nineteenth Century Class," the one graduating this year was entitled "The Twentieth Century Class." The speaker on Recognition Day was Chancellor E. Benjamin Andrews of the University of Nebraska, on the subject, "Problems of Greater America."

The season of 1902 was noteworthy from a visit of Bishop Vincent. It seems strange to read of a *visit* from the Founder of Chautauqua, but he was at that time living in Zurich, Switzerland, holding Methodist conferences all over Europe, in many languages through interpreters, and for several years had been absent from Chautauqua. We of the older generation always missed his presence, but to the younger troop of Chautauquans his was only a revered name. The Vincent whom they knew, and packed the Amphitheater to hear, was the Director George E. Vincent, the man at the wheel of Chautauqua. This year the announcement was made that the Chancellor was coming, and a royal welcome was prepared. A printed account of this event reads as follows:

> Arriving at Lakewood, the Bishop was met by members of his family, and the Board of Trustees. After the welcome greetings, the party took a special steamer for Chautauqua. At the Pier a fleet of craft of all descriptions—launches, sail-boats, and row-boats—awaited the arrival of the Bishop's steamer. As soon as it came within hailing distance, the larger boats dipped colors and all the people waved handkerchiefs, the chimes at the Point rang in a familiar tune, and as the steamer headed toward the Pier, the Chautauqua choir, gathered in the balcony, sang the old Chautauqua song, "Join, O friends, in a memory song."
>
> As the boat came to the wharf, the bank and the Park of Palestine were a mass of waving handkerchiefs. The Reception Committee, composed of officials of the Institution, stood on the Pier, and back of them an immense throng all eager to catch a glimpse of their beloved leader. Lines were formed on either side of the walk, and as the Bishop passed between them he was greeted with the salute of the white

handkerchiefs. In Miller Park were gathered the cottage owners, the Summer Schools, and the C. L. S. C. classes, with their banners and emblems, and the various clubs and children's classes. On the way to his cottage on Lake Avenue, the Bishop was escorted by about two hundred and fifty members of the Boys' and Girls' Clubs, whose sweet voices rang out clear and full in "Auld Lang Syne." From the veranda of his tent cottage, the Bishop made an eloquent address of appreciation, full of the joy of home-coming.

In 1904, Bishop Vincent was placed on the retired list, to dwell where he chose, free from episcopal service. From that year until 1918, he passed a portion of each summer at Chautauqua and took part in the program, but without the responsibility of supervision. Most of the time he was happy in his release, but there would come occasional hours when he longed to hold the reins once more.

In this year, 1902, a new charter was received from the Legislature of New York, giving a new title, "Chautauqua Institution." The Girls' Club and the Unitarian House were built this season, also the Disciples' Headquarters on Clark Avenue received its pillared portico. The Lutheran House was established during this season.

Senator Mark Hanna of Ohio, who was looked upon as "the power behind the throne" during the presidency of his friend, William McKinley, spoke at Chautauqua in 1902, also Mrs. Pennybacker of Texas, Dr. A. E. Dunning of Boston, editor of the *Congregationalist*, General John C. Black of Pennsylvania, Dr. Earl Barnes, Prof. Charles Zeublin, Dr. W. F. Oldham of India, afterward a Bishop, and the ever-welcome Frank Beard who had been absent for a number of years.

Chautauqua has always believed in the open and free discussion of vexed questions, and this year from August 4th to August 8th was held a most interesting conference on "The Labor Movement." The introductory address opening the subject was given by the Hon. Carroll D. Wright, U. S. Commissioner of Labor. Supplementary lectures, followed by discussion, were by President Harper on "The University and Industrial Education"; Mr. Frank P. Sargent, "Growth and Influence of Labor Organizations"; Mr. John Mitchell, "The Joint Conference between Employer and Employee." On both sides there was the frankest expression of opinion. I remember that when one speaker was asked whether he was an actual worker or a professional agitator, without a word he held out his hands that all might see they were the hands of a workingman.

This year was notable in the Department of

Music, by the entrance of Mr. Alfred Hallam as Director. His whole-hearted, absolutely self-forgetting labor, and his reach after the highest standards in his art, from 1902 to 1919, made Mr. Hallam dear not only to his choir, but to all Chautauquans.

The year 1903 was the twenty-fifth anniversary of the founding of the C. L. S. C. in 1878. That event in popular education was commemorated by a great meeting in the Amphitheater and the laying of the corner stone of a new Hall of Philosophy on the site of the old hall, which, being a wooden building, was decaying. The Class of 1882 planted some ivy brought from the Palatine Hill in Rome, other classes planted oak and pine trees. A sealed box, containing portraits of the Founders and copies of Chautauqua publications, was placed in the corner stone, which was then lowered into place and made secure with mortar, the trowel being handled in turn by Dr. George Vincent and Director Scott Brown. As the stone was put in place, a cablegram was read from Bishop Vincent at Helsingfors, Finland—"Remember the foundation is Christ." Vincent.

This year, 1903, the Arts and Crafts shops, which had been in various places over the ground, were brought together by the director, Henry

Turner Bailey, making the Arts and Crafts Village, in later years to become the Arts and Crafts Building. The Grange Building on Simpson Avenue was erected and presented as headquarters for that order by Mr. Cyrus W. Jones of Jamestown. This year, 1903, Dean Percy H. Boynton of the University of Chicago was made Secretary of Instruction, and placed in full charge of the Summer Schools, which by this time had grown to more than two thousand students. A few years later he received the title of Principal and gave to the summer schools his unremitting attention until 1917. To Dean Boynton's careful choice of instructors and watchfulness over details of management during those years the growth and success of the schools is largely due.

The Liquor Problem was the subject of the Conference on August 3–8, 1903. I find on the list of speakers and their subjects eight names to which might be added five times as many who participated in the discussions. Commander Frederick Booth-Tucker and his wife Emma Booth-Tucker, told of "The Salvation Army and the Liquor Problem." Mr. Raymond Robins, an eminent social worker of Chicago, spoke on "The Saloon and the World of Graft, Vagrancy, and Municipal Correction," although it may have been "municipal corruption," for I think he spoke on both subjects. Mrs. Lillian M. N. Stevens told of the work of the W. C. T. U.; Prof. I. P. Bishop showed "The Physiological Effects of Alcohol," Prof. Frederick Starr, the anthropologist, gave an interesting account of "Stimulants among Primitive Peoples." Other speakers were Rev. E. C. Dinwiddie, Mr. Frederick H. Wines, and Mrs. John G. Woolley.

Another Conference was held August 10th to 15th on "The Mob," and attracted the deepest interest. President William G. Frost of Berea College, Kentucky, told of "The Mountain Feuds"; Mr. John Temple Graves spoke in defense of lynching, and declared that the only solution of the negro problem in the south would be the enforced deportation of the negro back to Africa; but other Southerners present did not agree with him. Dean Richmond Babbitt gave "A Study of the Lynch Law"; Mr. D. M. Parry spoke on "The Mob Spirit in Organized Labor"; Mr. Thomas Kidd on "The Labor Unions and the Mob Spirit." Chief Justice Charles B. Lore of Delaware and Judge John Woodward gave "The Legal Aspects of the Mob Spirit." No discussion at Chautauqua awakened such feeling, although it was carried on with perfect courtesy by speakers on the opposing sides.

A Corner of the Playground

We can name only a few of the many lecturers in the regular program of 1903. One was Governor Robert M. La Follette of Wisconsin, soon to attract attention as an insurgent in the United States Senate. Another was Mr. George Willis Cooke, on social subjects. Mr. Hamlin Garland, the story-writer, gave a lecture, also General John B. Gordon of Georgia, Dr. Richard Burton, a course in literature; Hon. Wm. T. Harris, Dr. Moulton, and the Rev. R. J. Campbell of London. The platform during the season was fairly crowded, the speakers and concerts following in such close succession.

In 1904, Bishop Vincent having been relieved from the cares of the Episcopacy, went to live for a time in Indianapolis. He was now able to come with more or less regularity to Chautauqua, and gave the opening address of the season. The exercises of that year extended through sixty days beginning June 30th and ending August 28th. We note that the School of English included in its staff Prof. Richard G. Moulton and Edward Howard Griggs. The work in Nature Study was enlarged to include courses in Botany and Physiography. The courses for teachers embraced systematic work in all the grades from the kindergarten to the college. This year the new electric railway was opened from Jamestown to Chautauqua and thence to Mayville and Westfield on Lake Erie. Bishop Vincent was a passenger on the first car over the line. This improved means of transportation enabled people to come by rail every hour to Chautauqua, gave direct and speedy connection with the New York Central Railroad, and resulted in making the principal entrance to the grounds no longer by water but by land. Hence the crowds forsook the stores in the Pier Building and the Arcade, and a new business center grew up on the hill.

This year the new Hall of Philosophy was opened, of the same general plan as the old building, but with floor and pillars of concrete, a more durable material. The building was also somewhat larger than its predecessor and was in every way more convenient. In the concrete floor are inserted tablets in honor of the classes that contributed toward the building. The pillars also bear the names of their givers. The list of exercises in the Hall during any Assembly season would of itself make a long catalogue.

The Devotional Hour had now become a systematic order and called together large congregations. It was not altogether the fame of the great preachers, but also the strong religious atmosphere of the place that gathered every day at ten o'clock for five mornings of each week a thousand people for worship. How many churches could show a congregation as large, not only on Sundays, when the service was attended by five thousand people, but through the days of the week? Among the chaplains of this season, each serving a week, were Dr. S. Parkes Cadman, Dr. Hugh Black, Bishop Oldham, Dr. Daniel Dorchester of Pittsburgh, and the evangelist, Dr. J. Wilbur Chapman.

The Conference of 1904 was from July 24th to 29th on the subject of Missions, Home and Foreign. Among the speakers were Dr. Francis E. Clark of the Christian Endeavor movement, recently returned from an all-around the world visit to missions abroad, Dr. Frederick G. Stanley, Dr. George M. Boynton, Dr. Homer Stuntz from the Philippines—afterward a Bishop of the Methodist Episcopal Church—Bishop Oldham, and Mr. J. L. Joslin of India.

I remember hearing Dr. Stuntz tell of a native Filipino who came to him soon after the American occupation of Manila, and after carefully closing the door, and looking in closets to be sure that no one was in hearing, carefully unrolled a package, showed a small Bible in the Spanish language, and asked: "Would it be safe for me to be found reading this book? I have kept it hidden for years, for my life would have been the penalty if it had been seen." Dr. Stuntz led him to a window, pointed to the American flag flying over the castle, and said: "Do you see that flag? As long as that flag flutters over these islands, you can stand in the market place and read in as loud a voice as you choose out of this book and you will be safe. Wherever that flag flies, the Bible is an open book!"

Most of the men whom we have named gave lectures, as well as participating in the conferences. Besides these, we saw on the platform the massive form of William Howard Taft, then Secretary of War, after a few years to be President of the United States; Mr. Griggs also gave a course of lectures and taught classes in literature, and Prof. Frederick Starr was one of the speakers. Dr. George Adam Smith of Scotland was also with us during the season of 1904.

Some of the recitations this year were by Dr. S. H. Clark, Mrs. Bertha Kunz Baker, Mrs. Emily M. Bishop, Miss Marie L. Shedlock, and Prof. Henry L. Southwick.

## CHAPTER XX

### PRESIDENT ROOSEVELT AT CHAUTAUQUA

### (1905–1908)

THE notable event in the Assembly of 1905 was the fourth visit of Theodore Roosevelt. He was the President of the United States, not now by succession, but by direct vote of the people, for his first term, after the death of Mr. McKinley, had been completed. He had promised to maintain his predecessor's policies during the period for which Mr. McKinley had been elected, and through that term he had initiated no new movements. But his pledge having been kept and his administration ratified by the popular vote, Mr. Roosevelt was now free to bring forward his own plans. His address at Chautauqua on August 11th, five months after his inauguration, was the first public announcement of his principles and policies, and in its boldness, its candor, and its originality was fairly startling. Mr. McKinley was a cordial, but a reticent party leader. Every-one who talked with him was charmed, but no one could recall any definite promise or statement that he had made. Mr. Roosevelt was absolutely, unreservedly open; he would state to anybody his opinion on every public question. Lyman Abbott once said, "Mr. McKinley and Mr. Roosevelt were both great men and great statesmen, but between the absolute reticence of the one and the absolutely openness of the other, there is no half-way house."

The presidential party included his son Kermit, his nephew Paul Roosevelt, his cousin Philip Roosevelt, Mr. Jacob A. Riis, and a number of leading politicians, besides secret service men, and the inevitable troop of newspaper reporters. They were met at Lakewood by Bishop Vincent, his son the Principal, and representatives of the Chautauqua Board. A breakfast was served to the party and to some invited guests in Higgins Hall. I sat beside a prominent politician who said to me that on the train and boat he was absolutely amazed at the knowledge of President Roosevelt upon every subject, and his readiness to state his views upon even the deepest matters of State. At the table I noticed Dr. James M. Buckley sitting beside the President and in earnest conversation with him. As we passed out of the Hall, I mentioned to Dr. Buckley what the public man had told me of Mr. Roosevelt's outspoken candor, and Dr. Buckley said that the President had answered every question in utter frankness, evidently having nothing to conceal; and Dr. Buckley could ask searching questions.

The adage, "It sometimes rains at Chautauqua," was verified that day by a steady downpour, which with the umbrellas lifted over the moving procession made every avenue, seen from an upper balcony, look like an endless serpent with a series of bulging black knobs on his back. No words can express the jam of people in and around the Amphitheater and the breathless interest with which all listened to the President's address, which came like a revelation, with its outspoken utterances upon subjects hitherto held as State secrets. He talked of our relations with nations abroad, and of problems at home, the trusts, questions of capital and labor, and, indeed, every subject under discussion at that time. A statesman once said, "Language was invented to conceal thought," but that was certainly not the use of language by one eminent American. As Mr. Roosevelt was leaving the Amphitheater, he saw the Boys' Club standing together, on guard, and he gave them a short, appreciative, practical speech.

Some of the speakers at the Assembly of 1905

were District Attorney William Travers Jerome of New York, Governor Joseph W. Folk of Missouri, the Hon. Robert Watchorn, Commissioner of Immigration, President Charles Cuthbert Hall of the Union Theological Seminary of New York, recently home from giving addresses in India and China under the auspices of the Parliament of Religion, President Rush Rhees of the University of Rochester, President Herbert Welch of Ohio Wesleyan, Dean Charles D. Williams—on his next visit to be a Bishop—and Dr. Richard Burton. Mrs. Bertha Kunz Baker, Dr. S. H. Clark, Mr. Leland Powers, and others entertained us with readings and impersonations; but it should also be said that the leading elocutionists at Chautauqua made it a large part of their task to acquaint us with great literature, both in poetry, in prose, and especially in the drama.

In 1905 the Colonnade Building was built and became the business center of Chautauqua. During this season Mr. Scott Brown, the General Director under Principal George E. Vincent, called into the service of the Chautauqua Institution, as assistant, a young man to become in a few years his successor, Mr. Arthur E. Bestor. Mr. Bestor also began lecturing upon the platform in a course on "Studies in American Diplomacy."

In the report of the year 1906, I notice a custom that is mentioned for the first time this year, though it may have been observed before. On the opening night, June 28, signal fires were lighted at prominent points around the lake, notifying the summer residents, whose cottages by this year were girdling Lake Chautauqua, that the Assembly had now begun for another season. This illumination has been followed every year since 1906, and appropriately gives notice to every village between Mayville and Jamestown that the light of Chautauqua has begun to shine.

The program of July we find as full as that of August. During the earlier month were lectures and addresses by Professor F. Hyatt Smith on "Eminent Englishmen of the Nineteenth Century"—Coleridge, Macaulay, Carlyle, Matthew Arnold, and others; literary lectures by Leon H. Vincent, who was now "Doctor of Letters," Mr. Henry Turner Bailey, head of the Arts and Crafts, but lecturer on many subjects; Newell Dwight Hillis of Plymouth Church, Brooklyn; Dr. W. J. Dawson, an English preacher and author who had lately come to live in America, equally great in the pulpit and in literature; Dr. S. C. Schmucker, one who could make a scientific subject plain to the lay-mind; Dr. John T. McFarland, head of the Sunday School work of the Methodist Episcopal Church; Mrs. Donald McLean, President-General of the Daughters of the American Revolution, and other speakers.

During August a most interesting course of lectures was given by Mr. John Graham Brooks on "America Viewed by Outside People"—showing how the estimates of our country, especially by English writers, had arisen from almost contemptuous criticism (much of it deserved, it must be admitted) to high appreciation. Mr. Griggs gave a new course of literary lectures. Bishop Vincent gave a lecture on Martin Luther. Prof. Cecil F. Lavell spoke on historical subjects. Sir Chentung Lieng Chang, the Ambassador from China, graduate of an American college, Amherst, I think—was a visitor and spoke in excellent English. Prof. Edward A. Steiner, the great authority on immigration, lectured on "Our Foreign Population," and told a remarkable story of a journey that he had made through underground Russia, visiting nearly a hundred revolutionary centers. Mr. Ernest Thompson Seton talked on wild animals, to the enjoyment of both young and old.

On Recognition Day of the C. L. S. C., August 15, 1906, the new Hall of Philosophy was dedicated.

In 1907 Professor George E. Vincent was made President of the Chautauqua Institution. His father retained the title of Chancellor, but the active duties of the management were now entirely in the hands of the President. In the following year, Mr. Arthur E. Bestor was advanced to the place formerly held by Mr. Scott Brown, that of Senior Director in charge of all business administrations and assisting President Vincent on the educational side.

A man who made his mark deeply on Chautauqua came this year for the first time, Mr. Henry Turner Bailey of the Arts and Crafts School. He could not only teach, but could lecture on art or history in a most fascinating manner, all the time drawing pictures on the blackboard with both hands at once. Under his care the Arts and Crafts shops were assembled, grew into a village, and later found their home in a series of fine buildings on College Hill. He continued with us year after year until a new position in Cleveland, Ohio, compelled him to sever relations with Chautauqua.

Two great conferences were held this summer. The first was on "The Juvenile Problem," July 8th–13th. Speakers on the subject were Rev. W. Byron Forbush on "The Knights of King Arthur," an order of which he was the founder; Mr. W. R.

George, on "The George Junior Republic"; Judge Ben B. Lindsey of Denver on "The Juvenile Court." Mr. Melvil Dewey, Rev. Crawford Jackson, Judge Willis Brown and Mr. E. B. DeGrott spoke on "Public Playgrounds," "The Public Library," "The Child and the State," and kindred subjects.

The other conference was held July 29th to August 3d, on "The Social Unrest." A few of the speakers and their topics were: Mr. John Graham Brooks on "The Challenge of Socialism"; Mr. James Wadsworth, Jr., afterward U. S. Senator from New York, on "Politics"; Mr. R. R. Bowker on "The Corporation"; Mr. Henry Clews on "Capital"; Mr. J. G. Phelps Stokes and his wife, Rose Pastor Stokes, on "A Defense of Socialism"; Bishop Henry C. Potter, "The Church"; Mr. Charles Stelzle, "The Church and the Classes"; Miss Jane Addams on "The Settlement Movement."

On the regular lecture platform appeared Governor Charles E. Hughes of New York, Mr. William Jennings Bryan who had just returned from a trip around the world and spoke on "The Old World and Its Ways," President G. Stanley Hall a series on "Five Non-Christian Religions," President George E. Vincent on "Utopias," a series describing the ideals of men for the community and the state from Plato's *Republic* to the Community of Robert Dale Owen. Bishop Vincent also gave a lecture, the father and the son speaking on different days from the same platfrom. My recollection is that the Bishop spoke this summer on "Sidney Lanier and His Poetry," and placed him high on the roll of American poets.

Another lecturer who pleased us all was the bright essayist, Samuel McChord Crothers. His paper on "The Society for Polite Unlearning" was heard by a crowd in the Hall of Philosophy. Most of the audience caught the undertone of wisdom with the wit, but a few thought that it was only funny, in which they were mistaken. Dr. Shailer Mathews, Dr. C. F. Aked, and Bishop McDowell were among those who conducted the daily Devotional Services.

Grand Army Day was a dramatic occasion in the fact that before an audience of old Union soldiers, in their G. A. R. uniforms, the address was given by Mrs. LaSalle Corbell Pickett, the widow of General George Edward Pickett of the Confederate Army, who led the famous "Pickett's Charge" in the battle of Gettysburg—an attack that stands in history beside the "Charge of the Light Brigade," sung by Tennyson. Her story of that great day, deciding the destiny of a continent, was listened to, not merely with interest, but with outbreaking enthusiasm by an audience of Union soldiers, who honored the memory of a soldier whom they looked upon less as a foe than as a hero.

One little incident told by Mrs. Pickett we must make room for; in substance it was this: On Lee's march through Pennsylvania, Pickett's division passed a young girl who waved a United States flag, and then, fastening it around her waist, cried, "Traitors! come and touch this flag if you dare!" At this fierce challenge, a mingled stir of many voices went through the long gray ranks and many a rifle shifted uneasily. General Pickett rode in front of his men, and with true southern chivalry saluted her flag. Then he turned and faced his men. The soldiers followed his example, and as they passed by, every hat was swung aloft in honor of the girl and her flag. The little maiden was so overcome by this generosity that she cried out, "I wish I had a rebel flag; I'd wave that too!"

In October, 1907, the Colonnade Building, which had been standing only two years, was wholly destroyed by fire, causing a loss of $100,000, with an insurance of about $55,000. The indirect loss is not easy to estimate, for it included the contents of the stores and the issues of the Magazine ready for mailing, with much other printed matter of the Institution. This was the fourth fire which had occurred during the thirty-four years of Chautauqua; a remarkable record when one remembers how close together are many of the houses, and all built of wood. Plans for rebuilding the Colonnade were taken up immediately, also the beginning of a quadrangle of buildings for the Arts and Crafts Department and the erection of a Post Office Building.

In 1908 the July program included the names of Professor J. E. McFadyen of Knox College, Toronto, Principal James Robertson of Scotland, and Dr. W. L. Watkinson of England; all these in the Department of Religious Work, which was unusually strong that year. Dr. Watkinson looked the least like an Englishman that could be imagined. Long and lank and lean, he might have been taken for a Yankee of the Yankees, until he began to speak. His oratory is indescribable, original thoughts expressed in original language, with here and there a solemn witticism at which the hearer wanted to laugh but hardly dared to. Bishop Vincent gave a lecture on "An Old School House." Dr. H. W. Wiley, the food specialist and foe of misbranded packages of food, gave an address. Norman Hapgood of *Collier's Magazine*, Hon. Everett Colby of New Jersey, a leader in political reform, Prof. Graham Taylor, a sociologist and social reformer, were among the speakers.

In August of 1908, a notable English lady spoke on the Amphitheater platform, Mrs. Philip Snowden, wife of a member of Parliament. It was said that her husband owed his election to her power of public speaking, and especially to her skill in answering "heckling" questions—a political method quite common in England, though regarded as not quite proper in America. In our country when one party holds a meeting, it is not considered fair to interrupt the flow of oratory and disconcert the orator by disagreeable questions from the other side; but in Great Britain every political speaker must face such enquirers, and the one who put them to little Mrs. Snowden generally got the worst of the encounter. Though slight and seemingly fragile, speaking apparently without effort, every syllable of her speeches on the question of woman's enfranchisement could be distinctly heard from every seat in the Amphitheater. Other speakers in August, 1908, were Lieut.-Governor Chanler of New York, Edward Howard Griggs, Prof. Charles M. Cobern, an authority on Biblical archæology,

Dr. Leon H. Vincent in a course on "French Literary Celebrities," President J. D. Moffatt of Washington and Jefferson College, Pennsylvania, Charles Stelzle on social rights and wrongs, and George Riddle in some enjoyable recitations. Percy Alden, M.P., spoke on "Social and Economic Questions" in England and Charles F. Lavell gave a course on historical lectures. Dr. R. S. MacArthur and Dr. J. Wilbur Chapman were among the preachers and leaders of the Devotional Hour.

August 11, 1908, was Pennsylvania Day, with addresses in praise of the Keystone State by Governor E. G. Stuart, Ex-Governor and General J. A. Beaver, and others.

# CHAPTER XXI

## THE PAGEANT OF THE PAST

## (1909–1912)

THE thirty-sixth session of Chautauqua was epoch making in the development of material resources. The blackened ruins of the burned Colonnade Building were replaced by a new structure, the official headquarters of the Institution, the business center, and on its upper floor a rooming place for many employees in the offices. On the southern front of the Plaza arose the new Post Office Building, with the village public library, the presses and office of the *Chautauqua Press*. The first section of the projected Arts and Crafts quadrangle was built, to the great joy of Mr. Bailey, who had labored and almost fought for its construction. The Hall of Pedagogy arose at one end of the grounds and the Athletic Club House at the other. The Hall of the Christ was completed after many years of slow growth, and the Commons, a boarding-place for students, was opened through all the year for employees residing during the winter. As a venture, with some questioning, the New York Symphony Orchestra was engaged for a week of concerts, its leader being Walter Damrosch. Who would have dreamed in 1909 that in 1920 the same orchestra would sound its harmonies through six full weeks!

The keynote of the year, and indeed of Chautauqua through all its history, was expressed in President George E. Vincent's utterance in his annual report—that Chautauqua must "be kept in close and sympathetic connection with the great currents of national life. It must be a center from which the larger and more significant movements may gain strength and intelligent support." The season this year opened on Friday, July 2d, with a lecture by President Vincent on "Vocation and Culture."

To even name the speakers of the year and their subjects would necessitate the enlargement of our book, and to omit any of them may bring the author into peril of his life if he should meet any of those left out; but he must face the prospect of a martyr's end, by naming only a few. President Edwin Earle Sparks, of the Pennsylvania State College, gave a series of lectures on American history; Prof. Archer B. Hulbert on "The Military Conquest of the Alleghanies"; Prof. Stockton

Axson on "Literary Leaders"; Dr. Andrew Sloan Draper, Superintendent of Education for New York State, spoke, also Prof. George Albert Coe, Prof. Clyde W. Votaw, and Dr. Richard M. Hodge—these four on subjects relating to education; Mr. Earl Barnes gave a course of lectures, besides teaching in the schools; Booker T. Washington, President Frank R. Sanders, Dr. P. S. Henson, Prof. Henry F. Cope, Mr. Ernest Hamlin Abbott, of *The Outlook*, and many more were with us in July, 1908.

In August we heard Prof. Richard Burton in a course of literary lectures; Dr. George Adam Smith, Richard G. Moulton, and J. M. Thoburn, Jr., a nephew of Bishop Thoburn, also Bishop Samuel Fallows of the Reformed Episcopal Church, and the Rev. Samuel A. Eliot, a son of the Harvard President. Mr. S. S. McClure gave an offhand conversational address on "The Making of a Magazine," the story of his own experience.

The Devotional Hour was by this year firmly fixed in the Chautauqua system. The Chaplain preached on Sunday morning, at the great Amphitheater service, and at ten o'clock for five days following gave an address on some religious topic. Among our chaplains during the season of 1908 were Dr. Charles E. Jefferson of New York, Prof.

Herbert L. Willett of the University of Chicago, President Herbert Welch, and Dr. R. H. Conwell. The Recognition address to the graduating class of the C. L. S. C. was by President Faunce of Brown University on "Ideals of Modern Education."

This year a course in Esperanto, the proposed world-language, was conducted, and the second Esperanto Congress of America was held at Chautauqua. Not having studied the language and being too busy to attend the convention, the writer is unable to state whether the lectures were given in that tongue or in English, the inferior language which Esperanto is expected to displace. Probably two or three hundred years hence Shakespeare's plays, Milton's poems, and Mark Twain's stories will be known only in that language, English being a quarry for archæological research with about as many students as Greek or Sanscrit has to-day.

An event of 1901 which attracted crowds from all Chautauqua County and its surroundings was the historical pageant of scenes in the history of Chautauqua Lake. It included scenes from the Indian Wars before the Revolution, the French explorers, the British and American soldiers of the Revolutionary period, and the settlement of the shores. This was followed by the rendition of a play, *The*

*Little Father of the Wilderness*, by Francis Wilson and his company. The concerts of the preceding year by the New York Symphony Orchestra, under Walter Damrosch, had been so successful that the management brought them for a second visit in 1910.

One distinguished visitor in 1910 was the Right Honorable James Bryce, Ambassador of Great Britain to our country. His lecture was on "History and Politics." Dr. S. M. Crothers gave four lectures in his own inimitable manner on "The One Hundred Worst Books." He proposed as an interesting question, "Suppose that twenty centuries hence, when the English language may be as dead as Latin and Greek are now, what authors in English literature will be remembered?" Director Bestor found time in the midst of his labors to give us a fine lecture on "Gladstone." Paul Vincent Harper, son of President Harper, spoke on "Life in Palestine" after a visit to that land. Dr. Griggs gave a course on "Social Progress." Distinguished visitors from the old country were Sir William Ramsay, the highest authority in the English-speaking world on the church in the New Testament age, and Lady Ramsay. Both lectured, Lady Ramsay on "The Women of Turkey." Mrs. Philip Snowden gave another course of lectures, maintaining fully her popularity. She was strongly in favor of the suffrage for women but as strongly opposed to the methods of the militant suffragettes. Another speaker who attracted attention, although his views were not accepted by the majority at Chautauqua, was the Secretary of the American Federation of Labor, Mr. John B. Lennon. On the questions pertaining to trade unions and collective bargaining, however, one who talked with the Chautauqua constituency was surprised to find so large a number of progressive thinkers taking the side of labor against capital.

The Chautauqua Devotional Hour was represented in the season of 1910 by Dr. Hugh Black, Dr. J. Wilbur Chapman, Dr. G. A. Johnston Ross, and Charles D. Williams, who was now Bishop of Michigan.

It has been found that many are eager to enjoy the advantages of the Summer Schools at Chautauqua who are unable to meet the expense. To aid these, various gifts have been made from time to time. On old First Night in 1910 a system of fifty annual scholarships was established by setting apart the offering of that evening for this purpose, and the fund has since been increased from year to year.

In 1911, the Miller Bell Tower at the Point

beside the Pier was dedicated. For years the chime of Meneely bells had stood in the belfry of the old building on the Pier. But the piles beneath it were becoming decayed and the bells by their weight and their movement racked the old edifice. Their removal was necessary and the Tower was built adjoining the wharf. A fine clock presented by the Seth Thomas Clock Company, and the chimes, were placed in the summit of the Tower which received the name "Lewis Miller Bell Tower." These bells ring five minutes before the lecture hours, and at certain times, morning, noon, and night, the chimes play familiar music. After the night bell, which may be either at 10 or 10.30, silence is supposed to reign throughout the grounds. One of the original peal of four bells, afterward enlarged to form the chime of ten bells, is named the Bryant bell, and is rung precisely at twelve o'clock noon on the first day of October as a signal for beginning the readings of the Chautauqua Circle. The name is in honor of William Cullen Bryant, in recognition of his interest in the C. L. S. C.

During the season of 1911 a number of illustrated lectures were given by Prof. R. W. Moore on "The Rhine"; by C. L. Harrington on "Aerial Navigation,"—a lecture fully up to date at that time, surprising to many who heard it and looked at the pictures. But that was before the great war, and the same lecture would be hopelessly behind the times in 1921. Mr. Henry Turner Bailey showed us "A Dozen Masterpieces of Painting," and Mr. Jacob A. Riis, "The Making of an American," Dr. Henry R. Rose exhibited "The Oberammergau Passion Play," and Dr. H. H. Powers, "Venice." Both President George E. Vincent and Director Arthur E. Bestor gave lectures; also Edmund Vance Cooke and Mr. Earl Barnes, Mr. Leland Powers impersonated stories and plays as nobody else could. Mr. Frank A. Vanderlip gave three lectures on "Banking," which proved far more interesting than most of us had anticipated. Dr. H. H. Powers told in a series of lectures the stories of five great cities, Athens, Rome, Florence, Paris, and London. Dr. Gunsaulus gave a series of lectures on "Some of the Great Plays of Shakespeare"; Prof. S. C. Schmucker, a series mingling science with history on "American Students of Nature,—Audubon, Agassiz, Gray and Thoreau." Dean George Hodges in the Department of Religion lectured in a course on "Christian Social Betterment."

Among the chaplains of 1911 are the names of Bishop E. E. Hoss of the Methodist Episcopal

Church, South, Dr. John T. Stone of Chicago, Dr. Shailer Mathews, also of Chicago, Dr. C. F. Aked, then a pastor in San Francisco, and Rev. Silvester Horne of England. The baccalaureate sermon before the C. L. S. C. was this year given by the Chancellor, Bishop Vincent.

For twenty-two years William H. Sherwood was head of the piano department in the schools and untiring in his labors. He died in 1910, and in 1912 the Sherwood Memorial Studio on College Hill was opened and dedicated to his memory. A hospital, long needed, was this year established, named "The Lodge." The Department of Religious Work was reorganized, made more prominent, and placed under the charge of Dean Shailer Mathews as "Director of Religious Work." The headquarters of this department were established in the Hall of Christ.

The Independence Day address was given by Director Bestor on "The Old World and the New," the social, political, municipal, religious conception on the two sides of the Atlantic. Two stories from his lectures are worthy of being repeated. One was Theodore Roosevelt's retort when accused of wanting to become a king. "A king! what is a king? Why, a kind of perpetual Vice-President." The other was a conversation that Mr. Bestor had with an Englishman whom he met in Berlin. He asked "What would you do in England if the royal line should develop a William II. or a Roosevelt?" The Englishman answered, "Impossible! A man with any real political initiative is not to be thought of in the English kingship!"

For the first time, partisan political addresses were given on the Chautauqua platform. This was the year, it will be remembered, when Mr. Taft had been renominated by the regular Republican Convention, Mr. Roosevelt by the bolting Progressives, and Woodrow Wilson by the Democrats. It was decided to allow each of the parties to be represented. Attorney-General Wickersham spoke in behalf of the Republicans, Mr. Eugene W. Chafin, the candidate of the Prohibition Party, addressed a crowded Amphitheater, and seemed to give everybody great enjoyment from the constant laughter and applause. He said after the election that if everybody who applauded and cheered his speeches had voted for him, he would have been President!

But the great audience assembled, packing the Amphitheater to its utmost corner, with a great ring of people standing around it, to hear William Jennings Bryan. On account of an afternoon lecture in Ohio, he sent word that he could not arrive until 8.45 in the evening, and it was nine when at last he stood on the platform. But he held the crowd in rapt attention to the end of his plea in behalf of the Democratic Party and its candidate, who was indebted to Mr. Bryan more than to any other worker for his nomination and, as the result showed, for his election. I am not certain who spoke in behalf of Mr. Roosevelt, but think that it was Mr. William H. Prendergast, Comptroller of New York City.

Among the lecturers of 1912 we heard the Baroness Von Suttner, who had taken the Nobel Peace Prize by her book *Lay Down Your Arms*. She gave a strong plea for arbitration between nations, to take the place of war. There was also a lecture by David Starr Jordan, President of Leland Stanford University, on "The Case Against War," showing conclusively that the day of wars was past and that the financial interrelations of nations would make a great war impossible. How little we dreamed of the war-cloud within two years to drench the whole world in blood! There was, indeed, one warning voice at this Assembly, that of Mr. H. H. Powers, in his clear-sighted lecture on "International Problems in Europe." He did not predict war, but he showed from what causes a great war might arise. There was a debate on

Woman Suffrage. Mrs. Ida Husted Harper gave several lectures in its behalf, and Miss Alice Hill Chittenden on "The Case Against Suffrage." Professor Scott Nearing gave a course of lectures on social questions, showing powerfully the evils of the time, and setting forth his view of the remedy,—a socialistic reorganization of the State and of society in general. Some conservative people who heard Scott Nearing lecture, regarded him as a firebrand, in danger of burning up the national temple, but those who met him in social life were compelled to yield to the charm of his personal attractiveness. Dr. Leon H. Vincent gave a course of lectures on "Contemporary English Novelists." He began in the Hall of Philosophy, but was compelled to move into the Amphitheater. Mr. Charles D. Coburn of the Coburn Players gave a careful, critical address, summing up fairly the good and evil, on "The Drama and the Present Day Theater."

The Daily Devotional Service in the Amphitheater, and the addresses on "The Awakened Church," in the Hall of Christ, one at nine o'clock, the other at ten, drew large congregations. It could not be said that Chautauqua was losing interest in religion, Canon H. J. Cody of Toronto gave a series of talks on "Bible Portraits of Persons we Know: 1, The Average Man; 2, The Man in the Street; 3, The Man who Misapplies the Past; 4, The Man who is Dying of Things"; Prof. Francis S. Peabody of Harvard a series on "Christian Life in the Modern World." Bishop McDowell (Methodist) conducted the Hour for a week to the great spiritual uplift of the large audience. Dr. Shailer Mathews gave an interesting series on "The Conversations of Jesus," Dr. James A. Francis a course on "Evangelism."

Realizing how many worthy names I have omitted, I close regretfully the record of Chautauqua in 1912.

## CHAPTER XXII

### WAR CLOUDS AND WAR DRUMS

(1913–1916)

THERE have been visitors at Chautauqua who, listening to some of the lecturers and their radical expressions, were alarmed and inclined to believe that the woods were full of cranks, faultfinders of the general social order, wild agitators, and revolutionary reformers bent on reorganizing the world. Chautauqua has always favored the freest discussion of all subjects and has admitted to its platform spokesmen upon all the questions of the time and from every point of view, even some unpopular men airing their unpopular ideas, confident that in the conflict of opinions the right will triumph. In 1913 the living question under discussion was Socialism; what it means, its positive aims and the arguments both for and against it. Here are the names of some speakers on that controverted subject. Professor Scott Nearing, perhaps the most radical of any, spoke on "Social Sanity," although his conception of sanity was looked upon by many as absolutely insane. Mr. J. W. Bengough explained and advocated "The Single Tax" and almost converted some of us to his doctrine. Mrs. Rose Pastor Stokes, a most winsome speaker, without opinion as to her views, told us of "The Socialist's Attitude towards Charity," which was that much denominated charity is simple justice. Mr. Victor L. Berger of Milwaukee, who has several times been denied a seat in Congress to which he was elected on the Socialist ticket, stated the views and demands of his party. Dr. H. H. Powers spoke on "Present Day Socialism in Europe," John Mitchell gave us "The Trades-union Point of View." Earl Barnes took part in the discussion, and Dr. Charles R. Henderson of Chicago also touched upon it. Some speakers were openly for, others as strongly against the movement. Whether the Socialist Party gained voters may be doubted, but it certainly enjoyed a full and fair hearing.

Turning from politics to religion, which should have a more intimate friendship than most people give them, we notice the Devotional Hour during the season of 1913. The Chaplain for the first week was Dr. Charles F. Wishart of the Pittsburgh Theological Seminary, his addresses being on "The Christian View of Some Facts of Life." Dr. Lynn

Harold Hough, then a Methodist pastor in Baltimore, and Rev. Arthur C. Hill of London were on the list. Dr. S. M. Crothers of Cambridge, Mass., preached one Sunday and conducted the Devotional Hour a week in a series on "Gaining the Mastery." Bishop Williams was on the platform again, speaking on "Aspects of Personal Religion." Anyone who attended this service through the season—and the daily congregation was not far below a thousand—would obtain a pretty clear understanding of Christianity and the character of its advocates.

Every year the musical element grows at Chautauqua. There was this year, as had been the case for several seasons, a Musical Festival Week, with daily concerts. For many years there had been a quartette of the best soloists during July and another during August, supported by a chorus often of three hundred voices and the great Massey organ. Henry B. Vincent, who is the son of Dr. B. T. Vincent of the Children's Class, grew up at Chautauqua, in a sense, spending his summers there from early childhood. For many years he has been at the organ seat, except when conducting the orchestra which he organized and trained. In 1912 he gave an interesting course of lectures on "How to Listen to Music." Every Sunday afternoon a large audience assembles to hear Mr. Vincent for an hour in an organ recital. An oratorio of his composition and under his direction was given at Chautauqua some years ago, entitled "The Prodigal Son." With one Vincent Founder and Chancellor, his son the President, one nephew a lecturer every year or two on literature, the other nephew the organ and band master, and his mother the President of the Woman's Club for many years, the Vincent family has been worthily represented at Chautauqua.

While speaking of music we must not forget one course of lectures by Mr. Olin Downes, musical critic of the *Boston Post*, on "Musical Expression in Dramatic Form," a history of the music drama in general; early French operas; the German Romantic School; Richard Wagner; Verdi and Latter-day Italians.

Prof. Richard Burton gave an entire course of lectures on "The Serious Bernard Shaw," which caused a run upon the library for Shaw's writings, as I perceived, for I vainly sought them. Miss Maud Miner of the School of Expression gave some recitals and a lecture, packed full of suggestions on "Efficiency in Speech." Dr. George Vincent spoke to a crowded Amphitheater on "A National Philosophy of Life." A Serbian, Prince

Lazarovich Hvebelianovich, gave a lurid picture of the Balkan situation. Let me quote one sentence as reported in the Daily of July 11, 1913 (note the date):

"Within the next few months there will be a war; and such a war as has not stirred Europe since the days of Napoleon; a war that will involve all the principal nations on that side of the Atlantic."

Less than thirteen months after that prediction came the event in the capital of his own little nation which let loose twenty millions of armed men, filled the seas with warships, above and beneath the waves, and the skies with fighting aeroplanes.

Mrs. Percy V. Pennybacker of Texas, gave a series of addresses on the Federation of Woman's Clubs, of which she was at that time the President. We listened to a Chinaman, Ng Poon Chew, the editor of a Chinese daily paper in San Francisco, on "China in Transformation," a clear account of the new Republic of China in its varied aspects, spoken in the best of English. We noticed too, that the speaker showed an understanding and appreciation which foreigners are often slow to obtain of American humor and jokes.

Another lecturer from abroad, though hardly

a foreigner, for he came from England, Prof. J. Stoughton Holborn, wearing his Oxford gown (which we had not seen before at Chautauqua), gave a course on "The Inspiration of Greece,"—a view of that wonderful people in the different fields of their greatness. Think of one city which in the departments of literature, drama, philosophy, oratory, art, and public affairs could show more great men in two hundred years than all the rest of the world could show in two thousand!

We were treated during the season of 1913 to a sight new at that time, though common enough now. Mr. Engels brought to Chautauqua a Curtiss hydroplane, and day after day made flights, skimming over the surface of the lake, rising into the air, circling the sky and returning to the starting-point, to the amazement of the watching multitudes. A few, and but a few, dared to be strapped into the machine and take the flight; Director Bestor was one of them, and when Mrs. Bestor heard of it she said: "I told him that he must not do it, but I knew all the time that he would!"

Another event of the season was the production of a Greek play, in the original language, by a group of college students in Greek costume. Another fact worthy of remembrance was the opening of a completely furnished playground for the children in the ravine near the ball-ground. To stand on the bridge and look down upon that company of happy little people, is always a delight. Also it is not to be forgotten that this year for the first time natural gas for cooking and heating was supplied throughout the grounds.

The year 1914 was the fortieth anniversary of the founding of Chautauqua. One of the Founders was with us, hale and hearty, and still able to give an admirable address, although his memory of recent matters and people had failed. The other Founder was no longer among us, and even fifteen years after his departure we of the earlier days missed him; but his memory will ever be kept green at Chautauqua, while the white lilies are silently unfolded in his honor. On Friday, July 3d, the signal fires were lighted all around the Lake. The celebration of the anniversary did not take place until August, near the date in the month of the first Assembly. On Sunday, August 2d, Bishop Vincent preached in the Amphitheater with scarcely any lessening of his old power. At the anniversary service, Dr. Jesse L. Hurlbut—who was exhibited as one of the survivals of the prehistoric age, a sort of a dinosaurus or pleiosaurus, —gave an address on "Memories of Early Days," of which the reader may find the substance scattered through these pages. But we must give a paragraph or two from Mrs. Frank Beard's paper In reference to the interdenominational aspect of the Assembly, she said:

> The good Baptist brother, wandering down by the Dead Sea and Sea of Galilee to the Mediterranean, looked at the generous supply of water and was satisfied. The Presbyterian brother gazed into the cloudless sky above him, saw his favorite color, and felt that Chautauqua was foreordained for him. The lineal descendant of St. Peter croqueted his ball through the arch and rejoiced that he was on saving ground.
>
> We sat on the hard board seats with nothing to rest our backs upon but the salubrious atmosphere. We heard ponderous speakers who talked on ponderous subjects. Among the speakers was Joseph Cook, also Bishop Peck, 350 pounds. Some of the lecturers were recommended as cultured and highly finished. Mr. Beard said that he had attended these lectures, was glad that they were cultured and more than pleased that they were finished.

The music week had now become a permanent institution, bringing thousands to the Assembly. This year it began on Monday, July 27th, with Victor Herbert's orchestra through the seven days, the Chautauqua soloists, and the great chorus trained by Alfred Hallam. Some musical associations from Jamestown and elsewhere added their voices.

Among the lecturers, Mr. Griggs gave a course on "Dramas of Protest," the Book of Job, Shelley's "Prometheus Unbound," Galsworthy's "Justice," Calderon's "Life is a Dream," and some others. Bourke Cockran, the brilliant orator of Irish descent, gave a great lecture on "Abraham Lincoln —Original Progressive." Miss Mary E. Downey, Director of the Library School, spoke on "The Evolution of the Library," Dean Edwin Watts Chubb on "Shakespeare as a Moral Teacher." John Purroy Mitchel, the reform Mayor of New York, spoke on "Municipal Government" on July 18th; Dr. Lincoln Hulley of Florida gave a course on the leading American poets. Mr. E. H. Blichfeldt spoke most interestingly on "Mexico as I Know It," the results of a year of wide travel and close observation in that land.

During the month of July we read in the papers of complications in the political world beyond the ocean, but few looked for serious trouble and none for actual war. On the first of August, 1914, the storm burst, and nation after nation in a few hours assembled their hosts for the most terrible war in the history of the world. In accordance with the Chautauqua tradition of free and open discussion, a War Symposium was improvised and each of the contending nations had its speaker. On Tuesday, August 4th, Dr. Hans E. Gronow who had served his time in the German army gave "The German Point of View." On Thursday, August 6th, Mr. Sanford Griffith, a newspaper correspondent and a student of public affairs spending several years in Europe whom some of us had known as a boy at Chautauqua, spoke on "European Unrest Due to Shifts in the Balance of Power." On Friday, August 7th, Mons. Benedict Papot, formerly a soldier in France, gave "The French Point of View," and on Saturday, August 9th, Dr. W. S. Bainbridge, English in ancestry but American in birth and spirit, presented "The British Point of View." All the exercises of the crowded program were held, but amid all our efforts the war brooded above us, a darkening cloud.

The Department of Religious Work was carried on with a strong force of speakers and teachers under the direction of Dr. Shailer Mathews, its details supervised by his efficient assistant, Miss Georgia L. Chamberlin of Chicago, who also gave daily lectures. Among the instructors were Dr. Charles F. Kent of Yale, and Dr. James Hope Moulton, one of the richest minds of the age in

Biblical lore, who gave a series of lectures, learned yet simple, on "The Origins of Religion." None of us could have thought then that this noble life in its prime was destined to end in the Mediterranean by a shot from a German submarine.

The Devotional Hour and the Sunday services were led for a week by the Rev. C. Rexford Raymond of Brooklyn, who told in several chapters the old story of Joseph, yet seeming new in its application. The Rev. G. Robinson Lees, Vicar of St. Andrews, Lambeth, England, who had lived in Palestine and among the Arabs in the desert, had written a book forbidden by the Turkish authorities, and had been banished from the land, preached one Sunday morning and gave graphic pictures of Oriental life through the week. Dr. W. H. Hickman, a former President of the Chautauqua Board of Trustees, Rev. Peter Ainslie of Baltimore, Dr. C. F. Wishart, Dr. Washington Gladden, one who was ever welcome at Chautauqua; and a great-hearted man, Dr. George W. Truett of Texas, were also chaplains, each serving a week.

This year also the new golf course was opened on the field beyond the public highway, to the rejoicing of many patrons. At the close of the season the annual convention was held by the International Lyceum and Chautauqua Association, the union of bureaus and speakers in the "Chain Chautauquas" held all over the continent, of which we shall speak later. Their meetings were continued until September 10th, making 1914 the longest session in the history of Chautauqua.

In 1915, the war of the world was bringing its unspeakable terrors to Europe, and America was looking on, yet hesitating to plunge into the welter; but Chautauqua held on its even way, its courses of instruction as many, and its classes as large as ever. This year Dr. George E. Vincent felt constrained by the pressure of his duties as President of the University of Minnesota, with its eight thousand students and as large a number in its University Extension courses, to withdraw from the direct supervision of Chautauqua. He resigned his office as President of the Chautauqua Institution, and Dr. Arthur E. Bestor became President. But Dr. Vincent retained his membership on the Board of Trustees, was named Honorary President, and has continued to come to Chautauqua almost every year. Even for a few days, and with a lecture or two, his presence gives strength to the Assembly.

In 1917, Dr. Vincent resigned the presidency of the University of Minnesota to accept the same position with the Rockefeller Foundation, disbursing millions of dollars every year in the interests of world-wide education and health.

The lecture platform of 1915 was arranged under six great weeks, each making prominent one subject, while popular addresses and the devotional services went on parallel with them all. The first week was devoted to the study of community service. Mary Antin, whose book, *The Promised Land*, had been read by everybody, was greeted by an audience far beyond the reach of her voice, speaking in her ardent manner. Dr. Lincoln Wirt proclaimed "America's Challenge to the World"; Mr. E. J. Ward explained the why and the how of "Community Service," and Norman Angell set forth "American Leadership in World Politics." During this week Chancellor McCormick of the University of Pittsburgh conducted the services of the Devotional Hour.

The second week was devoted to the Drink Problem. Bishop Francis J. McConnell of the Methodist Episcopal Church preached on Sunday morning and spoke at the Devotional Hour each day. The opening address was by Governor George A. Carlson of Colorado, who set forth powerfully the methods and results of prohibition in his State. Dr. H. A. Gibbons spoke on "The

Prohibition Question in Europe." The Hon. J. Denny O'Neill, on "Booze and Politics." While the temperance question was discussed in the Hall of Philosophy, there were concerts and lectures in the Amphitheater, one especially by Mr. Sanford Griffith, who had been at the battle front as a war correspondent, on "Fighting in Flanders." Also Dr. Hamilton Wright Mabie, editor and essayist, spoke on "The East and West, Friends or Enemies?"

The third week was entitled "Justice and the Courts"—with such subjects as law, legislation, the administration of justice, and penology. Among the speakers were George W. Alger, Thomas Mott Osborne, Katharine Bement Davis, Judge W. L. Ransom of New York, and Dean James Parker Hall of the University of Chicago Law School. Mr. Charles Rann Kennedy, author of *The Servant in the House*, a drama with a sermon, recited the play, aided by Mrs. Kennedy. The play had already been read a year or two before by Mrs. Bertha Kunz Baker, and also enacted by the Chautauqua Players, so that we were familiar with it, but were eager to hear it recited by its author. Mr. Kennedy also gave some dramatic interpretations from the Bible. This week the Devotional Hour was held by Dr. Charles W. Gilkey, of the Hyde Park Baptist Church in Chicago, the church nearest to the University and attended by many of the faculty and students.

The music week was notable from the presence of the Russian Symphony Orchestra, led by a great player and delightful personality, Modest Altschuler. One of his company said of him, "He rules his orchestra by love." The Recognition Address this year was by President E. B. Bryan of Colgate University, on the all-important question: "Who are Good Citizens?"

The forty-third Assembly in 1916 found our country in the throes of a presidential election, party strife bitter, and the nation divided on the impending question of our entrance into the world war. The feverish pulse of the time was manifested in the opinions expressed by the different speakers. Dr. George E. Vincent gave a lecture on "What is Americanism"—a sane, thoughtful view which was needed in that hour.

The week beginning Sunday, July 23d, was devoted to the subject of Preparedness for War or Peace. The Ford Peace Expedition of that year will be remembered, the effort of a wealthy manufacturer to stop the war. Several who had taken part in that apparently quixotic movement spoke in defense or criticism of it, and also the question of preparedness was discussed by Governor Charles

S. Whitman, President Hibben of Princeton, Hon. Henry A. Wise Wood, Senator W. M. Calder, and others. Mrs. Lucia Ames Ward, of the Woman's Peace Party, was opposed to any participation in the war or preparation for it. The controversy waxed warm, for the opinions were positive on both sides.

On subjects aside from the war we had an enlightening series of addresses at the Devotional Hour by Dean Charles R. Brown of Yale; a course of lectures by Dr. Edwin E. Slosson on "Major Prophets of To-day," Bernard Shaw, G. K. Chesterton, H. G. Wells, and some others; a series of lectures by Dr. Percy F. Boynton on "The Growth of Consciousness in American Literature,"—as shown in Irving, Cooper, Emerson, Lowell, and Whitman. Raymond Robins gave four lectures on "The Church and the Laboring Classes." Dr. Griggs awakened general interest by his lectures on "Types of Men and Women," as illustrated in their autobiographies and letters, presenting John Stuart Mill, Benevenuto Cellini, George John Romanes, Marie Bashkirtseff, Sonya Kovalevasky (a new name to most of us), and Henri Frederic Amiel,—all possessing characters pronounced, some of them so peculiar as to be almost abnormal.

The Russian Symphony Orchestra, with its beloved director, Modest Altschuler, was with us again for another week, aided by the soloists and Chautauqua Chorus. In our rapid survey, we have only glanced at the prominent events in a great season.

# CHAPTER XXIII

## WAR AND ITS AFTERMATH

(1917–1920)

WHEN the forty-fourth session of Chautauqua opened on Thursday, June 26, 1917, it found the American republic just entering upon the Great War, which had already raged in Europe for over two years. Training camps had sprung up like magic all over the land, from ocean to ocean, and young men by the hundred thousand had volunteered, with others by the million soon cheerfully to accept drafting orders. Almost every university had been transformed into a war college. President Vincent was at the intensive military training school at Plattsburg, N. Y. Every morning before breakfast two hundred men at Chautauqua were marching and counter-marching, and learning the manual of arms with wooden guns, with President Bestor and most of the officials of the Institution in the lines. The young women every afternoon were receiving similar drill under a woman officer, and some said that they presented even a more soldier-like appearance than the men. The headquarters of several denominations had been commandeered for Red Cross work and training. A stranger could scarcely get into the Methodist House without being scrutinized as a possible German spy, with a pocketful of poison or powdered glass to sprinkle on the bandages. War was in the air as well as in the newspapers. No matter what was the subject of a lecture it was almost sure to be on the war before the finish. There were discussions on the platform and on the street about the League of Nations, some with President Wilson in favor of it, others as vigorously against it. A symposium on "Our Country" and a conference of "Organizations Engaged in Education for Patriotic Service" were held during the session; also a company of students from the Carnegie Institute of Technology, Pittsburgh, presented a brilliant pageant, "The Drawing of the Sword."

The Fourth of July address was given by the Hon. G. W. Wickersham, former Attorney-General of the United States. Captain A. Radclyffe Dugmore of the British Army spoke on "Our Fight for Freedom." Miss Ida Tarbell, who had won fame by a book showing the operations of the Standard Oil Company, and had also written a life of Abraham Lincoln, to be found in every public library and read more widely than any other biography of the Greatest American, gave some lectures. Her literary life, by the way, began in the office of the *Chautauquan Magazine*. Mrs. Percy V. Pennybacker this summer became President of the Chautauqua Woman's Club, which office Mrs. B. T. Vincent had relinquished after many years of leadership. Both these presidents were eminently successful in different directions and by different methods, the earlier having built up the Club by wisdom mingled with gentleness; her successor carried it onward by an energy that brought everybody into willing subjection to her far-reaching plans. Almost the first result of the new administration was the purchase of a club house fronting on the Lake, and holding in it almost a bewildering series of teas and receptions. While the public meetings of the Club crowded the new Hall of Philosophy every afternoon, Mrs. Pennybacker gave a stirring address on "What our Country Asks of its Young Women."

During the first week Dr. Harry Emerson Fosdick of the Union Theological Seminary was the Chaplain, and his addresses blended fervent patriotism and fervent religion in about equal measure.

The second week, from July 8th to 14th, was

denominated "Arts and Letters," with lectures on these subjects by Dr. Mitchell Carroll of Washington, Henry Turner Bailey of Boston, and others. But underneath the artistic and the literary, the echo of the war might still be heard in many of the lectures, and it sounded out in the Devotional Hour addresses of that soldier in the army of the Lord, the Chaplain, Bishop Charles D. Williams.

During the week of July 15th to 21st, the Methodist Bishop, William Burt of Buffalo, to whose "area" (for Methodists of course could not call it a "diocese") Chautauqua belongs, was the Chaplain. During this week we heard lectures by Admiral Peary, the discoverer of the North Pole; by Thomas Adams of Canada; by D. R. Garland of Ohio; by D. A. Reed of Michigan, and by George A. Bellamy of Cleveland.

July 22d–28th was Musical Festival Week, when we had with us once more the Russian Symphony Orchestra, conducted by Modest Altschuler, who was welcomed with sincere rejoicing by Chautauqua's multitude. Looking over the crowded Amphitheater during those daily concerts, the only reminder of a war in progress was that scarcely a young man was to be seen, although every seat was occupied.

From July 29th to August 4th, the Great War

was the theme on the platform. Mr. Earl Barnes gave a series of lectures on "Historical Backgrounds of the War," respectively in the British Empire, France, Germany, Austro-Hungary, the Russian Empire, and the Balkan Peninsular. Dr. Herbert Adams Gibbons presented some of the "Problems of the Peace Conference,"—though at that time nobody knew when the Conference would be held or whether anybody would be left alive to hold it. But the cheerful assumption was taken that Germany would be beaten, which proved to be correct, and also that the Allies would rearrange the map of the world, which does not now appear to be quite certain. Mr. Sanford Griffith, just from the front, gave us an inspiring word-picture of "Paris Reborn."

The concluding address of the symposium was given by President Bestor on "America and the War." It was considered by the National Security League as of sufficient value to be published in pamphlet form, and received a wide circulation.

From August 13th to 18th, Bishop Charles B. Mitchell (Methodist Episcopal), living at Minneapolis, held the post of Chaplain, and gave a number of heart warming addresses on "The Transforming Power of Divine Grace." During the week the Recognition Day exercises were held, with all pomp and ceremonial, the address being given by President George E. Vincent. His father was present and that afternoon, as Chancellor, gave the diplomas to the graduates, but none of us knew that it was for the last time, and that his face would not be seen again at Chautauqua, although he lived nearly three years longer.

In 1917, President E. B. Bryan of Colgate University accepted the position as Director of the Summer Schools. But to one who through the rest of the year has a college full of students to keep in order, and also a faculty to maintain in harmony—which one college president told me he found the harder task,—the burden at Chautauqua of a hundred and twenty-five teachers, two hundred courses of study, and forty-five hundred students during nearly all his summer vacation, proved too heavy even for Dr. Bryan's shoulders, and after three years, in 1919, he was compelled to relinquish it into the hands of President Bestor.

This summer, also, the new traction station of the Chautauqua Lake Railway was opened at the highway entrance to the grounds; a handsome pillared structure with more room than Chautauqua had ever before possessed for waiting room, ticket office, baggage, freight, and express, a convenience appreciated by every visitor. Also, by the shore a new bathhouse and the Jacob Bolin Gymnasium were built and opened, as well as the Fenton Memorial Home for Methodist Deaconesses on the Overlook addition.

In 1918,we were in the grip of the war, with our young men in camp by the million, overseas and on their way by the hundred thousand, and every woman "doing her bit" in the Red Cross work. Outwardly, Chautauqua seemed as flourishing as in other years, the hotels and cottages appeared to be full, the Amphitheater was crowded at the concerts and popular lectures, and the main streets before and after lectures were a continuous procession. But the gate receipts showed that the Institution, in common with every college in the land, was lessened in its attendance and its financial returns. Nevertheless, the program was not allowed to decline in its extent and its interest. Indeed, one added feature attracted attention. In the field of the Overlook a National Service School was held in coöperation with the Woman's Naval Service. A tented camp was maintained under the strict discipline of Mrs. George E. Vincent, with regular guards, and training for more than two hundred khaki-clad young women in agriculture, telegraphy, basketry, and canteen management. I am not sure about carpentry, though I saw a photograph of young women sawing boards and putting up a house.

The value of Chautauqua in national patriotic leadership was recognized, not only by our own government, but by the Allies as well. Great Britain, France, Belgium, Italy, and Greece sent official speakers, either through their embassies or their special war missions. It was a mark of distinguished favor that the French High Commission gave the French Military Band to Chautauqua for a week, their longest engagement in this country.

On the opening day, July 4th, President Bestor gave the oration on "Mobilizing the Mind of America." For nearly a year before, and until the Armistice in November of this year, Mr. Bestor was almost without intermission in Washington in government service as head of the Department of Publicity. He was Director of the Speaking Division of the Committee on Public Information, and also Secretary of the Committee on Patriotism of the National Security League, an organization which held in many places training camps for patriotic speakers. Dr. Bestor was carrying on more than double duty until the Armistice in 1918 gave him something of a breathing spell between the sessions of Chautauqua. During the week from July 7th to 13th, Bishop Edwin H. Hughes (Methodist Episcopal) was Chaplain, and gave addresses of a high character on "Varieties of Religious Experience." As samples of the type of lectures during this strenuous battle summer, this week President E. B. Bryan spoke on "War as a Schoolmaster," Mr. E. H. Griggs began a course on "The War and the Reconstruction of Democracy," and Dr. L. A. Weigle of Yale lectured on "Religious Education in War Times." One evening Dr. S. H. Clark read war lyrics in the Amphitheater.

The week from July 14th to 20th was "Women's Service Week," and among those who spoke on the subject were Anna Howard Shaw, who had been called by the President to be Chairman of the Women's National Council of Defense, in command of all the activities of women in aid of the war, Miss Helen Fraser of England, Mrs. Carrie Chapman Catt, Mrs. Ella A. Boole, Mrs. Pennybacker, and Mrs. George Thatcher Guernsey,—women whose voices had often been heard in behalf of woman suffrage, now as ardently speaking in aid of work to carry on the war. This week Dr. S. P. Cadman had been engaged as Chaplain, but he was unable to remain more than one day and other men were suddenly drafted to take his place on successive mornings, one of them, the writer of these pages, on fifteen minutes' notice called to conduct the Devotional Hour, immediately after an hour's teaching in class. This little incident, of no particular interest to anybody but the writer, is mentioned merely to illustrate the instant change of front which must be made frequently at Chautauqua, when a speaker is delayed by a railroad wreck or unexpectedly called home to conduct a funeral.

"Our Allies" was the title of the week from July 22d to 27th. Dr. Charles W. Gilkey of Chicago preached the sermon on Sunday morning and led in the devotions through the week. Prof. Robert Herndon Fife of the Wesleyan University, Conn., gave a series of lectures on "The New Europe." Not all of his forecasts have yet come to pass, for the new Europe is only slowly emerging out of the old. Mrs. Kenneth Brown—the name sounds American, but she is a Greek lady of rank, born Demetra Vaka—told a harrowing tale of her own experience and observation, "In the Heart of the German Intrigue." Dr. Mitchell Carroll of Washington gave an account of "Greece, our Youngest Ally," with Venizelos as the hero. Lieut. Bruno Roselli of the Italian army spoke; Miss Maud

Hayes of "England in War Time." On Friday evening, July 26th, there was a concert in the evening of national songs of the Allies; the flags of more than twenty nations being hung above the choir loft. On Grand Army Day in this week Lieut. Telfair Marion Minton spoke on "The Flags of a Thousand Years."

In the following week, July 28th to August 3d, while the Musical Festival was in progress, the French Military Band played every day, and concert followed concert, with Gaul's "Joan of Arc" sung one evening by the soloists and full chorus. Dr. Leon H. Vincent gave a course of lectures, showing "War in Literature," the stories called forth by the Wars of Napoleon, the Crimean War, the Franco-Prussian War of 1870, and the struggle in progress in 1918—a most interesting series. The Chaplain of this week was the Rev. Wm. S. Jacobs, D.D., of Houston, Texas.

Omitting a fortnight for lack of room, we must not omit "The Next Step Forward," the topic of the week from August 18th to 24th, a discussion of some movements to follow in the footsteps of war, such as "Theological Reconstruction," by Shailer Mathews; "Christianity in Foreign Lands," by Dr. J. L. Barton, Secretary of the American Board of Commissioners for Foreign Missions; "The

Sunday Evening Club" and "Church Advertising," by W. F. McClure, and "The Art of Motion Pictures," by Vachel Lindsay. There was also a course on "Art in Daily Life," by our English friend, Prof. I. B. Stoughton Holborn, of Oxford.

Bishop McConnell, who conducted the Devotional Hour, August 11th–17th, also gave the Recognition address to the graduating class of the C. L. S. C., on "Ideals of Leadership." The skies were clouded, yet we were able to hold the procession as usual (only once in forty-seven years has the march been broken up by rain), but the storm fell during the address, with such noise on the roof that the Bishop was compelled to pause for some minutes until its rage abated. We missed on this day especially the presence of Bishop Vincent and his son, and the diplomas were conferred by Dr. Bestor, the new President of Chautauqua. Not long after the closing of the Assembly, on November 11, 1918, "Armistice Day" was ushered in by the blowing of every steam whistle upon the continent, by all-day processions, by bands and horns, and a surrender of the nation to the universal joy, through the news that the most terrible war that ever desolated the world was over at last.

When the forty-sixth session of Chautauqua

opened in 1919, it found the land rejoicing over the conclusion of the war, happy in the return of two million men in khaki, apparently rich with high wages, booming business, and money in plenty. It was the top of a tide destined before many months to recede to normal conditions. But while the flush times lasted, Chautauqua shared in the nation-wide prosperity. This was the period of astounding financial drives. One great church commemorated the hundred years of its missionary enterprise by a centenary movement and a subscription of more than a hundred million dollars. Other churches followed with "New Era" and "Nation Wide" campaigns. It seemed to be the opportunity for Chautauqua to reap some benefits from the spirit of the time, and the trustees launched the "Comprehensive Plan" to raise half a million dollars, freeing the Institution from all debt and placing it on a safe, permanent, and prosperous basis. Here was a university of a hundred and twenty-five instructors, two hundred courses of study, and nearly five thousand students every summer, yet without a dollar of endowment;—what college in the land was doing so much with an income so small? Here was a property of three hundred and fifty acres, gradually accumulated, partly by the demands of the Institution's growth, partly from the necessity of controlling its surroundings. Debts had been incurred by enlargement of the grounds, a sewer system, a water supply, electric lighting, new buildings, new roads, and a hundred items of improvement. The overhead expenses of Chautauqua, in the form of interest that must be paid, were more than thirty thousand dollars every year. How much might be accomplished if every debt could be cleared away and the saving in interest be applied to the improvement of the property and the enlargement of opportunities? Mr. John D. Rockefeller made an offer of giving one-fifth of all that should be raised, up to the desired half-million dollars. The trustees assigned to themselves another hundred thousand of the amount, and a committee of the cottage owners pledged $150,000 from those having property on the ground. The plans were carefully laid, and during the season of 1919 every visitor at Chautauqua was called upon to make his contribution.

Of all the forty-six years of Chautauqua up to 1919, this was the most successful in its history. The attendance shown by the receipts at the two gates—one at the Pier where the steamboats landed their thousands, the other at the new station on the public highway where the trolley brought the tens of thousands—were far beyond that of any former year. The registration at the schools was sixty-two per cent. in advance of 1918, and eighteen per cent. beyond that of 1914, the best previous year. Every hotel and boarding house inside the fence was full, and pleas were made to cottagers to open their doors to incoming guests. Many who could not find lodging places on the grounds found homes in the hotels and hamlets around the Lake and came daily to the Assembly by trolley or by boat.

During the opening week, Mr. W. W. Ellsworth gave two illustrated lectures, one on "Theodore Roosevelt," the other "The Rise and Fall of Prussianism," and Prof. Thomas F. Moran of Purdue University gave an appreciation of "Mark Twain, Humorist, Reformer, and Philosopher." Miss Maud Miner gave a popular recitation of "Comedy Scenes from Shakespeare." It was noticed that in the very opening the Amphitheater was filled;—what would it become at the height of the season, the first two weeks in August?

The Devotional Hour from July 6th to 12th was held by Dr. Charles F. Wishart, in a series of studies in the book of Exodus, entitled, "A Free People in the Making," and from the story he drew frequent applications to the history of another "free people." During this week, Dr. Louis A. Weigle, Professor of Psychology at Yale University, began a course of lectures on "Character Building in the Public Schools" suggesting many thoughts—not all of them gratulatory—in those who heard them.

On Sunday morning, July 13th, the great congregation heard Dr. Wm. P. Merrill, of the Brick Church, New York, deliver a sermon on the topic as announced, "The League of Nations," of which he declared himself unreservedly in favor. On this question there were two parties throughout the nation strongly opposed to each other and fiercely debating it, and when a fortnight later the chaplain, Bishop Williams, who was never known to sit on the fence, also came out vigorously for the League, Mr. Bestor began to look around for some speaker on the other side, for it has been a principle at Chautauqua to give both sides a fair showing, even when the Chautauqua constituency as a whole might be opposed to a speaker. A speaker against the League was found in Mr. John Ferguson, but he evidently represented the sentiments of the minority. Among the speakers of the second week were several on "The Aftermath of the Great War," among them Dr. Katharine B. Davis, Major-General Bailey, who had been Commander of the Eighty-First Division of the A. E. F., and Attorney-General A. Mitchell Palmer. Prof. S. C. Schmucker also gave a course of lectures on "The Races of Man."

Musical Festival Week was from July 28th to August 2nd. The New York Symphony Orchestra of sixty instruments was with us in concerts daily, led in the absence of its conductor, Mr. Walter Damrosch (who was abroad) by René Pollain of France. During this and the following week Earl Barnes gave a course of lectures on "The New Nations of the World." We listened to a discussion of "Zionism," in a lecture on "Jewish Aims in Palestine" by Charles A. Cowen, of the Zionist organization, to which Mr. Earl Barnes gave a cool, dispassionate answer, showing the difficulty, amounting almost to an impossibility, of establishing a Jewish State in the land looked upon as holy, not only by Jews, but by Mohammedans and Christians of all the great churches. Another speaker in this symposium was Mme. Mabel S. Grouetch, the wife of the Serbian minister at Washington, who afterward became the Czecho-Slovak representative to Japan.

Old First Night on August 5th was devoted to the Comprehensive Plan of lifting Chautauqua out of debt. The elements seemed against the aim for rain kept some away,—though the Amphitheater was full—and its thunder on the roof made some speeches inaudible. But it could not dampen the ardor of the people. Practically every organization, club, or class at Chautauqua, besides many individuals, made pledges. Besides the chorus, there was a children's choir in the gallery, and one gentleman offered to give a dollar for every child in it, whereupon scouts were sent out, boys and girls were gotten out of bed and brought to the gallery, so that his pledge cost that gentleman considerably over $300.00. Before the close of the Assembly $375,000 had been subscribed, inclusive of Mr. Rockefeller's quota.

Americanization week was from August 11th to 16th, with timely addresses by Prof. Herbert Adolphin Miller, Prof. Thomas Moran, and a delightful lecture by Mrs. Beatrice Forbes-Robertson Hale, on "Reconstruction in England and America." As a practical illustration of Americanization, there was a wonderful pageant by the children of a public school in Pittsburgh, practically all of foreign lineage. The Recognition address on August 20th was by Bishop Charles F. Brent, who after heroic work in the Philippines had been translated to the Episcopal diocese of

Western New York. His subject was "The Opportunities of the Mind."

We must not forget that some lectures were given at this session by Dr. Charles A. Eastman, whose name does not suggest, as his complexion does, that he is a full-blooded Sioux Indian. He is a successful physician and a graduate of Dartmouth College,—which, by the way, was established in 1750 as a school for Indians, with no thought of Anglo-Saxon students. This year also Dr. E. B. Bryan was unable to remain as Director of the Summer Schools, and his work was added to the many tasks of President Bestor.

We come finally to the Assembly of 1920, the forty-seventh session, and at present the last upon our list, unless we undertake a prophetic look into the future. We met in sadness, for our great Founder John Heyl Vincent, who had lived to the age of eighty-eight years, died on Sunday, May 9th, at his home in Chicago. He had outlived his fellow-Founder, Lewis Miller, by twenty-one years. The two names stand together in the annals of Chautauqua and in the thoughts of all Chautauquans, for Chautauqua could not have been founded by either one without the other, and on Old First Night, for both together the lilies of the white handkerchiefs are silently and solemnly lifted, and as silently and solemnly lowered. A memorial service was held for our beloved Bishop and Chancellor on Sunday afternoon, August 1st, at the Vesper Hour, in the Hall of Philosophy as the appropriate place, and the writer of this story, as the oldest of living Chautauqua workers, was permitted to offer the tribute in his honor. In the evening another service was held in the Amphitheater, at which Dr. John H. Finley, Superintendent of Education for New York State, and Bishop Herbert Welch of the Methodist Episcopal Church, home for a few months from his field in Korea and Japan, gave addresses. During the past year Chautauqua had sustained another loss in the death of Mr. Alfred Hallam, who for nearly twenty years had been the untiring and wholly devoted leader of the Musical Department. It was felt that a musical service was his most appropriate memorial, and the oratorio "Hora Novissima," by Horatio Parker, was sung by the choir and soloists on Sunday evening, August 8th. During the session news came that Dr. Bethuel T. Vincent of Denver, long conductor of the Children's class and Intermediate class in the early years of the Assembly, had followed his brother the Bishop, into the silent land. He was remembered in an address by the writer at a memorial service. His wife, Mrs. Ella Vincent, for many years president of the Woman's Club, in a few months also joined the company of the church triumphant. Another voice often heard at Chautauqua was stilled this summer, that of Mrs. Frank Beard, always bright and sunny in her spirit, who fell asleep in the cottage where she was abiding, soon after the opening of the Assembly, fulfilling the wish expressed to a friend a year before that she might die at Chautauqua.

The most notable feature on the program this summer was the presence at Chautauqua for nearly six weeks, from July 26th to August 31st, of the New York Symphony Orchestra, with daily concerts, conducted by René Pollain and William Willeke,—a bold venture of the management but evidently successful.

This was the tercentenary of the landing of the Pilgrims, and the event was recognized by several addresses, one in particular by Mr. Charles Zeublin, on "1620 and 1920." Prof. Weigle gave a lecture on "Education of Children in Early New England"; Dr. Alfred E. Garvie spoke on "The Message of the *Mayflower* for To-day." Principal Alexander J. Grieve of the University of Edinburgh gave lectures on the "Leaders of the Pilgrims,—John Robinson and others."

Dr. Herbert Adams Gibbons, after an experience of years in Asia Minor and in France, gave a series of valuable lectures on "After the War," and Mrs. Gibbons narrated the thrilling story of herself in Turkey, during the massacres of 1908. Dr. Lynn Harold Hough was chaplain from July 4th to July 10th, and in the morning talks spoke on the spiritual experiences of St. Augustine, Martin Luther, and John Wesley, then summed them up in a conception of "The Christian Society." Prof. Richard Burton lectured in a course on "Modern Literary Tendencies,"—the essay, the novel, the drama, and other forms of literature. One of the great acquisitions this year was Prof. T. R. Glover of Cambridge, England, with a course of lectures on "The Jesus of History," the results of the deepest study of the New Testament and also of the contemporary Roman world. Dr. H. Gordon Hayes, just leaving Yale for the Ohio State University, discussed most ably "Factors in Labor Unrest." On Roosevelt Day, July 21st, Mrs. Douglas Robinson, his sister, gave "Recollections of Theodore Roosevelt." In the week from July 26th–31st, the subject was "Problems of the Present Day Civilization," discussed by Dr. E. H. Griggs, Rabbi Louis Wolsey of Cleveland, and Dr. Cornelius Woelfkin of New

York. "Woman and the New Era" was the theme of the week August 2d–7th, a discussion participated in by Mrs. Thomas G. Winter, President of the General Federation of Woman's Clubs; by Mrs. George Bass, who was the woman, for the first time in history to preside for a day at the Democratic National Convention which renominated Woodrow Wilson; and by Miss Mary Garrett Hay, the President of the Affiliated Women's Republican Clubs. August 22d–29th was the week of the Ministers and Church Workers' Institute, with addresses by Bishop McDowell (Methodist), Ozora S. Davis, Shailer Mathews, Mrs. Helen Barrett Montgomery, and Chancellor S. B. McCormick, of Pittsburgh.

This was a great year. Subscriptions to the Comprehensive Plan brought the amount up to $450,000, including Mr. Rockefeller's contribution, to be increased if other gifts warranted it. The Summer Schools were twenty-five per cent. in income and nearly twenty per cent. in numbers over 1919, the highest mark of past years. Provision was made for improving and enlarging the golf links, and for building a new club house on the grounds of the golf course.

## CHAPTER XXIV

### CHAUTAUQUA'S ELDER DAUGHTERS

CHAUTAUQUA, planted upon the shore of its Lake, grew up a fruitful vine, and within two years shoots cut from its abundant branches began to take root in other soils. Or, to change the figure, the seeds of Chautauqua were borne by the winds to many places, some of them far away, and these grew up, in the course of little more than a generation, a hundred, even a thousand fold. Many of these daughter-Chautauquas were organized by men—in some instances by women—who had caught the spirit of the mother-assembly; others by those who had heard of the new movement and saw its possibilities; some, it must be confessed, by people who sought to save a decayed and debt-burdened camp meeting, and a few with lots to lease at a summer resort. From one cause or another, immediately after the first Assembly had won success, Dr. Vincent began to receive pressing invitations to organize similar institutions in many places. As he was already fulfilling the duties both of an editor and a secretary for the rapidly growing Sunday School cause, he could accept but few of these many calls. But a number of younger men trained by a year or two of experience in teaching at Chautauqua were around him and to these he directed most of the enquirers. At least three Assemblies arose in 1876, two years after the founding of Chautauqua. Of these I possess some knowledge and will therefore name them, but without doubt there were others which soon passed away and left scarcely a memory.

So far as I have been able to ascertain, the first gathering to follow in the footsteps of Chautauqua was the Sunday School Parliament on Wellesley Island, one of those romantic Thousand Islands in the St. Lawrence River, where it emerges from Lake Ontario. This island stands on the boundary line between the United States and Canada, but the home of the Parliament was on the Canadian side of the line. The name "Chautauqua" has now become generic and almost any gathering in the interests of the Sunday School, or of general literature with a sprinkling of entertainment, is apt to be named "a Chautauqua." But in those early days the word Chautauqua was not known as the general term of an institution of the assembly type, and the new gatherings were named "Congress" or

"Encampment" or "Institute," and for this gathering the title "Sunday School Parliament" was taken, as smacking somewhat of English origin. Its organizer and conductor was the Rev. Wilbur F. Crafts, at that time a Methodist minister, afterwards a Congregationalist, and still at present working as the head of the International Reform Bureau in Washington, D. C. He was aided in the plan and direction by Mrs. Crafts, for both of them were then prominent leaders in Sunday School work. It was my good fortune to be present and conduct the Normal Class during a part of the time. As compared with Chautauqua, the Parliament was small, but its spirit was true to the Chautauqua ideal and it was maintained faithfully for ten or twelve years. The place had been established as a camp-meeting ground, but it shared the fate of many camp meetings in gradually growing into a summer resort for people in general. As cottages and cottagers increased the Chautauqua interest declined, and finally the attempt to maintain classes and meetings after the Chautauqua pattern was abandoned, and the island took its place among the summer colonies in that wonderful group.

The same year, 1876, saw another camp ground becoming a Chautauqua Assembly,—at Petoskey, near the northern end of Lake Michigan. Here a beautiful tract of woodland, rising in a series of terraces from Little Traverse Bay, about forty miles south of the Straits of Mackinac, had been obtained by a Methodist camp-meeting association, and laid out in roads forming a series of concentric circles. Here the first Bay View Assembly was held in 1876, and again in its scope were combined the camp meeting, the summer home, and the Chautauqua conception, three divergent aims that have rarely worked well together. It will be remembered that on its land side the original Chautauqua was shut off from the outer world by a high fence, and everybody was compelled to enter the ground through a gate, at which a ticket must be purchased. At Bay View, as at most camp-meeting grounds, access was open on every side. At first they undertook to support the Assembly by collections, but the receipts proved inadequate, and they placed a ticket window at each lecture hall and endeavored to induce the cottagers to purchase season tickets, a plan which has been pursued down to the present time. One of the founders of Bay View, perhaps the one who suggested it, was Dr. Wm. H. Perrine, an ardent and intelligent Chautauquan, the rebuilder of Palestine Park.

Other men came to the aid of the Bay View Assembly, some of them men of means, who gave liberally in the form of buildings, an organ, and to some extent an endowment. One of these was Mr. Horace Hitchcock of Detroit, another was John M. Hall, who organized the Bay View Reading Course, analagous to the C. L. S. C., and by his personal endeavor built up a reading and book-buying constituency. I was present at the second session in 1877, when it was a handful of people in a wilderness, and again thirty years later, when I found a beautiful city of homes in the forest, rising terrace above terrace, with good roads, fine public buildings, and a body of people interested in the best thought of the time. Chautauqua points with pleasure and pride to her oldest living daughter, the Bay View Assembly.

Mention should be made here of an Assembly established at Clear Lake, beside a beautiful sheet of water in northern Iowa, nearly midway between the Mississippi and Missouri Rivers. It was organized in 1876, with the Rev. J. R. Berry as superintendent. For some years, beginning in 1879, it was under the direction of the Rev. J. A. Worden, who, like some others of us, had learned the Assembly trade in apprenticeship to Dr. Vincent at Chautauqua. For ten years Clear

Lake was fairly prosperous, but in time it met the fate of most assemblies and dropped out of existence.

During the year 1877 three more Assemblies arose, one of which remains to this day in prosperity, while the two others soon passed away. The successful institution was at Lakeside, Ohio. Like many others, it was grafted upon a camp meeting which had been established some years before, but was declining in its interest and attendance. The name "Encampment" was chosen as an easy departure from its original sphere, but after a few years the name "Assembly," by this time becoming general, was assumed. The first meeting as a Sunday School gathering on the Chautauqua plan was held in 1877, with the Rev. James A. Worden, who had assisted Dr. Vincent for three years in the normal work at Chautauqua, as its conductor. Afterward Dr. B. T. Vincent was in charge for a number of seasons, and one year, 1882, Dr. John H. Vincent was superintendent. For many years all the Chautauqua features were kept prominent, the Normal Department, with a systematic course, examinations, and an Alumni Association; the C. L. S. C. with recognition services, Round Tables, camp fires, the four Arches, and all the accessories. Lakeside drew around it helpers and liberal givers, and still stands in strength. Lakeside has the benefit of a delightful location, on a wooded peninsula jutting into Lake Erie, near Sandusky City, and in sight of Put-in-Bay, famous in American history for Commodore Perry's naval victory in the War of 1812. It still maintains lecture courses and classes in the midst of a summer-home community.

Another Assembly began in 1877, with high expectations, at Lake Bluff overlooking Lake Michigan, thirty-five miles north of Chicago. It was confidently supposed that on a direct railroad line from the great city, Lake Bluff would draw large audiences, and Dr. Vincent was engaged to organize and conduct an Assembly upon the Chautauqua plan, with lecturers and workers from that headquarters. A strong program was prepared for the opening session. Among the lecturers was the Rev. Joseph Cook, at that time one of the most prominent and popular speakers in the land. I recall in one of his lectures at Lake Bluff a sentence, wholly unpremeditated, which thrilled the audience and has always seemed to me one of the most eloquent utterances I have ever heard. It was twelve years after the Civil War, and on our way to the Assembly we passed the marble monument crowned with the statue of

Stephen A. Douglas, the competitor of Lincoln for the Senatorship and Presidency, but after the opening of the war his loyal supporter for the few months before his death. Dr. Cook was giving a history of the forces in the nation which brought on the secession of the Southern States. He referred to Daniel Webster in the highest praise, declaring that his compromise measures, such as the Fugitive Slave Law, were dictated by a supreme love for the Union, which if preserved would in time have made an end of slavery, and he added a sentence of which this is the substance.

> Had it been given to Daniel Webster, as it was given to Edward Everett, to live until the guns were fired upon Fort Sumter, there would have been an end of compromise. He would have stamped that mighty foot with a sound that would have rung throughout the land, have called forth a million men, and might have averted the war!

Just then a voice rang out from one of the seats —"As Douglas did!" Joseph Cook paused a moment. His chest swelled as he drew in a breath, and then looking at the man who had interrupted him, he spoke in that powerful voice:

> The firmament above the massive brow of Daniel Webster was a vaster arch than that over the narrow

forehead of Stephen A. Douglas, and the lightning that rent the clouds from the dying face of one, would never have been needed to bring daylight to the other!

I was seated beside the Rev. Charles F. Deems of New York, a Southerner by birth and in his sympathies through the then recent war. He turned to me and said: "That was the most magnificent sentence that I have ever heard!" There was a moment of silence, and then a burst of applause from the audience.

The Lake Bluff Assembly never drew a large patronage, as no Chautauqua Assembly ever has which depended upon a great city whose inhabitants can hear the famous preachers and orators. The successful Assemblies have been located in fairly large towns, with villages and small cities surrounding, near enough to reach the Assembly, but so distant that to enjoy its benefits the visitors must stay more than one day. The support of a Chautauqua Assembly of the higher grade comes not mainly from the one-day excursionists, but from those who plan to enter the classes and remain at least a fortnight. These patrons constitute the backbone of the institution, and without them the transitory crowds soon lose their interest and the Assembly declines. Lake Bluff maintained an existence for ten or twelve years, but never obtained an extensive constituency.

The year 1878 was noteworthy in the establishment of two Assemblies, one still living after more than forty years, the other one of the largest, most steadfast in fidelity to the Chautauqua ideal, and most extended in its influence. The first of these was the Round Lake Assembly, at a camp ground near Saratoga in New York. We have narrated elsewhere (see page 44) the story of the "praying band leader" who undertook to hold a little meeting of his own at Chautauqua, and when called to order left in disgust, but later showed his manly spirit by asking Dr. Vincent to organize an Assembly on the Chautauqua plan on the grounds at Round Lake, of which camp meeting he was President. This Assembly began in 1878, and is still maintained both as a summer school, a camp meeting, and a Sunday School training institution. It was opened according to the Chautauqua pattern, with an evening of short speeches, of which some at least were supposed to blend humor with sense. Frank Beard was on the platform, and was expected to be the wit of the evening. To the blank perplexity of all, he made a serious speech, without a solitary funny allusion. The audience did not know whether to laugh or to look solemn, as he talked on, and at last brought us all "before the great white throne." The next morning at breakfast—for all the imported workers took our meals at one table in the Round Lake Hotel—Dr. Vincent freed his mind to Frank Beard, somewhat after this fashion:

> Now, Frank, I want you to understand that we bring you here to brighten up the program with a little fun. We don't need you to make serious speeches; there are plenty of men to do that; I can do it myself, a great deal better than you can. To-night I'm going to give you another chance, and I expect you to rise to the occasion with something to laugh at.

So, before the evening lecture, Dr. Vincent announced that Mr. Beard wished to say a few words. This was something of what he said:

> Dr. Vincent, he didn't like the speech I made last night. He told me this morning before all these fellers that it was too eloquent, and he said, "Mr. Beard, when you are eloquent you take the shine off from me, and these other men, and you mustn't do it. If there is any eloquence needed, I will do it myself, and you mustn't interfere with the regular program."

Then he went on, in his usual way, using some of the dear old jokes that some of us had heard at Chautauqua, but polished up for a new constituency. Everybody saw that he was guying the doctor, but there was a group of us present who knew just how Frank was twisting the breakfast talk of the Superintendent of Instruction.

On the shore of Round Lake, near the Assembly ground, a copy of Palestine Park had been constructed, and daily lectures were given there. It was just a few feet larger than the Park at Chautauqua, as we were informed by the President. Let me correct the report that a big Methodist bishop arriving late one night, and enquiring the way to the hotel, fell into the clutches of the most mischievous small boy in the region, who told him:

"The gates are all shut and you'll have to climb the fence yonder."

He did so, according to the story, and fell from the top of the fence into the Dead Sea, which at once swelled its waters and washed away the city of Jericho. The eminent divine, it is said, drenched with water and spattered with mud, walked up the Jordan Valley and over the mountains of Ephraim, destroying the cities and obliterating sundry holy places; one foot caught in Jacob's Well, and his head bumped on Mount Gerizim. He reached the hotel at last, but the next morning showed the land of Palestine in worse ruin than had been wrought by Nebuchadnezzar's army. All this I, myself, read in a New York newspaper that is said to contain "All the news that is fit to print"; but I here and now declare solemnly that there is not a shred of truth in the story, for I saw the Bishop, and I saw the Park!

The Round Lake meetings are held to this day, courses of lectures are given, and classes are held. But the Park of Palestine, which was to surpass Chautauqua's Park, is no more. It was built on swampy ground, after a few years sank under the encroaching waters of the lake, and was never restored.

The other institution founded in 1878 was the Kansas Chautauqua Assembly. It was organized by the Rev. J. E. Gilbert, then a pastor of a Methodist Church in Topeka, who was an active Sunday School worker and started other assemblies during his different pastorates in the Middle West. It was held for three years at Lawrence, then at Topeka for two years, and finally in 1883 located at Ottawa, about fifty miles southwest from Kansas City. Most of the Assemblies already named were held upon camp grounds, but the Ottawa Assembly was unique in its location upon the large Forest Park just outside the city, leased for this purpose by the authorities. Being public property, no cottages could be built upon it, but a city of three hundred tents arose every summer, and after a fortnight were folded and taken away. For nearly twenty years this Assembly was under the direction of the writer, and in every respect followed the lines laid down by its parent Chautauqua. Buildings were put up for classes, which served as well for the annual agricultural fair in the fall. In our first year at Ottawa, our normal class was held out of doors, the members seated upon the unroofed grand stand of the Park, and I was teaching them with the aid of a blackboard. Clouds began to gather rapidly and a storm seemed to be in prospect. I paused in the lesson and said:

"I am somewhat of a stranger here—how long does it take a thunder storm to arrive?"

"About two minutes!" responded a voice from the seats; and instantly there came a rush to cover, leaving the history of the Bible to care for itself. We were just in time, for a minute later it was blowing a hurricane, bending the great trees and breaking their branches. I had heard of Kansas cyclones, had been shown a "cyclone cellar," and only the day before had taken dinner in a house of which one end had been blown clean off by a cyclone. As we stood in a building which we had named "Normal Hall," I asked a lady by the window, "Is this a cyclone?" She glanced without and then calmly said: "No, this is a straight wind."

In ten minutes the tornado was over and we reassembled for the lesson. Kansas people seemed to accept occurrences like this as all in the day's work. One weather-story of Kansas reminds of another. On my first visit to that State in 1882, the last year of the Assembly at Topeka, I was standing in front of the hotel, thinking of the historic events in Kansas,—where the Civil War actually began, though unrealized at the time,—when I saw nearby a rather rough looking, bearded individual. Thinking that he might be one of the pioneers, with a story to tell of the early days, I stepped up and began in the conventional way by remarking:

"I don't think it's going to rain."

He looked me over and responded:

"Wal, strangers from the East think they know when it's goin' to rain and when it ain't; but us fellers who've lived in Kansas thirty years never know whether it'll rain in five minutes or whether it won't rain in three months."

The Ottawa Assembly was one of the best in the Chautauqua system. The people of the city built for its use a large tabernacle and halls for classes.

Beside the park flows the River Marais du Cygne, "the Swamp of the Swan," celebrated in one of Whittier's poems; and on a bank overlooking the river was erected a Hall of Philosophy, copying the old Hall at Chautauqua, except that its columns were lighter and ornamented, improving its appearance. We followed the Chautauqua programs as far as possible, having many of the same speakers on our platform and Professor Sherwin to lead the music, succeeded later by Dr. H. R. Palmer. The teacher-training work, then called the Normal Class, was maintained thoroughly, with adult, intermediate, and children's classes,—all wearing badges and following banners. The C. L. S. C., with all its usages of camp fires, Recognition Day, vigil, procession and arches, was kept prominent. We established a Chautauqua Boys' Club, and Girls' Club also. We could not conduct a summer school, as the meeting lasted only a fortnight, but we had lecture courses of high character upon literature. Kansas contained more old soldiers in its population than any other State in the Union, and the Grand Army Day at Ottawa was an event of State-wide interest. Some distinguished veterans spoke on these occasions, among them General John A. Logan, Major William McKinley, and General John B. Gordon of the Confederate Army; also Private A. J. Palmer of New York, whose "Company D, the Die-No-Mores," roused enthusiasm to its summit. One element in Ottawa's success was the steadfast loyalty of the city,—a place then of seven or eight thousand people, which enjoyed a special prohibitory law some years earlier than the rest of the State. Almost every family had its tent in Forest Park and lived there day and night during the fortnight of the meetings. Another cause of its prosperity was its able, broad, and continuous management. Its President for many years was the Rev. Duncan C. Milner, a Chautauquan from his boots up to his head, and laboring with untiring energy in its behalf.

I must tell an amusing story of our camp fire one summer. As the ground was by this time well occupied, we decided to have the bonfire on a raft out in the stream, while the crowd sang the songs and listened to the speeches from the Hall of Philosophy on the shore. But when we met at night for the services, the raft and the materials ready for lighting had disappeared! We were told that the janitor had thought it an improvement to have the fire lighted above, in a bend of the river, and float down to the Hall. We waited, not exactly pleased with the janitor's unauthorized action, and after a time we heard a mighty racket. The raft with the bonfire was floating down the stream, while around it was a convoy of about a hundred boats, loaded with boys, and each boy blowing a horn or yelling in the most vociferous manner. That put an end to any prospect of songs and speeches, for who could command silence to such a din? But that was not all nor the worst. The janitor tried in vain to anchor his raft, but it still floated downward. We saw our camp fire sail majestically down the river, until it approached the mill dam and the falls, when the boys desperately rowed their boats out of danger. Raft and contents went over the falls and the bonfire was quenched in the devouring flood. As we saw it going to its doom, I distinctly heard the word "dam" spoken, and I fear it was intended to include a final "n." But that was the last attempt at a camp fire. When I proposed one at the next season, the entire Round Table burst out with a roaring laugh.

The success of Ottawa led to the opening of many other Assemblies all over the State, and by degrees weakened this, the mother Chautauqua of Kansas. It is still maintained, but in a small way, as one of the chain Chautauquas.

In 1879, a Sunday School Congress which soon

grew into an Assembly was held at Ocean Grove, on the Atlantic Coast, almost the only place where the camp meeting, the summer resort, and the Chautauqua idea have lived together in mutual peace and prosperity. But even at Ocean Grove the Assembly has been overshadowed, almost out of sight, by the camp meeting and the summer boarding-house contingent. For several seasons I took part in the work, and in 1881 conducted the Children's Class. On the next to the last day I told all the children to meet me at our chapel, naming the hour when the tide would be at its lowest, every child to bring a pail and shovel, or a shingle, if his shovel had been lost. We formed a goodly procession of three hundred, marching down the avenue, myself at the head. At the beach I had selected a suitable area, and set the children to constructing out of the damp sand a model two hundred feet long of Palestine, the land of which we had been studying in the daily class. It was a sight to see those young nation builders, making the coastline, piling up the mountains, and digging out the Jordan valley with its lakes. Some Biblically inclined gentlemen aided in the supervision, and apparently a thousand people stood above and looked on. When it was finished I walked up and down the model, asking the children questions upon it, and was somewhat surprised to find how much they knew. Some whose conduct in the class gave little promise were among the promptest to exploit their knowledge. It was my purpose to leave the map that it might be seen by the multitude until the tide should wash it away. But the boys shouted, "Can't we stamp it down now?" and I rather reluctantly consented. Palestine has been overrun, and trodden down, and destroyed by armies of Assyrians, Babylonians, Turks, Crusaders, and many other warriors, but the land never suffered such a treading down by the Gentiles as on that morning at Ocean Grove.

In the year 1879, the wind-wafted seed of Chautauqua was borne to the Pacific Coast and an Assembly was founded at Pacific Grove in Monterey, California. I know not whether it remains, but the Grove has been the place of meeting for the California Methodist Conference year after year. Another Assembly combined with the summer resort was established this year at Mountain Lake in Maryland, a charming spot, whose elevation beside a lovely lake brings coolness to the summer air.

One more Assembly established in 1879 must not be forgotten. In the early years of Chautauqua we used to see a plainly clad man, who from his appearance might have been a farmer or a lumberman; in fact, he was the proprietor of a large saw and planing mill. This man was at every meeting, listened intently and took full notes, for he was intelligent, reading good books, and ardent in his devotion to Chautauqua. For years he was one of my friends, but, alas! I have forgotten his name. He lived in Northern Indiana, and in 1879 was able to interest enough people to start an Assembly at Island Park at Rome City, Indiana, not far from the Michigan line. He became its Secretary, managed its finances, and called upon the Rev. A. H. Gillet, one of Dr. Vincent's lieutenants, to conduct it. For many years Island Park was one of the foremost children of Chautauqua in its program and its attendance. It was situated upon an island in a lovely lake, with bridges leading to the mainland, where most of the tents and cottages were placed, and where buildings were erected for the normal classes and the kindergarten; the Tabernacle, seating 2500, being upon the island which was bright with flower beds amid winding paths. For years Island Park was a center of Chautauqua influence and strong in promoting the C. L. S. C., but like many other Assemblies, it failed to receive financial support and was abandoned.

Two great Assemblies, both closely following the path of Chautauqua, were founded in the year 1880. One of these was Monona Lake, near Madison, Wis. It was established by the State Sunday School Association, its founder and first president being the Hon. Elihu Colman of Fond du Lac. Like Ottawa in Kansas, it was an assembly of tents, not of cottages. The first session, a small gathering, was held in 1880 on the shores of Green Lake, one of the five hundred lakes of Wisconsin; but in the following year it was removed to Monona Lake, one of the five surrounding the capital city, Madison. After Mr. Colman, the Rev. F. S. Stein, D.D., became President, and for nearly a generation, Mr. Moseley, a bookseller of Madison, was its efficient secretary, business manager, and organizer of its programs. The standards of Monona Lake were high and its work was thorough, but for lack of adequate support, it was given up after nearly thirty years of usefulness and the point became an amusement park.

Among those prominent in the early seasons at Monona Lake was the Rev. O. P. Bestor, who was active in promoting the C. L. S. C. He brought with him his son, who began as a small boy attending the Assembly, and formed the assembly-habit so strongly that in the after years he grew up to be the President of the Chautauqua Institution—Albert E. Bestor, LL.D.

The other notable Chautauqua started in 1880 was the New England Assembly at South Framingham, Mass., originally in closer affiliation with the original Chautauqua than any other Assembly, for it chose Dr. Vincent as Superintendent of Instruction, and many of its speakers were also on the Chautauqua program. It drew from all the New England States, until its success led to the establishment of other Assemblies at Fryeburg, Maine, at Northampton, Mass., and at Plainville, Conn. One of Dr. Vincent's assistants at the Framingham Assembly was the Dr. A. E. Dunning, at first Congregational Secretary of Sunday School work, later Editor of the Congregationalist. Dr. Vincent, after a few years, gave the Assembly into the hands of Dr. Dunning and the writer, and sometimes we conducted it jointly; at other times in successive years. On an eminence overlooking the grounds and the adjoining lake arose another Hall of Philosophy, like the one at Chautauqua, and all the Chautauqua customs were followed—C. L. S. C., Normal Class, Children's Classes, and the rest. The first President was the Rev. William R. Clark, who was instrumental in locating the Assembly upon the ground of a camp meeting which it succeeded. It was continued for more than a generation, but at last succumbed to changing times. Perhaps it might have continued longer, if throughout its history it had not been encumbered by the debts of the former Camp Meeting Association.

Our chapter has already grown beyond bounds. We would like to tell the stories of Monteagle, Tennessee, of Mount Dora, Florida, of De Funiak Springs, also in Florida, of the Arkansas and Dakota and Southern California Assemblies. In fifteen years after Chautauqua began there were nearly a hundred Assemblies, each independent of all the others, yet all in friendly relation to the oldest and greatest of them all, the mother,—Chautauqua by the Lake.

## CHAPTER XXV

### YOUNGER DAUGHTERS OF CHAUTAUQUA

WE have seen how Chautauquas sprung up throughout the land, inspired by the example of the original Assembly beside the lake. All these were independent, arranging their own programs and securing their own speakers. Chautauqua never took a copyright upon the name or a patent for the idea. It was natural, however, for many of these Assemblies to combine their interests, for it soon found that half a dozen Chautauquas in the same section could save expenses by employing the same group of speakers and passing them on from one gathering to another. There were already lyceum bureaus offering lecturers and entertainers. At first the Assemblies secured a few of their speakers from these offices, and after a few years their entire programs were arranged in conjunction with the bureaus. Finally the lyceum agencies began to organize and conduct assemblies directly, and thus the Chautauqua circuit or the system of a Chautauqua chain was developed.

One office in Chicago, the Redpath Bureau, is said to conduct three thousand Chautauqua assemblies every year, others have charge of a thousand apiece, while there are lesser chains of fifty, twenty-five or a dozen assemblies. I have been officially informed that in the year 1919, ten thousand chain Chautauquas were held in the United States and Canada. They are to be found everywhere, but their most popular field is in the Middle West, where "the Chautauqua" is expected every year by the farming communities. These bureaus and the "talent" which they employ have been combined in an organization for mutual interest, to avoid reduplication in the same locality, to secure their workers and arrange their programs. This is named the International Lyceum and Chautauqua Association, holding an annual convention at which the organizers and the participants upon the programs come face to face and form their engagements. The circuit system has arisen largely through economic causes; the saving of expense by efficient organization, the elimination of long railroad jumps from Assembly to Assembly, guarantee of continuous engagement to attractive speakers, better publicity, and the concentration of responsibility. It is found that the most successful Chautauquas are held, not in cities, nor even in large towns, but in the smaller places. The town of a thousand, or even one as small as five hundred inhabitants, during its annual Chautauqua week will rally from the farms and hamlets two thousand people to hear a popular lecture, five or seven thousand during the week. In each place an advance agent appears, interviews the business men, the ministers, and the heads of any clubs or improvement societies, and obtains pledges of support by the sale of a definite number of tickets. College boys make up the tent crews; a Scout Master organizes the Boy Scouts; and trained experts arrange for the advertising. The "morning-hour men" give lectures in courses of uplifting nature on civic and national questions; the popular features of the program are supplied by entertainers, musical troupes, bands, artists, and dramatic companies. It is a fact of deeper significance than many recognize that political leaders find here the greatest forum for their messages. Many of these orators receive more than fees for their speeches; they come near the heart of the people, they reach their constituencies and disseminate their views more widely than through any other agency. Some political reformers have won not only prominence, but power through these chain Chautauquas.

It may be remembered that while the Hon. William Jennings Bryan was Secretary of State he received some criticism and even ridicule for "hitting the Chautauqua trail" and "going off with the yodelers." On that subject the *Baltimore Sun* said in an editorial:

If it could be demonstrated, we would be willing to wager that the average Chautauqua student has a far better knowledge of public questions than the average of those who sneer. And whether he likes it or not, no public official of to-day can afford to disregard the Chautauqua movement.

Mr. Bryan himself gave this testimony in the *Review of Reviews:*

The Chautauqua affords one of the best opportunities now presented a public speaker for the discussion of questions of interest to the people. The audience is a select one, always composed of the thoughtful element in the community, and as they pay admission, they stay to hear. I believe that a considerable part of the progress that is now being made along the line of moral and political reform is traceable to the influence of the Chautauqua.

A writer in *The Outlook* (September 18, 1918) says:

I have studied the Chautauqua speakers. They command the admiration of the honest critic. They deal with serious subjects as experts. They carry men, women and children on to the conclusion of the longest lecture by knowing when to lighten at the proper moment with a story or a lilt of humor, or sometimes a local reference. Said a village woman in my hearing of a fellow-speaker on the problems of patriotism, "I thought at first he would be hard to follow, but I surely hated when he had to stop." The thermometer was reported to be 105° in the tent. The speaker held the rapt attention of the people for an hour and a half in a philosophical presentation of the causes of the war and our responsibilities in consequence. It was like reading a solid book and condensing it with marked success into one hearing. It was typical, and twenty millions are reported to be listening to such addresses in Chautauqua tents the country over.

In the magazine *The World To-Day* (September, 1911), I read the following by George L. Flude:

A few years ago I saw Senator Robert M. La Follette address a crowd of eight thousand people at Waterloo, Iowa. For two hours and a half he jammed insurgent Republicanism into that crowd. He was at that time the only insurgent in the party and had not been named yet. The crowd took it all in. They were there to be instructed, not to hear a partisan speech. Hence their attitude, regardless of party affiliation, was a receptive one. He absolutely converted that crowd into insurgents and they did not know it. For five years La Follette crammed and jammed "non-partisan" talks into Chautauqua crowds through Iowa, Illinois, Missouri, Ohio, Nebraska, and Kansas. The average audience was probably about four thousand and he met sixty or more audiences each summer; 240,000 people inoculated with insurgency by one man.

Occasionally an audience finds that the lecture is not what was looked for. Some years ago a Western Assembly engaged Senator La Follette, and from the list of his subjects chose "The World's Greatest Tragedy," expecting a sensational attack upon the greed of capitalists. A great crowd assembled to see "Senator Bob jump on the trusts." He gave his well-known literary lecture on *Hamlet*, a critical appreciation, without a word on current affairs. The crowd sat, first puzzled, then baffled, and at last went away dejected.

A newspaper of wide circulation, *The Christian Science Monitor*, said:

By far the most active and keenly interested voters of the country, with their leaders, forceful in shaping progressive legislation, have come during the last decade from States where this Chautauqua method of cultivation of the adult population has been most steadily used, and the end is not yet, since now the system is being organized in a thorough-going way never known before. Public men, educators, artists, authors, pioneers in discovery of unknown lands or of secrets of nature, who get the ear of this huge audience season after season, come nearer to the heart of the nation and observe its ways of living better than by any other method.

The old mother Chautauqua by the Lake would not like to be held responsible for all the utterances under the tents of her ten thousand daughters. For that matter, she would not endorse everything spoken upon her own platform in the Amphitheater, where "free speech" is the motto and the most contradictory opinions are presented. But she must recognize that her daughters have wielded a mighty power in forming the political and moral convictions of the nation.

The bell which rang at Fair Point on August 4, 1874, to open the first Assembly, might be compared to "The shot heard 'round the world" from Concord Bridge in 1775, for in answer to its call ten thousand Chautauquas have arisen on the American Continent. The question might be asked, Why have none of the ten thousand rivaled the first, the original Chautauqua?

Many of these opened with a far better outfit of external accommodations, with more money expended upon their programs, with greater advertising publicity, with more popular attractions. Yet now at the period of almost fifty years, not another among the ten thousand, either of the earlier or the later Assemblies, holds a two months' program, conducts courses of study of a wide range, or brings together even one quarter of the assemblage which every year gathers upon the old Chautauqua ground. All the assemblies which were established with the highest promise have either been abandoned or are continued as chain Chautauquas, meeting for a week only. Let us endeavor to answer the question—Why does the mother-Chautauqua still stand supreme?

In the judgment of this writer, who has known Chautauqua almost from the beginning, and has taken part in fifty similar gatherings, the reasons for its supremacy are easily seen and stated. It was established by two men of vision, one of whom was also a practical man of business, and both men of high ideals which they never lowered and from which they and their successors have never swerved. In its plans from first to last, there was a unique blending of religion, education, and recreation. No one of these three elements has been permitted to override the two others, and neither of them has been sacrificed to win popularity, although on the other side, popular features have been sought for within just limits. Never has the aim of Chautauqua been to make money; it has had no dividends and no stockholders. It has opened avenues and leased lots to hundreds of people, but it has not sought financial gain. Neither of its Founders nor any of their associates have been enriched by it, for all profits—when there have been any—have been expended upon improvements or enlargement of plans. It has shown the progressive spirit, while firm in its principles, open to new ideas, willing to listen to both sides of every question. It has sought to attract and to benefit all classes in the community, not setting the poor against the rich, nor the rich against the poor, giving a welcome to scholars of every view and to churches of every doctrine. It has maintained a continuous, consistent administration, fortunate in finding able and broad-minded men to carry forward the conceptions of its founders. Few changes have been made in its management and these have been without a revolution or a renunciation of principles. Men at the head have changed, but not the policy of the institution. It has remained unshaken in its loyalty to the Christian religion and penetrated through and through with the Christian spirit, without flying the flag or wearing the badge of any one denomination of Christians. These have been the principles that placed Chautauqua at the front in its beginning and have kept it at the front through forty-eight years.

# APPENDIX

## DISTINGUISHED PREACHERS AT CHAUTAUQUA

Dr. Lyman Abbott
Dr. Charles F. Aked
Rev. Hugh Black
Bishop C. H. Brent
Bishop F. S. Bristol
Bishop Phillips Brooks
Dean Charles R. Brown
Prof. Sylvester Burnham
Bishop William Burt
Dr. S. Parkes Cadman
Rev. Francis E. Clark
Rev. R. H. Conwell
Bishop R. Cleveland Cox
Rev. T. L. Cuyler
Dr. E. W. Donald
Dr. Daniel Dorchester
Rev. Samuel A. Eliot
Bishop Samuel Fallows
Pres. W. H. P. Faunce
Dr. Harry Emerson Fosdick
Bishop Cyrus W. Foss
Bishop Charles H. Fowler
Dr. James A. Francis
Dr. Washington Gladden
Bishop D. A. Goodsell
Dr. George A. Gordon
Dr. F. W. Gunsaulus
Dr. John Hall
Dr. N. D. Hillis
Dr. P. S. Henson
Dean George Hodges
Bishop E. E. Hoss
Rev. Lynn Hough
Bishop Edwin H. Hughes
Dr. Charles E. Jefferson
Bishop A. W. Leonard
Dr. R. S. MacArthur
Dr. A. Mackenzie
Pres. W. D. Mackenzie
Bishop F. J. McConnell
Bishop W. F. McDowell
Dr. W. P. Merrill
Bishop C. B. Mitchell
Chaplain W. H. Milburn
Dr. Philip S. Moxom

Bishop W. F. Oldham
Bishop J. T. Peck
Bishop H. C. Potter
Rev. G. A. Johnston Ross
Bishop Matthew Simpson
Dr. T. DeWitt Talmage
Bishop Boyd Vincent
Bishop John H. Vincent
Bishop W. D. Walker
Bishop H. W. Warren
Bishop Herbert Welch
Dr. H. L. Willett
Bishop C. D. Williams
Dr. C. F. Wishart
Dr. Cornelius Woelfkin
Rabbi Louis Wolsey

## COLLEGE PRESIDENTS AND OTHER EDUCATORS

Prof. Herbert B. Adams
Pres. E. B. Andrews
Pres. J. B. Angell
Prof. H. T. Bailey
Pres. J. H. Barrows
Prof. B. P. Bowne
Prof. H. H. Boyesen
Prof. P. H. Boynton
Pres. E. B. Bryan
Pres. N. M. Butler
Com. E. E. Brown
Pres. J. H. Carlisle
Com. P. P. Claxton
Prof. A. S. Cook
Pres. W. H. Crawford
Prof. M. L. D'Ooge
Prof. A. S. Draper
Pres. C. W. Eliot
Prof. R. T. Ely
Pres. John Finley
Prof. Alcee Fortier
Pres. W. G. Frost
Pres. C. C. Hall
Pres. G. Stanley Hall
Pres. W. R. Harper
Dr. W. T. Harris
Prof. A. B. Hart
Mr. Walter L. Hervey
Prof. Mark Hopkins
Mr. James L. Hughes
Prof. William James
Pres. D. S. Jordan
Pres. Henry C. King
Prof. C. F. Lavell
Pres. H. N. MacCracken
Dean Shailer Mathews
Pres. J. E. McFadyen
Pres. Edward Olson
Mrs. Alice F. Palmer
Prof. George M. Palmer

Col. Francis W. Parker
Prof. F. G. Peabody
Pres. A. V. V. Raymond
Pres. B. P. Raymond
Pres. Rush Rhees
Pres. J. G. Schurman
Pres. Julius H. Seelye
Prof. Thomas D. Seymour
Prof. Morse Stephens
Pres. E. E. Sparks
Pres. C. F. Thwing
Prof. Moses C. Tyler
Dr. Herman Von Holst
Pres. Booker T. Washington
Prof. L. A. Weigle
Pres. B. I. Wheeler
Pres. C. D. Wright

## AUTHORS AND EDITORS

Dr. Lyman Abbott
Mrs. G. R. Alden (Pansy)
Mr. Norman Angell
Mr. John K. Bangs
Prof. Earl Barnes
Rabbi H. Berkowitz
Mr. John G. Brooks
Dr. J. M. Buckley
Mr. Richard Burton
Mr. Geo. W. Cable
Mr. Ralph Connor
Mr. G. Willis Cooke
Rev. S. McChord Crothers
Dr. W. J. Dawson
Prof. Henry Drummond
Dr. A. E. Dunning
Mr. John Fiske
Mr. John Fox
Mr. Hamlin Garland
Mr. H. A. Gibbons
Rabbi R. J. H. Gottheil
Mr. John T. Graves
Rabbi Moses Gries
Mr. Edward H. Griggs
Dr. Edward E. Hale
Mr. Norman Hapgood
Col. T. W. Higginson
Dr. R. S. Holmes
Mr. Hamilton W. Mabie
Mr. S. S. McClure
Mr. Donald G. Mitchell
Dr. R. G. Moulton
Mr. Thomas Nelson Page
Rear Admiral Peary
Prof. Bliss Perry
Miss Agnes Repplier
Mr. E. J. Ridgway
Mr. J. Whitcomb Riley

Mr. E. Thompson Seton
Mr. Elliott F. Shepard
Prof. E. E. Slosson
Judge A. W. Tourgee
Dr. Leon H. Vincent
Gen. Lew Wallace
Dr. Wm. Hayes Ward
Mr. Henry Watterson
Mrs. Kate D. Wiggin
Prof. C. T. Winchester

## LEADERS IN SOCIAL REFORM

Miss Jane Addams
Miss Susan B. Anthony
Mrs. Mary Antin
Mrs. Maude B. Booth
Mrs. Carrie C. Catt
Hon. Everett Colby
Mr. Anthony Comstock
Dr. Kate B. Davis
Mr. W. R. George
Mr. John B. Gough
Mrs. Julia Ward Howe
Judge Ben B. Lindsey
Mrs. Lucia A. Mead
Mr. John Mitchell
Prof. Scott Nearing
Mr. Thomas M. Osborne
Prof. Francis Peabody
Mrs. P. V. Pennybacker
Mr. Jacob A. Riis
Mr. Raymond Robins
Rev. Anna H. Shaw
Prof. E. A. Steiner
Rev. Charles Stetzle
Mr. J. G. Phelps Stokes
Mrs. Rose Pastor Stokes
Dr. Josiah Strong
Prof. Graham Taylor
Commander Booth-Tucker
Mrs. Booth Tucker
Hon. Robert Watchorn
Miss Francis E. Williard
Mr. Robert Woods
Mr. John G. Woolley
Prof. Charles Zeublin

## POLITICAL LEADERS

Pres. U. S. Grant
Pres. R. B. Hayes
Pres. J. A. Garfield
Pres. Wm. McKinley
Pres. Theodore Roosevelt
Pres. W. H. Taft
Hon. Geo. W. Alger
Gen. Russell A. Alger
Gov. G. W. Atkinson
Mrs. George Bass

Gov. J. A. Beaver
Gen. John C. Black
Hon. W. J. Bryan
Gov. Geo. A. Carlson
Hon. Schuyler Colfax
Lieut. Gov. L. S. Chanler
Senator J. P. Dolliver
Gov. Joseph W. Folk
Gen. John B. Gordon
Gov. H. S. Hadley
Hon. Murat Halstead
Senator M. A. Hanna
Miss Mary Garrett Hay
Gov. F. W. Higgins
Gen. O. O. Howard
Gov. C. E. Hughes
Judge W. T. Jerome
Gov. R. M. LaFollette
Gen. John A. Logan
Mayor J. P. Mitchel
Gov. B. B. Odell
Gov. R. E. Pattison
Hon. W. H. Prendergast
Gov. E. S. Stuart
Gov. R. L. Taylor
Hon. G. W. Wickersham
Gen. Leonard Wood

## DISTINGUISHED FOREIGNERS

The Earl of Aberdeen
The Countess of Aberdeen
Hon. Percy Alden
Canon S. A. Barnett
Rev. Joseph A. Beet
Ram Chandra Bose
The Right Hon. James Bryce
Rev. R. J. Campbell
Sir Chentung Lieng Chang
Mrs. L. Ormiston Chant
Dr. Marcus Dods
Prof. Henry Drummond
Mr. W. Aver Duncan
Principal A. M. Fairbairn
Mr. J. G. Fitch
Prof. T. R. Glover
The Bishop of Hereford
Mrs. Forbes-Robertson Hall
Prof. J. Stoughton Holborn
Prince Larazovich Hreblianovich
Charles Rann Kennedy
Prof. J. P. Mahaffy
Prof. Boni Maury
Rev. Mark Guy Pearse
Rev. Dr. Percival (Rugby)

Prof. William M. Ramsay
Mr. Owen Seaman
Rev. W. O. Simpson
Dr. George Adam Smith
Mrs. Philip Snowden
Lady Henry Somerset
Miss Kate Stevens
The Baroness Von Suttner
Rev. W. L. Watkinson

## CHAUTAUQUA RECOGNITION DAY ORATIONS

| | | |
|---|---|---|
| 1882 | Bishop H. W. Warren | "Brain and Heart" |
| '83 | Dr. Lyman Abbott | "The Democracy of Learning" |
| '84 | Dr. W. C. Wilkinson | "Literature as a Good of Life" |
| '85 | Dr. E. E. Hale | "Questions and Answers" |
| '86 | Pres. J. H. Carlisle | "Redeeming the Time" |
| '87 | Dr. J. T. Duryea | "The True Culture" |
| '88 | Bishop H. W. Warren | "The Possibilities of Culture" |
| '89 | Dr. David Swing | "The Beautiful and the Useful" |
| '90 | Mrs. Alice F. Palmer | "Education is Life" |
| '91 | Mrs. Mary A. Livermore | "The Highest Aristocracy" |
| '92 | Dr. F. W. Gunsaulus | "The Ideal of Culture" |
| '93 | Dr. Joseph Cook | "Columnar Truths in Scripture" |

| | | |
|---|---|---|
| 94 | Dr. E. E. Hale | "The Education of a Prince" |
| '95 | Dr. H. W. Mabie | "Literature as a Resource" |
| '96 | Pres. C. W. Eliot | "America's Contribution to Civilization" |
| '97 | Dr. J. F. Goucher | "Individualism" |
| '98 | Bishop J. H. Vincent | "The Chautauqua Idea" |
| '99 | Gov. G. W. Atkinson | "Modern Educational Requirements" |
| '00 | Pres. A. V. V. Raymond | "Education in its Relation to Life" |
| '01 | Pres. E. B. Andrews | "Problems of Greater America" |
| '02 | Mr. E. H. Griggs | "The Use of the Margin" |
| '03 | Hon. W. T. Harris | "University and School Extension as Supported by the Church" |
| '04 | Mr. E. H. Griggs | "Self-Culture Through the Vocation" |
| '05 | Miss Jane Addams | "Work and Play as Factors in Education" |
| '06 | Mr. E. H. Griggs | "Public Education and the Problem of Democracy" |

| | | |
|---|---|---|
| '07 | Pres. E. H Hughes | "Knowledge and Power" |
| '08 | Pres. H. C. King | "Revelation of Personality" |
| '09 | Pres. W. H. P. Faunce | "Ideals of Modern Education" |
| '10 | Mr. E. H. Griggs | "Literature and Culture" |
| '11 | Dr. G. E. Vincent | "The Larger Selfishness" |
| '12 | Dr. Earl Barnes | "Being Born Again" |
| '13 | Prof. S. C. Schmucker | "What Next?" |
| '14 | Dean Shailer Mathews | "Vocations and Avocations" |
| '15 | Pres. E. B. Bryan | "Who are Good Citizens?" |
| '16 | Mr. E. H. Griggs | "World-War and Ethics" |
| '17 | Dr. G. E. Vincent | "The Meaning of America" |
| '18 | Bishop F. J. McConnell | "Ideals of Leadership" |
| '19 | Bishop C. H. Brent | "The Opportunities of the Mind" |
| '20 | Dr. L. Howard Mellish | "The Way into Life's Greater Values" |

## CLASS DIRECTORY, CHAUTAUQUA HOME READING CIRCLES—C. L. S. C.

---

### Class 1882, "The Pioneers"

Motto—"From Height to Height."
Emblem—The hatchet.
President—J. L. Hurlburt, Bloomfield, N. J.
Secretary—Miss May E. Wightman, 238 Main St., Pittsburgh, Pa.
Treasurer—Mrs. L. J. Harter, Chautauqua, N. Y.

### Class 1883, "The Vincents"

Motto—"Step by step, we gain the height."
Emblem—The sweet pea.
President—Mrs. Thos. Alexander, Franklin, Pa.
Secretary—Miss Anne Hitchcock, Burton, O.
Treasurer—Miss M. J. Perrine, Chautauqua, N. Y.

### Class 1884, "The Irrepressibles"

Motto—"Press forward, he conquers who will."
Emblem—The golden rod.
President—Miss Anna McDonald, 630 Magnolia Ave., Long Beach, Calif.
Treasurer—Mr. F. A. Kinsley, 461 Ashland Ave., Buffalo, N. Y.
Secretary-Trustee—Mrs. Lizzie Wilcox, Chautauqua, N. Y.

### Class 1885, "The Invincibles"

Motto—"Press on, reaching after those things which are before."
Emblem—The heliotrope.

President—Mr. E. C. Dean, Delphi, N. Y.
Secretary-Treasurer—Mrs. T. J. Bentley, Springboro, Pa.

**Class 1886, "The Progressives"**

Motto—"We study for light to bless with light."
Emblem—The aster.
President—Miss Sara Soule, Chautauqua, N. Y.
Secretary—Mrs. M. V. Rowley, 112 Vassar St., Cleveland, O.
Treasurer—Miss Lucy Woodwell, 25 Indiana Ave., Somerville, Mass.
Trustee—Dr. Ili Long, 1339 Main St., Buffalo, N. Y.

**Class 1887, "The Pansy"**

Motto—"Neglect not the gift that is within thee."
Emblem—The pansy.
President—Mr. H. E. Barrett, Syracuse, N. Y.
Secretary—Miss Alice M. Bentley, Meadville, Pa.
Treasurer—Miss Letitia Flocker, Evergreen Road, R. F. D., N. S., Pittsburgh, Pa.
Trustee—Miss Adell Clapp, Chautauqua, N. Y.

**Class 1888, "The Plymouth Rock"**

Motto—"Let us be seen by our deeds."
Emblem—The geranium.
President—Mr. G. W. Bartlett, Hamburg, N. Y.
Secretary-Treasurer—Miss Agnes S. Chalmers, Amsterdam, N. Y.
Trustee—Mr. G. W. Bartlett, Hamburg, N. Y.

**Class 1889, "The Argonauts"**

Motto—"Knowledge unused for the good of others is more vain than unused gold."

Emblem—The daisy.
President—Rev. J. E. Rudisill, Columbus, O.
Secretary—Mrs. Mary C. Morris, Point Pleasant, N. J.
Treasurer—Mrs. D. F. Emery, Greenville, Pa.
Trustee—Rev. C. C. Creegan, Marietta, O.

### Class 1890, "The Pierians"

Motto—"Redeeming the time."
Emblem—The tube rose.
President—Rev. J. R. Morris, Homer City, Pa.
Secretary-Treasurer-Trustee—Miss Ada Benner, 5512 Center Ave., Pittsburgh, Pa.

### Class 1891, "The Olympians"

Motto—"So run that ye may obtain."
Emblem—The laurel and the white rose.
President—Mrs. George T. Guernsey, Independence, Kans.
Secretary-Treasurer—Miss Marie A. Daniels, New Britain, Conn.
Trustee—Mrs. George T. Guernsey, Independence Kans.

### Class 1892, "Columbia"

Motto—"Seek and ye shall find."
Emblem—The carnation.
President—Mrs. Clara L. McCray, Bradford, Pa.
Secretary—Miss Annie E. Jackson, Port Deposit, Md
Treasurer—Mrs. Chas. B. Adams, Zanesville, O.
Trustee—Mrs. Clara L. McCray, Bradford, Pa.

### Class 1893, "The Athenians"

Motto—"Study to be what you wish to seem."
Emblem—The acorn.

President—Mrs. J. J. Matthews, 623 N. Negley Ave., Pittsburgh, Pa.
Secretary-Treasurer—Mrs. Nettie C. Rice, Ebensburgh, Pa.
Trustee—Prof. Thomas H. Paden, New Concord, O.

**Class 1894, "The Philomatheans"**

Motto—"Ubi mel, ibi apes."
Emblem—The clover.
President—Dr. A. C. Ellis, Oil City, Pa.
Secretary-Treasurer-Trustee—Mrs. Sanford Lynn Porter, Chautauqua, N. Y.

**Class 1895, "The Pathfinders"**

Motto—"Truth will make you free."
Emblem—The nasturtium.
President—Mrs. George P. Hukill, Franklin, Pa.
Treasurer—Mrs. E. L. Ploss, Chautauqua, N. Y.
Secretary-Trustee—Miss Catherine Lawrence, 610 E. 23rd St., Brooklyn, N. Y.

**Class 1896, "The Truth-Seekers"**

Motto—"Truth is eternal."
Emblem—The forget-me-not. The Greek lamp.
President—Mrs. Margaret A. Seaton, 1943 E. 86th St., Cleveland, O.
Secretary-Treasurer—Miss Emily A. Birchgard, 1826 Penrose Ave., Cleveland, O.
Trustee—Mr. John R. Connor, Chautauqua, N. Y.

**Class 1897, "The Romans"**

Motto—"Veni, Vidi, Vici."
Emblem—The ivy.

President—Mrs. Harriet M. Dunn, Brooklyn, Mich.
Secretary-Treasurer—Mrs. Anna Heilman, Greenville, Pa.
Trustee—Mrs. Harriet M. Dunn, Brooklyn, Mich.

**Class 1898, "The Laniers"**

Motto—"The humblest life that lives may be divine."
Emblem—The violet.
President—Mrs. G. E. Tanner, Chautauqua, N. Y.
Secretary-Treasurer-Trustee—Miss Fannie B. Collins, Grandview, O.

**Class 1899, "The Patriots"**

Motto—"Fidelity, Fraternity."
Emblem—The flag.
President—Mrs. E. E. Sparks, 444 Macon St., Brooklyn, N. Y.
Secretary—Mrs. M. Barnard, 1637 E. 66th St., Cleveland, O.
Treasurer—Mrs. J. V. Ritts, Butler, Pa.
Trustee—Mrs. Ella Richards, Chautauqua, N. Y.

**Class 1900, "The Nineteenth Century"**

Motto—"Faith in the God of Truth; hope for the unfolding centuries; charity toward all endeavor."
Emblem—The evergreen.
President—Mrs. J. H. Montgomery, Chautauqua, N. Y.
Secretary-Treasurer—Mrs. L. B. Watts, 5740 Cabanna Ave., St. Louis, Mo.
Trustee—Mrs. J. H. Montgomery, Chautauqua, N. Y.

**Class 1901, "The Twentieth Century"**

Motto—"Light, Love, Life."
Emblem—The palm.
President—Mrs. Lucy Mendell George, Wellsburg, W. Va.
Secretary—Miss Elizabeth J. Steward, Westwood, N. J.
Treasurer—Mrs. Clara Lawrence, 610 E. 23rd St., Brooklyn, N. Y.
Trustee—Miss Margaret Hackley, Georgetown, Ky.

**Class 1902, "The Altrurians"**

Motto—"Not for self, but for all."
Emblem—Golden glow.
President—Mrs. J. A. Walker, Brownwood, Tex.
Secretary-Treasurer-Trustee—Miss Frances Davidson, Chautauqua, N. Y.

**Class 1903, "The Quarter Century"**

Motto—"What is excellent is permanent."
Emblem—The cornflower.
President—Mr. Edward E. Sparks, 444 Macon St., Brooklyn, N. Y.
Secretary—Miss Ida M. Quimby, 20 Spring St., East Orange, N. J.
Treasurer—Miss Evelyn Dewey, 20 Spring St., East Orange, N. J.
Trustee—Mr. Edward E. Sparks, 444 Macon St., Brooklyn, N. Y.

**Class 1904, "Lewis Miller"**

Motto—"The horizon widens as we climb."
Emblem—Clematis.

President—Mrs. Laura Johnston, 30 W. 4th St., Oil City, Pa.
Secretary-Treasurer—Miss Louise Nicholson, 89 Union St., Blue Island, Ill.
Trustee—Miss Grace E. Beck, 424 Mahoning St., Monongahela, Pa.

**Class 1905, "The Cosmopolitan"**

Motto—"A man's reach should exceed his grasp."
Emblem—The cosmos.
President—Dr. James Babbitt, Philadelphia, Pa.
Secretary-Treasurer—Mrs. J. J. Bowden, Johnstown, Pa.
Trustee—Miss Minnie Edgerton, 104 Prospect Ave., Buffalo, N. Y.

**Class 1906, "John Ruskin"**

Motto—"To love light and seek knowledge."
Emblem—Easter lily.
President—Mrs. Theo. Hall, Jr., Ashtabula, O.
Secretary-Treasurer-Trustee—Miss Irena Roach, Box 126, Round Lake, N. Y.

**Class 1907, "George Washington"**

Motto—"The aim of education is character."
Emblem—The scarlet salvia.
President—Mrs. Geo. Coblentz, 1045 W. 9th St., Erie, Pa.
Secretary-Treasurer—Mrs. A. H. Marvin, Oberlin, O.
Trustee—Miss Rannie Webster, Chautauqua, N. Y.

**Class 1908, "Tennyson"**

Motto—"To strive, to seek, to find, to yield."
Emblem—The red rose.

President—Prof. Samuel C. Schmucker, West Chester, Pa.
Secretary-Treasurer-Trustee—Miss Sarah E. Ford 169 Court St., Binghamton, N. Y.

### Class 1909, "Dante"

Motto—"On and fear not."
Emblem—The grapevine.
President—Mrs. O. B. Shallenberger, Beaver, Pa.
Secretary-Treasurer—Mrs. Hiram J. Baldwin, Falconer, N. Y.
Trustee—Mrs. Thos. B. Hill, Chautauqua, N. Y.

### Class 1910, "Gladstone"

Motto—"Life is a great and noble calling."
Emblem—The beech.
President—Miss Nannie S. Stockett, Annapolis, Md.
Secretary—Mr. James Bird, 1028 Ann St., Parkersburg, W. Va.
Treasurer—Mr. J. J. McWilliams, 11500 Euclid Ave., Cleveland, O.

### Class 1911, "Longfellow"

Motto—"Act, act in the living present."
Emblem—The young Hiawatha and the hydrangea.
President—Mrs. M. L. Chattin, Temple, Tex.
Secretary—Mrs. Effa Brown, McKeesport, Pa.
Treasurer—Mrs. L. B. Yale, Chautauqua, N. Y.
Trustee—Mrs. Walter King, 323 W. 83rd St., New York City.

### Class 1912, "Shakespeare"

Motto—"To thine own self be true."
Emblem—Eglantine.

President—Mrs. S. F. Clarke, 4th St., Freeport, Pa.
Secretary—Miss M. E. Phillips, Marion, Ala.
Treasurer-Trustee—Mrs. S. F. Clarke, 4th St., Freeport, Pa.

**Class 1913, "Athene"**

Motto—"Self-reverence, self-knowledge, self-control, these three alone lead life to sovereign power."
Emblem—The owl.
President—Rev. W. C. McKnight, Birmingham, Mich.
Secretary—Mr. Robert Adams, Warren, Pa.
Treasurer—Mrs. Alice J. McKnight, Birmingham, Mich.
Trustee—Mrs. J. H. Knepper, 924 Michigan Ave., Buffalo, N. Y.

**Class 1914, "Dickens"**

Motto—"The voice of time cries to man, 'Advance.'"
Emblem—Wild rose.
President—Prof. Chas. E. Rhodes, 507 Potomac Ave., Buffalo, N. Y.
Secretary—Miss Rose Webster, Chautauqua, N. Y.
Treasurer-Trustee—Miss Eleanor Clark, 1101 King Ave., Pittsburgh, Pa.

**Class 1915, "Jane Addams"**

Motto—"Life more abundant."
Emblem—American laurel.
President—Mr. W. H. Hamlin, Tougaloo, Miss.
Secretary-Treasurer—Mrs. A. F. B. Morris, 6716 Thomas Bldg., Pittsburgh, Pa.
Trustee—Mrs. Ida B. Cole, Chautauqua, N. Y.

**Class 1916, "The Internationals"**

Motto—"Knowledge maketh all mankind akin."
Emblem—The holly.
President—Miss Laura Hamilton, Chautauqua, N. Y.
Secretary-Treasurer-Trustee—Miss Amelia H. Bumstead, St. Petersburg, Fla.

**Class 1917, "Emerson"**

Motto—"Let us know the truth."
Emblem—The cat-tail.
President—Mrs. John Orr, Hotel San Remo, New York City.
Secretary—Mrs. T. D. Samford, Opelika, Ala.
Treasurer—Mr. Louis H. Walden, Norwich, Conn
Trustee—Mrs. O. G. Franks, Chautauqua, N. Y.

**Class 1918, "The Arthurians"**

Motto—"Live pure, speak true, right the wrong, follow the King."
Emblem—The gladiolus
President—Miss Emma T. McIntyre, Eustis, Fla.
Secretary—Miss Margaret M. Chalmers, Hagaman, N. Y.
Treasurer-Trustee—Mrs. Chas. E. Rhodes, 507 Potomac Ave., Buffalo, N. Y.

**Class 1919, "America"**

Motto—"Peace and Democracy."
Emblem—The American Beauty rose.
President—Mrs. S. E. Booth, 700 N. Harrison Ave., Wilmington, Del.

Secretary—Mrs. Ethel M. Vanderburger, 70 Melrose St., Rochester, N. Y.
Trustee—Mrs. Anna M. Fay, Brocton, N. Y.

**Class 1920, "The Optimists"**

Motto—"Nothing less than the best."
Emblem—The pink aster.
President—Dr. George Hobbie, 600 Delaware Ave., Buffalo, N. Y.
Treasurer—Miss Jessie M. Leslie, Chautauqua, N. Y.
Secretary-Trustee—Mrs. Chas. C. Taylor, Akron, O.

**Class 1921, "The Adelphians"**

Motto—"Omnia vincit amor." "Love conquers all."
Emblem—The woodbine.
President—Prof. Frank E. Ewart, Colgate University, Hamilton, N. Y.
Secretary—Miss Harriet Sheldon, The Seneca, Broad St., Columbus, O.
Treasurer-Trustee—Mrs. Frances Akin, Chautauqua, N. Y.

**Class 1922, "The Crusaders"**

Motto—"Be not content to read history, make it."
Emblem—The oak leaf.
President—Mr. O. C. Herrick, 6028 Rodman St., Pittsburg, Pa.
Secretary—Miss Alameda Edwards, 750 Mt. Hope Road, Cincinnati, O.
Treasurer—Mr. Robert Cleland, 5809 Northumberland Ave., Pittsburgh, Pa.
Trustee—Mrs. Evalyn Dorman, Chautauqua, N. Y.

### Class 1923, "The Victory"

Motto—"Victory."
Emblem—The poppy. The flags of the Allies.
President—Miss Elizabeth Skinner, Dunedin, Fla.
Recording Secretary—Mrs. R. W. Johnston, 1649 Shady Ave., Pittsburgh, Pa.
Corresponding Secretary—Mrs. John W. Hanna, 803 Fourth St., Braddock, Pa.
Treasurer-Trustee—Mrs. R. I. Park, Chautauqua, N. Y.

### Class 1924, "The New Era"

Motto—"Enter to learn, go forth to serve."
Emblem—The blue larkspur and the marigold.
President—Mrs. F. M. Beacom, 1312 W. 10th St., Wilmington, Del.
Secretary-Treasurer—Mrs. F. N. Prechtel, Cherokee, Ia.

## THE TRUSTEES OF CHAUTAUQUA

N. B.—The Sunday School Assembly of 1874 and 1875 was held under the direction of a committee from the Sunday School Union of the Methodist Episcopal Church, the grounds at Fair Point being owned by the Erie Conference Camp Meeting Association. In May, 1876, the property was transferred to the Board of Trustees of the National Sunday School Assembly.

### THE FIRST CHAUTAUQUA TRUSTEES (SUNDAY SCHOOL ASSEMBLY)

C. Aultman, Canton, O.
A. Bradley, Pittsburgh, Pa.
Clinton M. Ball

Frank C. Carley, Louisville, Ky.
W. P. Cooke
Adams Davis, Corry, Pa.
George W. Gifford, Mayville, N. Y.
J. C. Gifford, Westfield, N. Y.
J. J. Henderson, Meadville, Pa.
Herman Jones, Erie, Pa.
C. L. Jeffords, Jamestown, N. Y.
Isaac Moore, Mayville, N. Y.
Lewis Miller, Akron, O.
Jacob Miller, Canton, O.
H. A. Massey, Toronto
Hiram A. Pratt, Chautauqua, N. Y.
John W. Pitts, Jamestown, N. Y.
David Preston, Detroit, Mich.
F. H. Root, Buffalo, N. Y.
E. A. Skinner, Westfield, N. Y.
Sardius Steward, Ashville, N. Y.
John H. Vincent, Plainfield, N. J.
Amos K. Warren, Mayville, N. Y.
W. W. Wythe, Chautauqua, N. Y.

## THE FIRST TRUSTEES OF THE CHAUTAUQUA INSTITUTION (1898)

### General Officers

John H. Vincent, Chancellor
W. H. Hickman, President of Trustees
George E. Vincent, Principal of Instruction
Joseph C. Neville, Chairman Executive Board
Ira M. Miller, Secretary
Scott Brown, General Director
Warren F. Walworth, Treasurer

### Trustees

Noah F. Clark, Oil City, Pa.
William J. Cornell, Chautauqua, N. Y.
W. A. Duncan, Syracuse, N. Y.
E. G. Dusenbury, Portville, N. Y.
C. D. Firestone, Columbus, O.
James M. Guffey, Pittsburgh, Pa.
W. H. Hickman, Greencastle, Ind.
Frank W. Higgins, Olean, N. Y.
J. Franklin Hunt, Chautauqua, N. Y.
Frederick W. Hyde, Jamestown, N. Y.
Julius King, Cleveland, O.
Chester D. Massey, Toronto, Canada
Ira M. Miller, Akron, O.
Joseph C. Neville, Chicago, Ill.
S. Fred. Nixon, Westfield, N. Y.
Frank M. Potter, Chautauqua, N. Y.
F. H. Rockwell, Warren, Pa.
A. M. Schoyer, Pittsburgh, Pa.
W. H. Shortt, Youngsville, Pa.
Clement Studebaker, South Bend, Ind.
William Thomas, Meadville, Pa.
George E. Vincent, Chicago, Ill.
Warren F. Walworth, Cleveland, O.

### Local Officers

George W. Rowland, Superintendent
William G. Bissell, M.D., Health Officer

## BOARD OF TRUSTEES—1920

Arthur E. Bestor, Chautauqua, N. Y., President Chautauqua Institution
Ernest Cawcroft, 48 Fenton Building, Jamestown, N. Y.

Noah F. Clark, 803 Magee Building, Pittsburgh, Pa.

Melvil Dewey, President Lake Placid Club, Essex Co., N. Y.

George W. Gerwig, Secretary Board of Education, Pittsburgh.

E. Snell Hall, 127 Forest Ave., Jamestown, N. Y.

Louis J. Harter, Chautauqua, N. Y.

Fred W. Hyde, American Bankers Association, Washington, D. C.

J. C. McDowell, 1321 Farmers Bank Building, Pittsburgh.

Vincent Massey, Massey Harris Company, Ltd., Toronto, Canada.

Shailer Mathews, Dean Divinity School, University of Chicago.

Ira M. Miller, Akron, O.

Mrs. Robert A. Miller, 17 West 45th St., New York City.

S. I. Munger, Dallas, Tex.

Mrs. Percy V. Pennybacker, 2606 Whitis Ave., Austin, Tex.

Frank M. Potter, Mayville, N. Y.

William L. Ransom, 120 Broadway, New York City.

A. M. Schoyer, Pennsylvania Lines, Pittsburgh

Alburn E. Skinner, Warren-Nash Motor Company, 18 West 63rd St., New York City

Clement Studebaker, Jr., South Bend, Ind.

H. A. Truesdale, Conneaut, O.

George E. Vincent, President Rockefeller Foundation, 61 Broadway, New York City.

Charles E. Welch, Welch Grape Juice Company, Westfield, N. Y.

### Honorary Trustees

Scott Brown, 208 South La Salle St., Chicago.
E. G. Dusenbury, Portville, N. Y.
George Greer, New Castle, Pa.
W. H. Hickman, Montpelier, Ind.
Julius King, Julius King Optical Company, Cleveland, O.
Chester D. Massey, 519 Jarvis St., Toronto, Canada.
Z. L. White, Columbus, O.

### Educational Council

Lyman Abbott, Editor *Outlook*, New York City.
Jane Addams, Hull House, Chicago.
Percy H. Boynton, University of Chicago, Chicago.
Frank Chapin Bray, League of Nations Union, New York City.
John Graham Brooks, 8 Francis Ave., Cambridge, Mass.
Elmer E. Brown, Chancellor New York University, New York City.
Richard T. Ely, University of Wisconsin, Madison, Wis.
W. H. P. Faunce, President Brown University, Providence, R. I.
J. M. Gibson, Linnell Close, Hampstead Gardens, London, England.
Frank W. Gunsaulus, President Armour Institute, Chicago.
G. Stanley Hall, President Clark University, Worcester, Mass.
Jesse L. Hurlbut, 74 Park Ave., Bloomfield, N. J.

F. G. Peabody, Harvard University, Cambridge, Mass.
Sir George Adam Smith, Principal Aberdeen University, Aberdeen, Scotland.
Charles David Williams, Bishop of Michigan, Detroit, Mich.

# INDEX

Printed in the USA
CPSIA information can be obtained
at www.ICGtesting.com
CBHW082325010424
6241CB00017B/262

9 781018 612